Japanese Girl
at the Siege of Changchun

The author at age 5, standing beside the Shinkyo ether storehouse in Changchun. This is the clothing she wore when entering the Qiazi no-man's land.

Japanese Girl at the Siege of Changchun

How I Survived China's Wartime Atrocity

Homare Endo

Translated by Michael Brase

Stone Bridge Press • *Berkeley, California*

Published by
Stone Bridge Press
P. O. Box 8208, Berkeley, CA 94707
TEL 510-524-8732 • sbp@stonebridge.com • www.stonebridge.com

 Publication of this book has been supported by
a generous grant from The Japan Foundation.

Originally published in Japan in 2012 as *Chazu: Chugoku kenkoku no zanka*
by Asahi Shimbun Publications, Inc. English-language translation rights
arranged by IBC Publishing, Tokyo.

First English-language edition published 2016.

Cover design by Linda Ronan, incorporating a map of the city of
Changchun prepared by U.S. Army Map Service in 1945 (Library of
Congress).

Printed in the United States of America.

p-ISBN: 978-1-61172-038-9
e-ISBN: 978-1-61172-925-2

Contents

Introduction   7

CHAPTER 1   :   The Red Glass Bead   *19*

CHAPTER 2   :   Changchun: A City without Hope   *75*

CHAPTER 3   :   The Free Earth   *151*

CHAPTER 4   :   Liberated Yanji   *178*

CHAPTER 5   :   Alive Again   *191*

CHAPTER 6   :   Outbreak of the Korean War   *221*

CHAPTER 7   :   The Wavering Light of Tianjin   *237*

Afterword   *291*

Note and Acknowledgments   *303*

Introduction

On October 1, 2012, China Central Television (CCTV) was showing the festive celebrations commemorating the sixty-third anniversary of the People's Republic. It would be the last such celebration in which Hu Jintao would preside as General Secretary.

Sixty-seven years earlier, on August 15, 1945, the day Japan surrendered to the Allied powers, the Chinese Communist Army led by Mao Zedong (Mao Tse-tung) and the Nationalist Army (Guomindang [Kuomintang] Forces) led by Jiang Jieshi (Chiang Kai-shek) resumed their fight for national hegemony, a struggle that is often referred to as the Chinese Civil War.*

During the Sino-Japanese War of 1937–45, instigated by Japan's invasion of China, the Communist Army and the Nationalist Army sometimes collaborated, but with the defeat of Japan, all relations between the two combatants ruptured, and in 1946 civil war broke out in earnest.

At the time China was called the Republic of China, and Jiang

---

* Chinese words and names are presented throughout this book in modern pinyin romanization, without diacritical marks to indicate tones. Japanese words and names are similarly presented in Hepburn romanization, without macrons to indicate long vowels. Some Chinese proper names may be more familiar in the West in their older romanized forms; these are displayed in parentheses after the name's first appearance in pinyin. Particularly notable among these are Mao Zedong (Mao Tse-tung), Jiang Jieshi (Chiang Kai-shek), Guomindang (Kuomintang), Manzhouguo (Manchukuo; in English, Manchuria).

Jieshi was the chairman of the national government. Thus, in the sense that the Communist Army was in rebellion against the national government, it can be said to have created a revolution. This explains why in modern-day China this struggle is often referred to as the Revolutionary War.

The Communist army emerged victorious and gave birth to today's People's Republic of China. This occurred on October 1, 1949.

I myself was caught up in the Chinese Civil War and struggle even today with ambivalent feelings toward China.

Until just recently, whenever I heard the opening notes of the Chinese national anthem, the "March of the Volunteers," I instinctively stopped whatever I was doing and came to attention. This ingrained reaction was implanted in me when I was small. Whenever this happened, I couldn't help but shed sad tears over what I was doing.

There were days when Chinese children called me a Japanese Dwarf, a Japanese Devil, or a Japanese Dog, threw rocks at me, spit on me. It was as if I was the one who had invaded China. All this hatred and anger was directed at a little girl only ten years old or so. Their pent-up anger came in a furious barrage, as if to say it's all your fault because you're a Japanese. There was nothing I could do but stand there, shrinking into myself.

"My parents are not invaders, and neither am I," I wanted to say.

Wanting somehow to prove my innocence, I would raise my voice loudly when singing the "March of the Volunteers" and other revolutionary songs. And somewhere in the back of my mind, I harbored the faint hope that the new China would bring a brighter tomorrow.

Even though a great deal of time has passed since then, I would still come to attention, shouldering the burden of several decades, crying as I sang, my body trembling from sheer sadness.

* * * * *

But now it's different.

Now I can be coldly objective; now I can feel an emotion close to wrath rise irresistibly within me.

In particular, the recent scenes on Japanese TV showing the anti-Japanese riots of September 2012, the figures of Chinese youths running amuck, has put even further distance between me and China. Seeing those faces twisted in hate, hearing the cries of Japanese Dwarf, Japanese Devil, Japanese Dog, I couldn't help but return to my ten-year-old self and feel as though I had been stabbed in the heart.

Although more than sixty years have passed since the war, young Chinese with no firsthand experience of the Japanese invasion are becoming more and more vehement and destructive in their anti-Japanese sentiments.

How long do they plan on prolonging this historical chain of events?

Then in October, as if someone had thrown a switch, CCTV suddenly began broadcasting a series of programs in which ordinary citizens were asked, "Are you happy?" Day after day it was this same question.

Many interviewees answer, "What, am I happy? That goes without saying, doesn't it? After all, here I am, living a prosperous life in this wonderful country. My children and grandchildren have plenty to eat; they're getting a good education, and . . ."

I realize that CCTV has purposely focused on what the Chinese government wants to hear. But still, listening to one proud smiling face after another say, "I'm happy, so happy," I can't help but have mixed feelings.

Then, all of a sudden, the announcer turns to the camera and asks the TV audience, "Are you happy?"

I immediately spring to my feet. "Unhappy—that's what I am. How could I be anything else?" Facing the TV, I shout this out in Chinese, challenging the announcer.

I had never reacted in this way before. It was unexpected, sur-prising even myself.

* * * * *

My life has been a long, continuous, agonizing struggle between China and Japan. But now I have had enough.

I was born in the city of Changchun, Jilin Province, in 1941, then called Xinjing, the capital of the Japanese puppet state of Man-zhouguo (otherwise known as the State of Manchuria or the Great Empire of Manchuria).

In 1946, owing to the intervention of U.S. special envoy George Marshall, the escalating Civil War was brought to a temporary halt and large numbers of Japanese were repatriated. This is known as the "One Million Repatriation." It is said that the motive for American intervention was the fear that the Japanese remaining on the main-land would eventually come under the control of the Chinese Com-munist Party and be converted to Communism.

At this time Changchun was occupied by the Nationalist Army. In 1947 the Nationalist Party (Guomindang; Kuomintang) decided that all Japanese should be repatriated except for technicians with vital skills, who were to be detained. Since my father was a techni-cian, he was not allowed to return to Japan. As a result of this policy, Changchun lost almost all of its Japanese residents.

When this repatriation had come to an end, Changchun abruptly came under siege by the Eighth Route Army (later the People's Lib-eration Army). Electricity and gas were cut off, drinking water un-available. This was the beginning of the food blockade.

In 1983 I produced a piece of nonfiction writing called *Fujori no kanata* (Beyond the Unthinkable), which won the Yomiuri Women's Human Documentary Excellence Award. In one short week I had dashed down the thoughts that rushed to my mind. This was my first literary work for public consumption.

In 1984, in response to a request from the *Yomiuri Newspaper*, I published a book titled *Chazu: Deguchi naki daichi* (Qiazi: The Land of No Escape). The Chinese word *qiazi* (卡子, pronounced "chya-zuh") generally refers to a military checkpoint or sometimes to an area that is sandwiched on two sides.

In this case, "Qiazi" referred to the no man's land separating the Nationalist Army that was occupying Changchun and the Communist Army that had encircled the city in a double ring of barbed wire.

The entire city of Changchun was placed under a food blockade, and countless people died of starvation. Among them were my older and younger brothers. Most of the dead were innocent civilians; not a single Nationalist soldier died from lack of food.

There were a number of escape routes from the city. In September 1948 my father decided to try one of them to forestall further deaths in the family. Going through the Qiazi gate, we were faced with a second ring of barbed wire and another gate, the Communist gate, which was closed. Civilians attempting to leave the city were caught in between the two rings of wire and left to die. The ground was littered with corpses. The number of deaths is said to have reached several hundreds of thousands.

Seven years old at the time, I spent the nights on top of these bodies.

Among the Chinese trapped in Qiazi, there were those who fed on the bodies of the newly dead. Caught in this hell on earth, my memory fails me.

The Communist soldiers, who were eating their full, could see what was happening on the other side of the fence, but they chose to leave the dying to their fate.

* * * * *

In the early 1990s I had *Qiazi: The Land of No Escape* translated into Chinese, but every Chinese publisher I approached said it was a delicate matter and declined to handle the book.

As it happened, the book *Xuebai xie hong* (White Snow, Red Blood), written by Zhang Zhenglong of the literary section of the People's Liberation Army and published in August 1989, was suppressed by General Secretary Jiang Zemin in 1990 and the author arrested. *White Snow, Red Blood* depicts the siege of Changchun exactly as I experienced it, although it shows an undeniable tendency to favor Lin Biao. It was Lin who attempted to oust Mao in a coup during the Cultural Revolution of 1966–76.

Learning from the suppression of *White Snow, Red Blood*, I excised some of the scenes depicting "atrocities committed by the Eighth Route Army," but Chinese publishers still refused to publish the book, fearing government reprisal.

I made my last attempt in 2011. I plucked up my courage and approached a highly placed Chinese government official. It was then I learned for the first time that some of his relatives had been at Qiazi. But even he said, "You should wait a little longer. Just a little longer. Then, for sure . . ."

Just a little longer . . .

Simply to bring one historical fact out into the open, how many long years was I supposed to wait?

A central principle of the country where I was born and raised was supposed to be *Shi shi qiu shi* ("Seek the truth from the facts"). The truth of Qiazi is a historical fact, pure and simple, to anyone who had experienced it. Bringing this fact before the public to serve as a lesson for all humanity—was this not to be permitted in the country where it took place?

* * * * *

In 1946, you—the Communist Party—made a promise to the Chinese people during the Revolutionary War.

This war of liberation, you said, was being fought to create a brighter, freer, more democratic future for the people. It was being fought to free the suffering masses. Therefore, fight with us, you said. You made us believe in the future.

And we believed you, and we fought with you. Even if we were struck by a stray Communist bullet and crippled or maimed, we told ourselves it was for the revolution, for the suffering masses. Even if we had to spend the night on the hard ground littered with skeletal bodies on the outskirts of Changchun, even if our memory should be wiped clean by this hellish experience, even then, in anguish and pain, we told ourselves it was for a brighter, freer, more democratic future. We believed in you.

But what about now?

Undoubtedly China has become a more affluent country. Economically it has grown. There is nothing wrong with that.

But the big question is: Are you, the Party, standing on the side of the suffering masses? Hasn't the power you have accrued, thanks to the blood and sweat of the people, turned your upper echelons into profit-making machines? What has happened to the country whose constitution declares, "The people are the masters"?

But still you call yourself a socialist state. Implausibly you describe yourself as "a socialist state with Chinese characteristics," hoping to sidestep inherent incongruities. What has been the result? The abuse of power by high-ranking Party cadres. And to suppress criticism you have clamped down on freedom of speech. What is the difference between this and the bureaucratic capitalism of the Republic of China before the Revolutionary War?

And I am not saying that economic reform and change (*gaige kaifang*) is bad.

In order to achieve the national goal of creating a stable society, and in order to maintain the absolute authority of the Party, haven't you sacrificed the promise made to the people during the Revolutionary War? What has happened to the freedom that you promised then? What has happened to freedom of speech?

What in fact are you afraid of?

What is "authority" when you can only maintain it by concealing your mistakes in the shrouds of history?

I am now seventy-three, and I don't have that much time left.

* * * * *

"Are you happy?"

I would like to respond to CCTV's question one more time.

No, I am not.

I will not be happy until you recognize the injustice of Qiazi as a historical fact. Toward that end I will devote the rest of my life. With mixed feelings toward the country where I was born and bred, with feelings both of love and resentment, I have fought over the years to bring that fact to life. Here, once again, I would like to record what happened at Qiazi. If I don't do it now, I may leave this life before China decides to make this fact public.

I will leave a memorial to the dead.

Not only to my family but to all the people who starved to death in Changchun in 1948, who were tossed aside like trash, who have been effaced from history as if somehow dying from starvation was a heinous crime. The present Chinese reality is that those who died at Qiazi can only be discussed in whispers, as you would speak of a family member who is a convicted criminal. To record this in writing is my memorial to the dead, a memento of my fight to make the truth known.

* * * * *

On the TV, after the national anthem has finished, CCTV cameras focus on the nine members of the Chinese politburo as they make their solemn way to the Monument to the People's Heroes in Tian'anmen Square, followed by representatives of various ethnic groups and other eminent figures. The monument was erected to honor those fallen in the Revolutionary and Sino-Japanese War (or the War Against Japan, as it is referred to in China). On the front of the monument, in Mao Zedong's handwriting, are the words, "Eternal glory to the people's heroes!" Engraved on the back are tributes by Zhou Enlai (Chou En-lai), one reading: "Eternal glory to the heroes of the people who laid down their lives in the people's war of liberation and the people's revolution in the past three years!"

Judging from the date following the final commendation on the monument, September 30, 1949, the time period being referred to here is the three years of Revolutionary War preceding the birth of the new Chinese nation on October 1, 1949.

From 1946 to 1949 . . .

These dates cover the dates of the Qiazi tragedy, from 1947 to 1948.

However, the reported 300,000 to 600,000 deaths by starvation at Changchun are not included among the heroes who fell during the Revolutionary War.

Behind the prosperity of present-day China lie the countless bodies and souls of those who were treated like sacrificial lambs at Changchun. How many Chinese know that when they sing praises to prosperity, they are standing on the bones of those who died at Changchun?

In 1988 a monument was erected in Changchun to commemorate the fortieth anniversary of the city's liberation. The inscription on the monument refers only to the sacrifice made by soldiers of the People's Liberation Army. The people who were driven to starvation in the cause of the Revolutionary War are not counted among the victims. Even to mention this fact is considered a crime.

Just as with the young people who were shot down by the People's Liberation Army as they called for democratic rule in Tian'anmen Square on June 4, 1989, it is a sacrifice not to be spoken of. The reason is simple—the defenseless lives lost were felled by the People's Liberation Army, the supposed friend of the people.

It is not my intention to pass from this life hiding the truth. It is not my intention to lead a life of lies. Telling the truth is a matter of human dignity, the human spirit.

There is not much time left. Those who know the truth, the aging survivors, are growing fewer day by day.

Is that what China is waiting for? Is it waiting for the day when only the dwindling few who directly experienced this horrendous tragedy will feel any genuine anger or sorrow? It may take a hundred years or two hundred years for people to forget, but is that what China is waiting for?

The Chinese people have a right to learn from the past. But to exercise this right in China today is to put one's life at risk. I know that full well.

Sitting at my desk, looking out the window at the lingering light of the setting sun, I find myself filled with unbearable sadness.

Japanese Girl
at the Siege of Changchun

CHAPTER I

The Red Glass Bead

The evening sun in Changchun was beautiful. A flaming, almost transparent red.

When it suddenly settled on the horizon like a huge red bead of glass, the sun turned everything to gold—the trees on Xing-an Boulevard, the windows, and even me myself. Its golden red light flowed into the glass factory behind the house, fusing with the red-hot glass in the large crucible there. The glass would meld with the golden red sun, transform itself into a huge bead, and float up into the sky, shaking my soul to the roots. If I stretched out my hand, I felt I could grasp it. If I had golden wings, I felt I could fly up and pass through the red bead hanging in the sky. My world was within that golden-haloed glass bead; beyond it was the vast incalculable future.

Time and space stretched out to infinity. Looking through this glass bead, I tried to fathom what the nebulous future held.

* * * * *

Until the end of the war, this glass factory was located between Jilin and Changchun in a place call Xiajiutai. After Japan's defeat, a mob totally wrecked the place. Aside from an older craftsman who saved himself by hiding in the chimney, everything simply disappeared.

Originally, it had been part of our escape plans to take refuge at Xiajiutai.

On August 9, 1945, the Soviet Union declared war on Japan, and Changchun was immediately enveloped in fear and apprehension.

Rumors spread that Russia had broken through the borders of Manzhouguo and that on the 13th Changchun would be bombed by the Soviets, placing the city in the center of the fighting. Other rumors contended that the borders of Manzhouguo had only been breached by Soviet tanks and so aerial bombing couldn't occur any earlier than the 20th.

Then on August 11, sparks suddenly flew up from near the Changchun headquarters of the Kanto (Kwantung, Guandong) Army, with its majestic castle-like roof, and smoke billowed up and shrouded the sky. Seeing this, the people of Changchun realized that their apprehensions and fears were now becoming reality. They now knew that the Soviet entry into the war, which had seemed so far away and so unrelated, had thrust itself into their daily lives.

It was on this day, August 11, that Father received a message from the Horse Administration Bureau of the Agricultural Reform Department of the puppet Manzhouguo government.

"Early morning of the 13th a military truck or horse-drawn wagon will be sent around to your house for evacuation to Tonghua. Make preparations with utmost speed."

At the time Father was supplying the Horse Administration with some ten types of injection drugs, including Ringer's solution and camphor.

The war in the Pacific had begun to deteriorate in 1944, and units of the Kanto Army had been dispatched to that front. Japanese residing in Manzhouguo were mobilized down to the last man. The Kanto Army was suddenly sapped of its former strength and glory. The puppet government of Manzhouguo, which relied on the Kanto Army for its very existence, began to crumble from its foundations, and the Agricultural Reform Department fell into financial crisis. The department's Horse Administration Bureau, which was continually in arrears in its payments to Father, seemed to have finally reached a tipping point and asked him for a loan: "In the name of the state of Manzhouguo, you will be reimbursed without fail. The money is needed to get the Horse Administration Bureau back on its feet." Then, in passing, they asked if he could also loan money to the needy Manzhouguo Equestrian Association, which he did.

It was perhaps in acknowledgment of these loans that a military truck or wagon was to be sent around to our house, something that was entirely unheard of for a mere civilian.

Since he was responsible for the workers in the pharmaceutical factory, Father said he would remain in Changchun. Mother and we five children, together with wives and children of factory workers, would evacuate to Tonghua.

Tonghua was fortunately located near the border of Japanese-controlled Korea, but even so, if something should happen to Father, his children would end up being fatherless. Mother was bothered by the thought that when the children grew up, they would undoubtedly ask, "Why did you leave Father by himself and try to escape on your own?" Thus she opposed the idea of leaving Changchun for distant Tonghua. In any case, she didn't want to be separated from her husband.

Then the idea was proposed that Mother and we children go to Meihekou, which was located between Changchun and Tonghua. But still Mother wouldn't agree. It was finally decided that we would go to the glass factory in Xiajiutai. It had convenient company housing, and it would be easy to join up with Father if need be. Preparing for the worst eventuality, all of us had funeral apparel in our backpacks, and Mother had enough potassium cyanide for six people.

On the morning of the 13th we anxiously waited for the promised truck or wagon, but no matter how long we waited, neither showed up.

Just as we had reached a peak of anxiety and fatigue, Father said,

"Things may have taken a turn for the worse. I'll go to Headquarters and see." He immediately set off for the Kanto Army Headquarters, which he expected to find a hive of activity as it drew up strategy for repelling the Russians. But when he stepped inside the building, he couldn't believe his eyes.

The building was completely empty—not a soul to be seen, not a sound to be heard.

But that wasn't all. In the section dealing with war relief funds, an even more astounding sight met his eyes. "Relief funds" in this case refers to goods and money donated to the war effort. Even though most Japanese had scarcely enough to eat, they were expected to relinquish whatever they had for the brave soldiers fighting for the country. If they didn't, if they kept anything for their own use, they were considered traitors and liable to punishment, even imprisonment.

What Father saw was a room whose floors were littered with paperwork from corner to corner, leaving scarcely space to walk. Cabinet doors were agape, with more documents cascading from them. Drawers had been left open, revealing heaps of jewelry. In one corner of the room Father saw a familiar figure, a veteran clerk. He was sitting in a chair, a blank look on his face.

Father had visited this office any number of times to make donations. He knew this clerk, and he knew what the room usually looked like.

What on earth had happened, he thought. Making his way through the litter, he approached the clerk and asked him, "Where has everyone gone?"

But the clerk didn't answer; he just kept staring into space. Father shook his shoulder and asked again, but the clerk remained silent, his shoulders moving whichever way they were pushed like a puppet. Finally he forced some words from his lips: "To Tonghua. They've evacuated to Tonghua."

"To Tonghua? All of them? That can't be. Why, Tonghua is in the south. If the Kanto Army withdraws to the south, what is to become of the Japanese in Changchun? And what about the people living even further north? With all due respect, you must be mistaken."

Father threw an anxious glance at the jewelry-filled drawers.

Without buying what they needed, without eating decent meals, ordinary Japanese had donated these things to the war effort, for the country's sake. Could it be, he asked himself, that senior army officers had quickly stuffed as much money and jewelry as they could into valises and pants pockets before vacating the building? In the midst of the surrounding chaos, this is what Father said he imagined, and then he caught himself, and he shuddered.

He left Headquarters, passed by the smoldering ashes of burnt documents in the rear of the building, and headed for the Horse Administration Bureau. His hopes of borrowing a truck were dashed when he learned that the Kanto Army had not only commandeered the trucks but all the wagons that the Agriculture Reform Department had managed to muster. By the time he reached home, he had come to feel that his earlier thoughts about Kanto senior officers weren't wrong.

"I'm afraid the Horse Administration Bureau won't be coming for us after all," he told Mother.

Hearing this, Mother jumped for joy.

"Is that true? Then we can all stay together with you? Oh, how lucky! How very lucky!"

Paying no attention to Father's gloomy face, she cheerfully began to unpack.

For Mother the safest place was by Father's side. In fact, if the Horse Administration Bureau had come as promised and we had gone to Xiajiutai, the whole family, except for Father, would have perished in the riot there. The decision to stay with him had been the right one after all. We had to thank the Kanto Army for thinking of themselves first and foremost.

But another fear began to dominate Father's mind, pushing aside any thoughts of the Horse Administration Bureau. This was a fear that any patriotic Japanese would hesitate to put into words. Looking in the direction of the Headquarters, he muttered, "Our fortress has been breached, Mother. With the Kanto Army like that . . . Japan, it may just lose the war."

His face had the same blank expression as the clerk in the War Relief Funds.

"Father, what are you saying? Of all things . . . ," Mother chided him.

But in fact, affairs were already proceeding swiftly toward that end.

Two days later, on August 15, it became an undeniable reality. Another two days after that, the glass factory in Xiajiutai was razed by a mob.

On the 15th, throughout the city of Changchun, Japanese factories, stores, and homes were destroyed and plundered one after another. Then the news spread that the Manzhouguo Army had staged a revolt in the Imperial Palace at Changchun, and the reality of defeat pressed even more heavily on us.

Fortunately, the Shinkyo pharmaceutial factory that Father owned in Xing'an was spared. The Chinese and Korean workers had formed a human barricade around it, declaring "This is our factory," and thus protected not only the factory from the mob but Father as well, who was there at the time. The fact that Father was a very religious man may also have played a role.

* * * * *

Father developed an interest in religion when in his mid-twenties. Until then, he had operated a store in Oita in Japan and had invested heavily in the rice market. When he made a financial move, it is said that the whole market moved. There was an amazing amount of money to be made if you read the market accurately. But somewhere along the line, he began to think it was not so amazing or wonderful after all. This change of mind occurred when he actually saw the people who suffered when rice prices spiked.

It might be wonderful that one's pockets were filled with money, but that meant that others were suffering a loss. It was as if he was growing fat by taking food from their mouths. While his mind was struggling with this dilemma, his eye for reading the market began to fail him. He decided it was time for a change, and he went to the warehouse and emptied it of rice to give to the poor, every single grain. All his personal property he turned over to the needy, and entered the world of religion.

This was just before the rice riots of 1918, when farmers violently protested the huge gap between the consumer and the wholesale price of rice, not to mention city dwellers suffering from spiraling inflation.

Father thought: "I want to live a life that will benefit others. What can I do to be of service?" In his search for a new way of life, he meditated while sitting on seaside boulders, drenched by the waves; he meditated under waterfalls while being soaked to the skin, striving to bring his mind to a finer degree of concentration.

Finally he discovered a kindred spirit in the founder of the religion known as Konkokyo. He became a wandering missionary, singing the blessings of Konkokyo while playing a biwa, mostly in the fishing villages of Kitakyushu. He particularly liked the fact that Konkokyo didn't stress unfounded myth but focused on how human beings should live and think.

After spending seven years searching for a new way of life, Father finally found what he wanted and began to devote himself to pharmaceutical research. Eventually, as the result of some ten years of study, he developed a medicine called Giftol that was effective in treating drug addiction. Its main ingredient was pine resin.

In China there were many morphine and opium addicts. If he went to China and manufactured the drug there, he could save many lives. Father looked upon this as a sacred mission, and he crossed over to the Chinese mainland in 1937.

Father was forty-eight at the time and Mother twenty-nine. They had a sixteen-year-old son by Father's previous marriage and a one-year-old girl of their own. Mother had a round, refined face with a fair complexion. Father was directing a group in *kibigaku*, a type of classical music associated with Konkokyo, and Mother was in charge of the stringed *koto*, which was considered a woman's instrument. That is how they met. Father was particularly adept at the wind instrument called the *sho*, and the deep, melancholic sounds the instrument produced overlapped with the irresistibly alluring image Mother had of him.

Apparently at the time that Mother developed her one-sided attraction for Father, his first wife was still alive, though sickly. When she passed away, out of respect for her Father initially kept his associations with other women to a minimum. However, Mother's father, my grandfather, realizing her passionate feelings, made them subtly known to Father, who then abandoned his previous inhibitions, and the two were married.

Grandfather was the fifteenth-generation direct descendant of Chosokabe Motochika of the Tosa domain, Kyushu, a warlord during the Warring States period in the sixteenth century. In the normal course of events, Mother would have been the sixteenth-generation "princess" of the family. She loved literature, was a gifted poet, and was enthralled by the simple elegance of the *koto*. But she also had a strong character. Lord Motochika was eventually defeated by the great warlord Toyotomi Hideyoshi, so in our family Hideyoshi was not kindly regarded.

According to a story passed down in the Chosokabe family, and often repeated by Mother, seven woodsorrel leaves had been placed in a cup of tea that Motochika received from the emperor at an imperial party, and this led to the family crest being a stylized combination of seven woodsorrel leaves. Further, we were told that the roots of the Chosokabe family could be traced back to Qinwang Zheng, the First Emperor of the Qin, a descendant of whose had come to Japan as a Buddhist missionary. Since Mother loved telling incredible tales to us children, such as Akutagawa's *Rashomon*, it is hard to tell how much truth there is in this.

Once in China, Father hurried from one drug rehabilitation center to another with his precious Giftol, centering his activities on Changchun but also including Haerbin (Harbin), Shenyang (then Mukden), and other places. At these centers he saw swarms of pale-faced addicts, some writhing on the floor with withdrawal symptoms, others drooling at the mouth like the near-dead, their debilitated hearts beating their last. The air was filled with bestial cries and the stench of loose bowels.

Even with such patients as these, however, only five days after taking the medicine they were transformed from beasts back to human beings once again, the withdrawal symptoms beginning to ease. The same clinical results were observed at every rehabilitation center. The medicine was undeniably effective.

* * * * *

Government approval for the medicine was soon forthcoming, but there was one curious condition.

> The efficacy of the medicine is recognized. Therefore, commercial sale is approved. However, advertisement of any kind is forbidden. This does not apply to reports spread by word of mouth.

The rationale behind this was as follows:

> The State of Manzhouguo is now implementing a five-year plan to eliminate narcotics. If advertising via the written word were

officially approved for Giftol, this could be construed by foreign powers as meaning that Manzhouguo cannot successfully execute its five-year plan without the help of private enterprise. This would be an insupportable disgrace for the state. Furthermore, if advertising via the written word for Giftol were allowed, it would in effect mean that the government of Manzhouguo admits that drug addicts still exist in the country. The honor and authority of the state would be irreversibly damaged if addiction was acknowledged as an irredeemable problem.

And this from a country whose rehabilitation centers were overflowing with addicts! Even the empress, Wan Rong, was seriously afflicted, a fact that was a widely known secret.

Depending on the nature of the narcotic, it was true that withdrawal symptoms could be temporarily alleviated. But if the treatment had to be repeated, the interval between the appearance of withdrawal symptoms became shorter and the amount of narcotics smoked or injected at one time grew larger. As a result, the heart was damaged, the face grew deathly pale, the body weakened, varicose veins appeared, and the addict became disoriented and eventually died.

As Empress Wan Rong entered this final stage of withdrawal, the Manzhouguo government gave up all pretense of maintaining its dignity and honor and sent a messenger from the imperial household agency to ask for my father's help. This was just before the Soviet Union declared war on Japan. Treatment had just started when the empress and the Emperor Puyi boarded an imperial train for Tonghua, embodying the final hours and fate of Manzhouguo.

The dignity and honor of a nation can be both ludicrous and cruel.

Due to certain conditions associated with this work, all mention of the Tongren Chemical Research Center on Xing-an Boulevard in Changchun (later Shinkyo Pharmaceutical Company), which had been established to manufacture medicine for drug addicts, was completely erased from public record.

At the time many Chinese smoked opium as casually as they might smoke a cigarette. In various forms, opium, morphine, and heroin had spread throughout the country. But even in this dire situation it was amazing how fast the news spread of a drug alleviating withdrawal symptoms. Once the medicine was known, word spread like wildfire among addicts throughout Manzhouguo, crossed the Great Wall into Beijing, and then reached Shanghai. In 1939 the Republic of China approved Giftol for commercial sale, and almost immediately afterward it spread to Southeast Asia. Demand spiraled, and even the manufacture of 2,000,000 tablets a day wasn't enough.

No matter how much was made, supply still couldn't meet demand. New facilities were added as quickly as possible, including the Qing He factory on Qi Hua Road within Changchun, the Erdaohezi factory in the suburbs, the Xiajiutai glass factory, and the purchase of 100 square meters of land in the Tongren industrial zone in Dadonggou. Branch offices were added in Beijing (Peking) and Shanghai. Even then, supply could not keep up with demand, and there was a rush of people making payments for Giftol, causing further delays.

At the beginning, the price of the medicine was set so as to assure our family of a minimal standard of living, and it was never raised after that. Even so, the result was the accumulation of an enormous fortune, almost against Father's will.

This wasn't the only thing that didn't go as Father intended.

In a country overrun with drugs, it was only natural that underground organizations should become involved in the drug trade—the so-called Chinese mafia. As people were relieved of the aftereffects of withdrawal and vowed never to touch narcotics again, the demand for narcotics diminished and hurt the pocketbooks of these illegal organizations.

Eventually this led to Father's life being put in jeopardy. Mother feared this more than anything and begged him to stop producing Giftol and return to Japan.

"There's nothing to worry about," Father told her. "God is watching over us. Don't fret about it." And he kept on producing Giftol.

Before long, however, a situation arose that he could never have imagined. The magic of Giftol turned into black magic.

The mind is weak and the body strong, so people soon forget the pain they have been through, it seems. With the passage of time and physical recovery, addicts who had triumphed over the pain of withdrawal and had vowed to never touch narcotics again, were caught up once more by its sweet allure. The web that drugs throw over an addict is much stronger than ordinary people can ever imagine. Even if they should become addicted once more, recovering patients thought, they could take Giftol and give it up again. Apparently this removed any concern about relapsing and made it easy to revert to old habits.

The winners in all this were the underground organizations, the mafia. Father even received a bizarre "letter of thanks."

"Go ahead, make more Giftol. We'll just sell more and more drugs. As long as Giftol exists, our business is safe. Your life is in no danger from us, Doctor."

Father agonized over this. It had never occurred to him that things would take this terrible turn. His choices were to quit manufacturing Giftol or to produce a powerful anti-addiction drug to assist in the rehabilitation process. Father chose the latter.

He read the latest research, perused ancient texts, and had trial drugs clinically tested at rehabilitation centers. During this period he apparently got only three hours of sleep a night. He often said, "There is a clock in the human body made by the gods." He believed that all the body's basic functions, including pulse and respiration, reached their lowest ebb around 2:00 AM, and that's why he went to bed around 12:00 and got up at 3:00.

In the end he succeeded in making an improved version of Giftol and producing a powerful anti-addiction drug.

Until then, the overwhelmingly predominant method of treatment had been the coercive cessation of drug usage in either a complete or gradual manner. In this method, addicts were forced to go through unimaginable withdrawal symptoms while, in most cases, confined to small barred cells. Complete cessation called for all access to narcotics to be cut off, and the addict was required to bear excruciating pain, hopefully giving rise to a higher sense of self-awareness that would prevent future relapse. Another method was the sleep cure, in which the addict was put into a deep sleep and made oblivious to the effects of withdrawal. This was effected by the repeated administering of sleep medications to the utmost degree allowed by the physical condition of the addict, who was undoubtedly already suffering from a weakened heart. This method was the riskiest of all. Most patients did not survive, or the treatment was halted at the last minute. The gradual treatment, which called for the tapered diminution of narcotic usage, required a lengthy period of treatment, and the number of successful cases was few. As a result, the predominant method of treatment was the complete cessation or cold turkey method, which was accompanied by the most excruciating pain. Tranquilizers and anesthetics were also a possibility—"fighting fire with fire"—but they introduced the danger of further addiction.

Giftol, on the other hand, could be administered at home, obviating the need for entering one of the dreaded rehabilitation centers. Addicts hoping to return to a normal way of life looked upon Giftol as a blessing from heaven.

Furthermore, in the case of Giftol, if more than three-tenths of previous narcotic intake was exceeded, the addict would immediately experience headaches, dizziness, and nausea, adding to the medicine's anti-addiction properties. This almost completely eliminated the incidence of relapse for serious addicts. Giftol was found to be effective for opium, morphine, heroin, methamphetamine,

Pantopon, oxycodone, cocaine, and others, making it peerless as an anti-addiction drug. Giftol received high praise from the public welfare division of the government of Manzhouguo and the hygiene section of the metropolitan police department: "Since Giftol possesses heretofore unseen antagonistic properties that are anti-addiction and anti-smoking, the prognosis for the course of treatment is not only favorable, but the medicine is also effective in preventing relapse of former addicts and the emergence of new ones. Giftol represents a new ray of hope in Manzhouguo's stated policy to eliminate addiction from the state." Giftol was the only anti-addiction medicine approved by the government for commercial sale.

The word "Giftol" is a combination of German and Japanese. The German word for poison is "Gift." In Japanese the verb for "removing" something is *toru*. Combining the two produces "Gifttoru" or "Giftol." In Chinese it was called "Jifudelu." In Manzhouguo it was sold through the government agency Fulu Trading Company, and in the Republic of China through the Beijing Tongren Pharmaceutical Company.

At first the Manzhouguo government did not look kindly on Father's endeavors, but it eventually came to rely on him for the manufacture of medical supplies. Over time he began supplying the Horse Administration Bureau with injections of Ringer's solution, Locke's solution, Brom's calcium, and persic oil.

* * * * *

No matter how many transformations the company went through, Father remained a seeker after truth. Every morning he would get up exactly at 3:00, tie a towel tightly around his head like a pirate's headband to keep the sweat off his face, and begin making medicine at the crucible. Mother would do the same.

It was 7:00 before the factory hands began to show up, and a little after 8:00 when they had all assembled. But that didn't bother Father. He thanked the gods that he was healthy enough to continue the routine of awaking at 3:00, and grateful that by making even one more tablet of Giftol, he was able to save one more person from ruin. He was not adding to the suffering of the world; he was contributing to the general welfare. It was this knowledge, this sense of joy, that his life was founded on. He was living life to the full, overflowing with energy.

Among the factory hands there were some Japanese, but there were also many Chinese and Koreans. Father treated them all the same. Or rather, strictly speaking, he gave the Chinese first priority, the Koreans second, and the Japanese last.

The reason he gave the Chinese precedence was clear—this was their country. He had not come to China to exploit its people, he said, but to be of some help in saving suffering addicts. He was simply putting that thought into practice.

The reason he gave Koreans second priority was that he hated the way Japanese looked down on Koreans and made them the butt of their jokes. He continually told the Korean hands, "Study while you're young, so nobody can look down on you."

Accordingly, Father had the young Koreans attend night school. Every evening as 5:00 approached, Father would have Mother prepare an early dinner and send off the Koreans to Korean night school. And whenever there was some trouble between the Koreans and his son by his previous marriage, he would side with the Koreans and reprimand his son. On such occasions he would say, "You should treat all the employees with respect. It is because of them that we can live the life we are living now."

Father's fair-handed treatment would later have unforeseeable consequences, actually saving us from grave danger. The first instance of this occurred during the chaotic rioting immediately following the defeat of Japan.

* * * * *

On August 20 the Soviet army began to enter Changchun.

Despite doubts about the conduct of the Russian soldiers, the citizens of Changchun expected that law and order would return to the city once military rule had been imposed. The Chinese and Korean factory hands all left for their hometowns. Most of them had been driven from home by the Japanese and had sought shelter at Father's factory. They were replaced by detained Japanese who had lost their jobs following the defeat of Japan and by refugees from the north, abandoned by the Kanto Army and driven south by the Soviets. The Shinkyo factory was packed with people from stem to stern.

Almost all of the major pharmaceutical companies in Changchun had their home offices in Japan and lost contact with them in the postwar turmoil, leading to their collapse. Pharmacists from these companies showed up at Shinkyo Pharmaceuticals, bringing with them what they could salvage from the chaos, and began making inverted sugar such as "Wakamoto" and Takecho's "Lodinon" at the Xing-an factory.

Wives of even captains and other professional soldiers, as well as the wives of men working for the South Manchurian Railway, also came to the Xing-an factory to eke out a living by washing dishes.

At this time Mother and Father had five children of their own, the eldest a girl and the youngest a boy named Chiyoji, who was born in January 1945. After begetting four girls, Mother and Father were overjoyed to have a son, continually calling out, "Little Chiyo! Our little Chiyo!"

I was the third oldest child. Born in the middle, I was more or less taken for granted. I was born on the second floor of the Xing-an factory.

Shinkyo Pharmaceuticals was located at 412 Xing-an Boulevard. It had originally been called the Tongren Chemical Research

Center, but the year I was born it was renamed the Shinkyo Pharmaceutical Company. On the first floor was a reception room, an office, and one part of the factory. On the second floor was the family's living quarters. Behind the backyard were storehouses for diethyl ether and pharmaceuticals. Further behind them was a line of company housing, which abutted Xing-an Hutong. *Hutong* means backstreet or alley. On the right of the factory facing Xing-an Hutong there was a three-story dormitory, and the glass factory was situated in the rear of that.

Originally the dormitory had apparently belonged to the branch office of a certain life insurance company, and when the evacuation orders of August 13 came down, the employees of the company departed for Tonghua, leaving a key with Father and asking him to look after their things. Some of the people who evacuated to Tonghua at this time eventually returned to Changchun, but it seems that many stayed in Tonghua and were later repatriated to Japan. The insurance people were apparently among this group, because wait as we would, they never returned. In the meanwhile, refugees from the north came flooding into Changchun to escape the Soviet army, to be housed in Muromachi Elementary School and elsewhere. Soon after, however, there wasn't space to handle them all, and the refugees began moving into the houses left vacant by the Tonghua evacuees. In this situation it would not do to leave the dorm permanently vacant, and so using the key left in his care, Father opened the doors of the building and made it available for refugee use.

These refugees generally arrived with only the clothes on their backs, and Father undertook to give them some kind of paying work to do, thereby providing them with a means of making a living. That's how the building became what we called the Shinkyo dorm. There were times when there were too many people and too little work to go around. There were some refugees who had exhausted themselves making their way down from the north and were unable to work. Father took it upon himself to look after these people. Among them were those who could make a living on their own, and their finances were kept separate from the company's.

* * * * *

Meanwhile, the hopes and expectations of the citizens of Changchun were betrayed by the Soviet army. Far from establishing law and order, the Russian soldiers plundered and raped like evil demons, springing up out of nowhere, striking fear into the hearts of the people. They smashed all industrial machinery, and it was they who were the principal disrupters of civil order.

Of course, this rampant violence eventually reached Shinkyo Pharmaceuticals.

On the first day only a few soldiers showed up. They said they wanted to inspect the plant and took a tour of the Xing-an factory. They then went to the reception room and had a pleasant chat with Father.

One said, "A wonderful establishment!"

Another, "Absolutely amazing!"

Father thanked them.

Father entertained them with vodka, whiskey, and various hors d'oeuvres. They seemed quite pleased when they departed.

Father felt a sense of relief: they weren't as bad as rumor had depicted them. Then, two or three days later, they came again. This time there were five of them, and they came bearing presents: vodka, American canned food, and other things. Father felt so reassured that he complied with their request to see Shinkyo's records, and he explained the purpose and the present state of company affairs. Father wasn't conversant in Russian, so he had a former member of the Horse Management Bureau, who was staying with us, act as interpreter.

At first the soldiers reading the records were repeating "Da, da, da" among themselves, but then the superior officer of the group suddenly banged his glass of vodka down on the table. With this, everything went silent, and the soldiers seemed to straighten their shoulders.

Father immediately smelled blood in the air and started to get up. Before he knew it, five guns were pointed at him. They were submachine guns known as mandolins.

Two of the soldiers practically skated over the floor to take up positions behind Father. Two assumed positions at his side. This left the superior officer standing in front of Father, glaring at him.

The muzzle of the foremost gun was pressed up against Father's chest. The guns in back and at his sides did likewise. Father raised his arms in the air to show he was not resisting. The guns pressed even harder against his torso.

Were they all going to go off at the same time? But the next sound came not from the guns but from the mouths of the soldiers. "Hand over all your money," they said.

So it was money they were after. If that were the case ...

On August 13, after witnessing the ugly scene at the Kanto Army Headquarters and getting a strong sense that the war would soon be over, Father went around to the banks and withdrew almost all of his money. There was so much that he had to put it into trunks and cardboard boxes, later to be stored in closets on the second floor or hidden in the attic.

Careful that he didn't disturb the balance of the guns pressed against him, Father began quietly to move a step at a time toward the second floor. The five Russians were as tense as he was. If the Russians made a misstep going up the stairs and mishandled their guns, someone might get hurt.

Upstairs, unaware of all this, Mother and we five children were in Father's room enjoying some starch-syrup "water candy." Water candy was used in the manufacture of medicine, and there was always a plentiful supply in the pharmaceutical warehouse.

I was sitting with my back to entrance to the room, just about to put my spoon into a bowl of water candy. Sensing something strange in the air, I looked over at Mother, who was sitting across from me. Her mouth was half open, her eyes huge, fixed on the entrance to the room.

I whirled around to look.

"Ah!"

Terrified by what I saw, I ran to Mother's side. The muzzles of the guns followed me as they might follow a small animal of prey.

No eyes! They had no pupils!

I was used to seeing people with black pupils, and looking at the huge Russian soldiers with light gray eyes, I was stunned.

Then Father—he was hanging from the Russians' rifles, dead.

But, no, he wasn't dead. Instead he spoke to Mother.

"Mother . . ." His voice was hoarse. But, oh, he was still alive.

But what on earth had happened? Father's face, which was usually suffused with dignity and a gentle kindness, was now deathly pale. The defenseless hands he held up barely reached the chins of the two-meter-tall Russians. His dark-skinned compact body now looked as flimsy, as insubstantial, as a thin sheet of pallid brown wrapping paper. He appeared small and shrunken. He would be killed, for sure.

I was just on the point of crying out when my oldest sister, nine years old, screamed out.

"Ohhh, Father's going to be killed." Then she burst out in violent tears.

Two mandolins were quickly trained on her.

But she didn't stop. The mandolins took aim at her head, ready to fire.

Suddenly Father's frail body sprang into action, and he put his hands over the guns' muzzles.

"Shut up!" he told his oldest daughter.

At exactly the same instant there was a slapping sound.

The second youngest daughter, seven, had slapped her older

sister on the cheek with all her might. Startled at this turn of events, the crying stopped. The mandolins, just as surprised, loosened their grip.

Once again with five rifles pressed against his body, breathing heavily, Father turned as slowly as he could toward Mother. Any quick movement drew the attention of the mandolins.

"Mother . . . the trunk, where would the trunk be?"

Management of the second floor was in Mother's hands.

"Oh, the trunk . . . ," she quavered.

At the sound of Mother's voice, all the mandolins turned in her direction.

It was as if the Russians saw with their mandolins, heard with their mandolins, and conversed with their mandolins.

Faced with the gun muzzles, Mother choked up. The hand that held her less-than-one-year-old son on her knee trembled like a leaf. She had to say where the trunk was, but she couldn't get a single word out of her mouth. Finally she raised her right hand and tried to indicate where the trunk was. But her arm just circled in the air like a top, no help at all. It wouldn't do to keep the mandolins waiting, and Father decided on a mean direction and, hands still in the air, began walking slowly toward it.

The mandolins were losing patience.

Father put his hand on the closet door to open it.

There was a sudden flurry of activity among the mandolins. A burly, white, hairy arm impatiently pushed aside Father's dark bony hand and opened the door. Like ravenous beasts they soon spotted their prey and pulled the trunk out onto the floor.

The superior officer made to open the lid. For an instant the mandolins stopped all movement, holding their breath.

The lid came off.

"Ohhh!"

The trunk was crammed with large bills. The predators let out a roar and pounced on their prey.

Their guns were no longer important. They were tossed aside on the floor, transformed into mere objects.

Ten big hands grabbed fistfuls of paper money and stuffed it into their pockets. When their pockets were ready to burst, they unbuttoned their collars and began filling the chests of their coats. You could see their straggly brown hair. Their sleeves were rolled up as if it were hot, and their arms had three or four wristwatches on them, between which you could see tattooed numbers and symbols.

Having completely emptied the trunk, they appeared satisfied and slung their guns over their shoulders. They threw out their chests and assumed a dignified posture. That's when I noticed Father kneeling on the floor, his hands still held up in the air. The fingers of his raised hands were trembling.

The storm having passed, freed from fear and intense excitement, we were all completely exhausted and for a while couldn't utter a word. From the next day we children didn't leave Mother's side, and Mother didn't leave Father's. The family was always together. As Father went about his business in the factory, he was continually followed by his family brood. But a day finally came when we could feel safe separated from him. The plundering Russians came so often that we finally got used to them.

Faced with the muzzle of a mandolin, Father would say, "That doesn't scare me anymore. Put your guns down." He would put a hand over the muzzle and have them lower the weapon. He was now treating their plundering exactly as he would a commercial transaction.

It was then I realized what had frightened us at first was not the tall Russian soldiers but Father's groveling, defeatist attitude.

* * * * *

Directly across Xing-an Boulevard from Shinkyo Pharmaceuticals was the office of the Soviet military police, the GPU.

Officially it was called the State Political Directorate under the People's Commissariat for Internal Affairs of the Russian Soviet Federative Socialist Republic, which was generally shortened to the State Political Directorate. In essence, it was a secret police whose job was to expose anti-government individuals and movements. We simply called it the GPU, and the terrible sound of those letters became indelibly imprinted on our minds. One after another, the GPU arrested people suspected of war crimes as well as former officials of Manzhouguo, and its reach even extended to ordinary citizens.

Before the war came to an end, foods such as rice, sorghum (kaoliang), and rock salt were distributed by a rationing system, together with such daily necessities as soap and anything containing rubber. Among Japanese employing Chinese and Korean workers, there were some who expropriated their rations, and others who treated anyone who was not Japanese as less than human, not to mention the many who physically abused their employees. Most of these people received their just deserts during the postwar riots, but it didn't end there. Former employees and others in the know informed on these people as members of the exploitive class, and one after another they were spirited away by the GPU. The GPU encouraged informing of this type, and informers were reimbursed for their trouble.

Father not only passed on all the employees' rationed goods to them, he even shared the family portion. Again, food he bought on the black market to make up for shortages was handed out fairly to one and all. The workers' pay was also higher than elsewhere, leading to complaints from the neighbors: "Your pay is so high, it's leading to dissatisfaction among my workers. For the good of everyone, don't you think you could lower it a bit?" Thus, even though Father was a member of the propertied class, not a single person ever informed on him. He was undoubtedly one of the few Japanese who escaped being seized by the GPU.

Just about the time that our fear of the Russian soldiers had dwindled, I asked Father something that had been bothering me.

"How come the Russian soldiers don't take away the boxes and trunks full of money, instead of stuffing it into their pockets?"

"Well, you see, that's because they're doing something they shouldn't. If the GPU found out, they'd be in deep trouble. In a former life they were robbers and thieves. They were sent to Siberia, and that's where they got the numbers on their arms."

That made sense. Those white burly arms grabbing bundles of bills . . . The tattooed numbers peeking out between the arrays of wristwatches were prisoner numbers.

These thieves came to seem not only ludicrous but ignorant as well. They were ridiculously fond of fountain pens and wristwatches on the one hand, and on the other they would try lighting matches by striking them on lamps or the headlights of cars. When that didn't work, they'd get mad and shoot at the offending object. And then they would proudly make off with worthless government bonds and rice rationing books, thinking they were as good as money.

Our family had a lot of government bonds. Until the end of the war everyone was forced to buy bonds, and a certain portion of salaries was even paid in bonds. Since they couldn't be immediately converted into money, anyone existing on a scanty salary had a hard time making a living. This led to a good many people coming to Father and asking if he would buy their bonds, which he did with cash at face value. In the end, the monthly neighborhood association meetings turned into veritable bond exchanges, and the bonds Father accumulated grew and grew.

Next, Russian army officers sporting flashy military capes, whose job it was to keep the thieves under control, would pull up in American-made jeeps and "requisition" valuable factory machinery and boldly send it off to Russia.

With the end of the war, the blackout theretofore enforced in Changchun was lifted, but the citizens of the city hardly had time to rejoice before another strict blackout was ordered by the occupying Soviet army. What could its aim possibly be? One day, in the middle of the night, there was so much noise from vehicles going down Xing-an Boulevard that Mother opened the curtain a few centimeters and peeked out. An amazing sight met her eyes. Mixed in with some tanks, truck after truck formed an endless line heading north, piled high with requisitioned machinery and equipment.

* * * * *

Still, Shinkyo Pharmaceuticals never lost hope. Near the end of the war, the ingredients for making medicine were under strict control, and Giftol suffered in output. But after the defeat of Japan, controls were relaxed, making increased production possible. Consequently, there was a flood of pent-up orders from addicts, and the sales of Giftol surpassed what they had previously been. In addition, with the disappearance of the state of Manzhouguo, its exclusive control over the sale of Giftol also disappeared, giving Father the freedom to sell on the open market. However, since Father never once raised the price of Giftol from the very beginning, the income from sales couldn't keep pace with the rise in the cost of living. In the end, the fact that the price continued unchanged actually boosted sales. Every day, so many bundles of bills came in that there was hardly a place to put them all. Using this money, Father looked after the people who had sought a safe haven at Shinkyo Pharmceuticals and donated the rest to the Japanese Resident Association for the relief of refugees.

The GPU was in the habit of demanding that the Resident Association supply it with sums of money in amounts of 1 million or 2 million yen. When they learned that Father was the ultimate source of the funds, they began coming directly to him and demanding money which they said was for the Resident Association. Father wasn't sure how much he could trust what the Russians said, but if he didn't comply with their demands they would simply go to the Resident Association. In any case, the Soviets had no legitimate rationale; they just took what they could. Realizing it was a hopeless case, that the Soviets would never be satisfied, he decided to act as a bulwark on behalf of the Association and agreed to GPU demands.

Yet even Father didn't have unlimited resources. And the number of people under his wing kept growing. Some of the workers who had taken their leave and gone back to their hometowns returned, saying they couldn't make a living back home. Father accepted almost anyone who said they were experiencing hard times.

One day five men who said they were former Japanese soldiers came looking for work. They didn't have a place to stay and asked Father if he could provide them with space to bed down. The dorm and company housing were full to capacity, so it was decided they would spend the nights on the second floor where the family living area was. We children became attached to them and referred to them as our older brothers. Father gave them a warm welcome and expressed his gratitude for their efforts on behalf of the country.

Then one day one of the five came to Father and said he had something serious to discuss.

"And what would that be?" asked Father.

The man went on to say that, in actual fact, the five of them belonged to a gang of thieves made up of some three hundred former Japanese soldiers who had their base in a former Japanese barracks in a place called Luyuan, northwest of Changchun. They planned, in collusion with people both inside and outside of Shinkyo, to raid the company. The five of them had been sent ahead to study the layout of the place.

"I had heard Shinkyo was defenseless, but that very defenselessness has given me second thoughts. Rather than suspecting our motives, you treated us kindly, and you have worked hard to help displaced wanderers like us. I didn't take up this way of life because

I wanted to. It's because of the war, that's why things turned out like this. I feel thoroughly ashamed."

To prove he was telling the truth, he said that there was gunpowder and firearms hidden in the factory and the medicine storehouse, and that Father should check for himself.

When Father looked into it, it was just as the man had said. Ammunition, pistols, and rifles emerged in troves from the places he had mentioned. Father was aghast. The possession of firearms was illegal, and if the GPU got wind of it, he could face a firing squad. Late at night that very day, everything was consigned to the bottom of a nearby pond. The fact that Shinkyo was no longer as rich as rumored might have been a lifesaver.

If he raised the price of Giftol, money could be made, without a doubt. But to Father Giftol was like a living thing. He had created it in his search for truth. Thus he had no intention of raking in profits from it. But on the other hand, to meet the demands of the Soviets and to continue to provide aid to the refugees, there was no end to the money he needed.

It was at this juncture that an unintended helping hand appeared.

During the war Father had received an order from the Kanto Army. It directed him to manufacture the amino acid cystine. "We hear cystine promotes muscle growth. The idea is to make the ground troops stronger and show up the navy. Under no circumstances should this be divulged to anyone connected with the navy. The development of cystine injections should be carried out in the utmost secrecy."

This was the gist of the order issued to Father by the Kanto Army ground forces.

At the time Father wondered if Japan could win the war with this kind of thinking. If the army believed that cystine could promote physical strength, there was no need to keep it secret from the navy. Why couldn't all the armed forces use it? He had heard that there was fierce competition between the army and navy, but if they were going to fight among themselves over something as trivial as this, how could they hope to emerge victorious in the war? Reading the Kanto Army's request, he felt a shiver go down his spine.

But neither Father nor anyone else could turn down a request from the Kanto Army. Following the instructions that it be made as cheaply as possible, instead of trying chemical synthesis he decided to treat hydrolyzed human-hair waste, and he therefore strove to produce a crystal deposition. With time he succeeded in obtaining good crystals and in creating a water-soluble solution of generally insoluble cystine. He delivered the 2cc ampoules of the cystine injection to the Kanto Army. With the end of the war and the disbanding of the Kanto Army, there was no particular need to keep cystine secret.

In the course of time, talk of cystine leaked out from the factory workers, and was whispered from mouth to mouth as if it were somehow a top secret. The word was that "Shinkyo has produced a medicine that's wonderfully effective against typhus and cholera."

At the time typhus and cholera were running rampant. All the refugee camps in Changchun were filled to the brim with refugees from the north who had been abandoned by the Kanto Army or Japanese who had evacuated to places near the Korean border and then returned to Changchun. Typhus and cholera were widespread among them. How cystine got into their hands is uncertain, but a number of these afflicted people got hold of some of the ampoules of cystine that Father had provided the Kanto Army and injected themselves. They reported that the results were very positive. This, among other things, fed the rumor mill.

Following this, Chinese began showing up at Shinkyo Pharmaceuticals asking to buy some cystine. At first Father was hesitant to do so. "It wasn't especially made for typhus or cholera," he explained. But the demands were so insistent, and Changchun city hall even asked him to increase production, that he ended up making 5cc ampoules.

They sold like wildfire.

When the seller is hesitant to sell, those who succeed in making a purchase return happily home as if they have just won a hard-earned trophy. This makes other people even more eager to buy. A strange phenomenon, indeed.

One day a man showed up who said he wanted to buy Shinkyo's entire stock of cystine. From the looks of him, he was apparently the leader of a gang of bandits. He said that almost all of his men had fallen to typhus or cholera.

Father felt sorry for him and told him out of kindness: "The truth is, cystine wasn't particularly made to treat typhus or cholera."

Contrary to Father's expectations, this just made the man angry.

"You think I'm a fool or something? How can you sell to others and not to me? Isn't my money good enough for you?"

The man whipped out a dagger and plunged it into a block of wood in front of Father. At almost the same instant several more bandits rushed into the room, all dangerously wielding knives or pistols. Father had grown used to being threatened, but he decided that further rejection of the man's demands would just lead to trouble. That it would be better to give him what he wanted. Father got out all available stock and handed it over. The man paid up, every last cent, loaded up his trophies on a horse-drawn wagon, and left with a satisfied look on his face.

This incident spurred sales of cystine even further, much to Father's chagrin. They continued until August of the following year, 1946, when the first case of cholera appeared at Shinkyo.

Meanwhile, this illegitimate child of the Kanto Army filled the coffers of Shinkyo Pharmaceuticals, and as a result saved the lives of many refugees and thus changed the destiny of any number of people.

* * * * *

On November 25, 1945, the army of the Nationalist People's Party (Guomindang) entered Changchun. Basically, it was a small makeshift unit created from Chinese remnants of the Manzhouguo Army just before Japan's defeat. The citizens of Changchun referred to it as the Central Army or Local Central Army.

After a brief interrogation, Shinkyo Pharmaceuticals was requisitioned by the Nationalist government, and as of December 1 became the First Manufacturing Depot of Changchun City, Father being named its leading technician. Since the pharmacists of the major pharmaceutical companies had already been making their patented and principal medicines at Shinkyo, the new company could provide almost any type of medication. The profits, however, all went to the government, and Father was paid a salary.

Nationalist sentries were placed around Shinkyo on a twenty-four-hour basis and continually patrolled the grounds of the factory. Thereafter, the plundering and looting by the Soviets in the name of requisition came to a halt.

Among the Nationalist soldiers were some Japanese and Koreans, and although they were not very neatly dressed, most of them were very friendly. They didn't look particularly soldierly, and in fact many of them carried an extra set of plain clothes into which they could quickly change if the military situation turned to their disadvantage, enabling them to mix in with the civilian population. Although they were armed, never once did they threaten or menace anyone. They thought highly of Father.

That winter the number of large, two-wheeled man-drawn carts on Xing-an Boulevard suddenly became conspicuous. They were headed for the Dafangshen public cemetery in a northwestern suburb of Changchun. On the bed of the wagons were piled heaps of almost naked bodies, covered with straw mats. Perhaps because they were frozen stiff, their arms and legs stuck out from the wagons like the branches of a tree. They were being carted off because the grounds around the refugee camps were already full of corpses. We heard that more and more of these bodies were those of Japanese, who, hoping at least to save their children before dying themselves, had left them in the custody of Chinese as they fled from the Soviet army or after they had arrived in the refugee camps. Whenever these wagons passed by, Mother would quickly draw the curtains over the frosty windows, trying to keep the sight from the eyes of her children. No one would have thought then that three years later we would join their number.

In February of 1946 the number of Russian soldiers suddenly diminished, and in April the GPU headquarters across the street was abandoned, leaving Changchun devoid of a Soviet presence.

* * * * *

While the Soviet army was there, the Asian population formed a kind of nucleus.

The Soviets were so ruthless in their treatment of Japanese residents that feelings of sympathy arose among the Chinese and Koreans, outweighing their hatred of Japan. In time the Soviets began looting the Chinese and Koreans as well, giving them good reason to hate the Russians.

Among the factory workers there were such voices as this:

"It took a long time, but it was we Chinese who won back our land from the Japanese. It was we Chinese who did it. The Russians, the Big Noses (*dabizi*), hardly fought at all, but they made off with the booty of war in Manzhouguo. Japanese came to China and built a lot of factories. We worked in those factories. Those factories are permeated with our sweat. They are permeated with the sweat of Japanese too. But they don't have one drop of Russian sweat. The Japanese took our land; the Russians took our things. What is taken and who takes it is different, but the victims are always we Chinese."

Among the workers were some people like this, who condemned

both Russia and Japan equally. Anti-Russian feelings existed side by side with the hatred of the Japanese army and the people who worked for the Japanese. However, as long as the Soviets were there, the Asians were intricately bound together in being anti-Russian.

Once the Soviet presence was removed, it became very clear how weak, ephemeral, and superficial that bond had been.

The Asian link began slowly to dissolve, and a chilly atmosphere that was more convoluted and complex then the original bond began to course through the Asian population.

The Chinese split into two groups, as did the Koreans. The splinter groups then came together to form a new nucleus and began to gather energy in ways we had no knowledge of.

In time some of the Chinese and Koreans working in the factory quit and left the company. The factory was enveloped in a shroud of silence and undefinable tension.

One day Father said to Mother, "We have to keep on our toes. The Eighth Route Army may soon launch an attack."

The Eighth Route Army?

Hearing this, I felt a chill run through my body. Grownups referred to the Eighth Route Army as Communist bandits (*gongfei*). Most Chinese in Changchun were terrified of them. While I didn't really understand what was going on, I had heard that the Eighth Route was more frightening than the Kanto Army.

Are they scarier than even the Soviet soldiers? What kind of faces do they have? Are they carrying mandolins? Are they going to say, "Hand over your money"? What is going to happen to us next?

It wasn't long before the answers to these questions arrived wearing hideous faces. Just how hideous, just how terrible, just how awful, would take years and years to be fully brought home to me.

* * * * *

On April 14, 1946, the eerie atmosphere was finally broken by distant gunfire. The sound came from the northwest and southwest of Changchun and gradually grew nearer. Finally it became a confluence of violent noises like the simultaneous explosion of a myriad of firecrackers. It was as if two nuclei had collided and exploded in a burst of enormous energy.

"Quick! Take the children down into the basement," Father ordered.

Wearing a headband, Father rushed about the factory. He told the people on the first and second floors of the dorm and those in company housing to put straw mats up against the windows.

The diethyl ether storehouse was the place most in danger. Ether was flammable at even below-zero temperatures. In the crucible in the factory there were pharmaceuticals in the process of being made that contained ether. If these ignited, a sea of flames would result. Many precious lives would be lost. And in Changchun there was nowhere to take refuge. Father concentrated all his energy on seeing that the ether didn't ignite.

We children spent our days in the basement. The gunfire didn't let up even at night. Father got no sleep.

Gwaarrr!

The earth suddenly shook with the heavy reverberating sound of an earthquake. Was it a hand grenade? Was it a cannon? Had the ether storehouse exploded? Father, was he all right? If Father got blown to bits, what would we do?

The gunfire continued without break, rattling on like a sewing machine stitching people's lives together.

I could hear the sound of glass breaking somewhere.

I wanted to see what Father was doing. When there was a letup in the gunfire, I climbed up the basement steps and stuck my head out to see if Father was there. But before I could catch sight of him, a bullet hummed through the air. I hurried back down the steps. Silence fell.

The silence felt full of danger. In the tension-stricken air I held my breath, determined not to be fooled by its quiet deception.

The soundless intervals grew longer, and just as I was growing tired of doubting their reality, a bugle sounded in the distance. It was a long, gentle sound, as if a call for an end to the shooting.

Just then Father came down the basement steps.

"Ohhh, Father!"

We children ran to him and clutched at his body. We hung from his arms and clasped onto his back, happy to see him safe. From head to foot he was covered in black. His cheeks were sunken, his beard grown out.

"Father, you're alright then?"

"I'm alright. I hope I didn't cause you any worry. The ether storehouse made it through too."

Rubbing each of us on the head, he explained the situation to Mother.

"At first the Nationalist Army took up positions in the Inner City in the east and near Xinjing Station in the north. Rumor had it that the Eighth Route Army would attack there, but instead the main force suddenly attacked from the west. Then the Nationalist Army shifted its forces and tried to bolster its position there. The Eighth Route attempted a pincer movement from the northwest and Mengjiatun in the south. That's how Xing-an Boulevard seems to have become the center of the fighting. The street is littered with window glass and fragments of brick. Every building is riddled with bullet holes. The overhead electric wiring for the city is shredded and dangling down to the ground. But everything should be all right now. The center of the fighting has moved elsewhere. . . . Well, I think I'll just take a bath and rest up a bit."

Father loved a Japanese bath more than anything.

There was a boiler room and a bathing room in the basement. I also loved taking baths. It was the only time in the day that I could have Father to myself.

Just about the time of my first birthday, my little sister was born. Immediately I was separated from Mother. This somehow led me to seriously believe that it was Father who had given birth to me. People thought this was funny, and would teasingly ask me, "Hobo-chan, who gave birth to you?" Hobo-chan was my nickname.

I always gave the same answer, just as everyone expected. That's how I came to take baths with Father from an early age. The practice became a custom that continued long after.

Father liked to use some bath salts called Mutohappu. It had a faint yellowish-green color and a sulfurous aroma. When Mutohappu was put in the water, it spread out in a lovely pattern, filling my heart with Father's presence.

"Such cute little hands," he would say, placing my two hands on one of his. Then he would stroke the palms with his other hand. That's why I liked the basement so much.

But now, being closed up in the basement day after day, it was terribly boring. I wanted to see the sky! I wanted to see the setting sun!

One day, when Mother was busy looking after Father, I sneaked up to the second floor.

The first room on the second floor was at the top of the stairs on the right. This room had the best view of the setting sun. It was usually occupied by a young woman who was bedridden with tubercular myositis; she had come to our house seeking a place to stay. When the fighting in the city had escalated, she had been carried down to the basement, where she lay now.

Mother had strictly forbidden us to go into this room. Even though the young woman didn't have tuberculosis, Mother was afraid of us catching something. Since she was busy helping Father with his work, the care of us children was largely the responsibility of the maids. But having too many people who were responsible meant that virtually no one was. It wasn't difficult for me to skirt the maids' watchful eyes and go up to the forbidden room.

Behind the door to the room existed a fascinating multicolored world. Looking out the window revealed a sight of such beauty that it surpassed even that of a kaleidoscope. It was my red glass bead.

Quietly opening the shutters and looking out on the central garden, I could see the light of the sun on the other side of the curtained window, highlighting in red the weaving of the curtain's thick cloth.

Carefully, oh so carefully, I drew the curtain.

The frosted glass of the window, like granulated sugar, was aflame in a madder red, and in the bright diffused light of the rough surface I could see small golden angels dancing.

Steadying myself, I opened the window. And there it was!

My huge red bead in the sky!

I reached up with both hands toward it. I wanted to fly up on golden wings. If I reached out far enough, I could grasp it, my red glass bead, and hold it to my chest.

That's when it happened. The sound of a rapid series of gunshots hit my ears. In the same instant there was a thudding sound and I lost consciousness.

When I came to, my right elbow was bandaged, and I was lying in the basement. At first I didn't know what had happened. Then I remembered I had tried to squat down when I heard the gun go off. If they couldn't see my face, I couldn't be shot. With that in my mind, I had tried to draw the curtain. The window frame was just about chest high. My right arm was on the frame when it was hit by a stray bullet. The elbow was gouged out to the bone.

Father was taking a bath when he heard the shots. He immediately jumped out of the tub, grabbed some towels, and raced up the basement steps, naked as the day he was born.

When he got to the back garden, where the shots had come from, he saw a number of Eighth Route soldiers hiding on the left side of the ether storehouse. They were aiming their guns up toward the northeast, oblivious to the fact that Father was stark naked. Then, from the rooftop to Father's right, three guns fell to the earth. The Eighth Route soldiers lowered their weapons.

Up to the right from the direction Father had come, two Nationalist soldiers on a rooftop were holding up their hands in surrender, facing toward the western sun. Another of them had apparently already been killed. The Eighth Route soldiers had used the sun at their backs to good advantage. In effect, this meant that the ether storehouse had been protected by the Eighth Route soldiers and had emerged unscathed.

Some of the Nationalist soldiers in Changchun changed into plain clothes and disguised themselves as ordinary citizens; others quickly surrendered; the fighting was basically over. But some soldiers, trying to escape their fate, hid in civilian homes on Xing-an Boulevard, waiting for an opportunity to sneak away. To root out the last of these Nationalist soldiers, the Eighth Route Army began a search of each and every house on the boulevard.

It was about this time that the wife of a doctor taking refuge on the third floor of the dorm was hit between the eyes by a stray bullet and died instantly. It apparently happened when, thinking that things had quieted down, she was removing the tatami mats propped up against the window and took a peek outside. With the war coming to a close, the family had evacuated to Xiajiutai but were caught up in the riots there and had made their way back to Changchun. Before evacuating, the husband had been our family physician. Whenever he gave us children a shot, he would distract us by saying the nonsense words "Churuchuru dondon churu dondon" as he inserted the needle. That's how he came to be affectionately called Dr. Churuchuru Dondon. He was one of those people who kept his accounts separate from Shinkyo. His wife was an exceptionally beautiful woman.

With this last shot the street fighting came to an end, and the Eighth Route Army established complete control over Changchun.

Some time passed before I was discovered. Dr. Churuchuru

Dondon was busy with his wife, so it was Father who removed the bullet from my elbow. Again Father had missed his chance to get some sleep, and just as it seemed he might be able to do so, some thirty Eighth Route soldiers showed up at the house. They were members of the medical corps.

"We're not going to take anything," they said. They just wanted a place to stay and something to eat.

It was now the fifth day since Father had taken up his watch over the ether storehouse, without rest or sleep. His training as a wandering missionary after abandoning the rice business now stood him in good stead; his heart was strong. But he had reached a limit, and Mother forced him to get some sleep in the basement while she dealt with the terrifying Eighth Route soldiers herself.

They were all dressed in dirty, ragged clothes.

But as they had said, they didn't threaten us with their guns or ask for money. Much less did they, like the Soviet soldiers, persistently make sexual advances and ask, "Madam, sell? Madam sell?" As she always did when the Soviet soldiers came, Mother quickly hid the young women in the hallway closet on the second floor, but she was so reassured by the soldiers' attitude that she let the girls out of the closet. She led the soldiers up to the second floor, had the women cook a meal in the kitchen there, and prepared a room suitable for thirty people with the best futon. Once again the family made their beds in the basement.

This continued for two or three days before the soldiers decided to leave. When we went down to the first floor to see them off, we were struck speechless.

Instead of the ragged, filthy cotton garments they had come in, they had changed into clean, neat clothing. Most surprising of all, these clothes belonged to my father, brother, and the refugees staying with us, which had been kept in a closet. Even their socks were brand new. At the moment they were taking shoes out of the cabinet on the first floor and trying them on to see which fit.

The soldiers had broken their promise. They then proceeded to go into the medical room and began taking anything connected with the medical corps: chemical balances, emergency supplies, boxes of Ringer's solution, and glucose. They wrapped them in blankets taken from the second floor and tied them to the ends of their rifles with wire from my sister's *koto*, shouldering their guns as they left.

On the back of one of the departing figures could be seen the beautiful brocade tassel of the *koto*, gracefully swaying back and forth.

Mother suddenly had a premonition, and she rushed up to the second floor. What she saw there left her speechless.

Sister's *koto* was broken into shreds. In the kitchen the canned food and portable provisions to meet the needs of more than a hundred people had disappeared, down to the last item. Father's large household shrine had been smashed to bits. All the damask futons had been soiled by urine and feces.

With tears in her eyes Mother gathered up the soldiers' lice-infested clothes and burned them in an oil drum.

That very same day Father was taken off to the office of public security. As the leading technician of the First Manufacturing Depot under the Nationalist city government, he was naturally presumed to have collaborated with the Nationalists in manufacturing pharmaceuticals and was interrogated on that subject. However, he was soon released and came home in great spirits.

He told Mother, "There are some very impressive men in the Eighth Army. I've taken a liking to their way of thinking. The medics who came here were farmers without proper training, and I received an apology and was asked to forgive them. Mother, if you can, please excuse their behavior this time."

In effect, Father apologized to Mother on behalf of the medics.

The next day and the day after that, people from the security office came to look over Shinkyo's books and tour the factory, and as a result Shinkyo was taken over by the Communist Party and given the name First Pharmaceutical Depot of Changchun City. In reality, the only change was that "Manufacturing" had been replaced by "Pharmaceutical." As the leading technician, Father was essentially made responsible for supplying medication to the Eighth Army.

Then one day a horse-drawn wagon showed up carrying a number of Eighth Route soldiers. "The commander has died," they said. "He was a very important person, and we want to give him a proper burial. For the accompanying banquet we need a lot of sugar. We'd want all the sugar you have."

So saying, they filled up the wagon in the blink of an eye.

In his dealings with the Public Security Office Father came into contact with many senior army officers, and he knew their usual way of doing business. Something was wrong here. The difference in attitude was too great.

"If you're going to do this, give me a receipt," Father told them. That wasn't necessary, they replied.

"That won't do," Father said. "This is materiel to be delivered to the city government. I can't let you take it without a proper receipt. Until you provide one, I can't let you go."

Holding out his arms, Father stood in front of the wagon, a receipt slip in one hand.

A curious crowd began to gather.

"What's that? Anyone disobeying army orders gets shot, you hear," a soldier on horseback shouted, unholstering his pistol.

"Ah, go ahead and shoot," Father shouted back. "Every bottle, every single gram of sugar, is reported to the city. If a whole wagon of sugar disappears, I'll get shot anyway. It's just a matter of when. Go ahead, shoot!"

The murmuring crowd suddenly grew quiet, holding its breath, watching to see what would happen next. Every eye was pinned on this mortal game. Witnesses were many. It would be difficult to deny what transpired.

The soldier on horseback grabbed the slip from Father's hand with a look of disgust and wrote his name and the name of his unit, returning it to Father.

Father took the receipt to the Communist Public Security Office to have it verified. Just as he had thought, there was no soldier by that name in the Eighth Route Army, and no commander had died. Immediately a warrant was issued throughout Changchun, but it was too late. The culprits had vanished into thin air. It was a new type of banditry making use of the name of the Eighth Route Army.

The security office found this situation intolerable. The next day they sent a soldier to stand permanent guard at our house.

When this young Eighth Route soldier laughed, his eyes became as thin as a thread, and he was very friendly. His name was Zhao. He hung a rifle from his shoulder, a pistol from his hip, and carried three hand grenades. He spoke good Japanese. Now we had a sentry, and a twenty-four-hour watch was kept on the factory.

Zhao told me a lot of things.

"Our flag, the *hong qi*, is colored in red. Do you know what that red stands for?

What came to my mind was the setting sun, but I didn't say anything, just kept looking at him intently.

"It's the color of blood."

That gave me a start. How disgusting!

"You see, it's the blood of the people, that color. It's dyed in the color of the people's blood who fought for the revolution. You also lost blood in the fighting this time. I feel really bad about that. But this is a fight to free the Chinese people. It's a fight for the great revolution. You didn't fight with a gun, but still you're a soldier.

"You're a little hero, a *xiaoyingxiong*.

"You can think of your blood as being part of that red. You can think that you helped dye the *hong qi*. That makes you one of us. A comrade. You understand?"

I didn't really understand, but I realized that Zhao was trying to cheer me up. And that was enough.

Zhao also liked the sunset.

With his rifle resting on his shoulder, he would sit by the window in the waning light, sometimes whistling a tune for me. The melody was sorrowful, but it had something beautifully grand about it. His eyes were perfectly clear. At times like this I could think of Zhao as a friend and companion. But on the other hand, I also felt that I was somehow losing the setting sun; that it no longer belonged to me alone.

Zhao also told me, "The sun is the Communist Party. The sun is the great comrade Mao Zedong. Just like the sun always rises, Mao Zedong will rise shining in the sky and make us all happy. You know Mao Zedong, don't you?"

I didn't know him. I had never heard the name before.

The setting sun was mine. It was my glass bead. The setting sun was my world; it had to be. The idea that some man named Mao Zedong would be part of that world . . .

My glass bead had to be pure, transparent, and red. Otherwise, there would be no room in it for me, no room for myself.

In fact, though, from the moment when I had reached out to the setting sun and been shot in the arm, the glass bead that so enraptured my soul had lost its perfect brilliance. The nebulous future I had seen looking through that glass bead now came to be shrouded in a disturbing shadow.

*****

As mid-May came and went, the Chinese and Korean workers began to grow restless, and one after another left the factory. Even Zhao looked as though he might up and leave at any minute.

On the evening of May 22, an Eighth Route Army officer arrived with a cart and a dozen or so soldiers following behind. The officer was a big, burly man. He had clean-cut features and an intelligent face. Father was pleased to see him, thinking, "The Eighth Route Army has some pretty imposing men in its midst."

His name was Lin Feng, and he then held the eminent position of secretary to the Changchun City Committee of the Communist Party, the most important man in the city. He would later become a standing member of the Northeast Bureau of the Central Committee of the Communist Party and, after the new government came into being, a member of the Central People's Government Committee.

This was the man who was now standing before us, someone whom Father was apparently on friendly terms with. At the age of five I was meeting a future member of the Central Committee of the Communist Party.

Lin Feng and Father shook hands in a friendly way.

"We'll be leaving Changchun today. I have come to say goodbye," he said. "By the way, Doctor, I wonder if you could spare some of your Giftol."

His face looked rather tense, and I noticed that he had referred to Father rather formally as "Doctor."

"Please take as much as you need. If it will be of any help, you can take it all."

"I really appreciate it. I won't forget your kindness."

After filling the cart with Giftol, Lin handed Father some military scrip. Tomorrow, with the army gone, it would not be worth the paper it was printed on. Father knew that, but he still appeared happy to receive it, and Lin, who was also aware of that fact, was happy to repay Father in some form or other. They said nothing for a moment, just looked intently at one another.

We'll definitely be coming back, though," Lin finally said. "Please wait for that day. If you are ever in one of the liberated areas and have any trouble, please show this. Anyone should be happy to help you out."

On a piece of cloth Lin wrote his name and rank and stamped it with a large square seal just below his signature. Lin later served as secretary to Liu Shaoqi, president of the People's Republic of China, who was later jailed during the Cultural Revolution (1966–76). Liu was well known as a great reader, and it may have been his reading, I hear, that brought about his downfall.

At that time, we had in our possession a decorative screen that had once belonged to the Empress Dowager Cixi. It was composed of six panels and was almost two meters in width, made of jade, agate, coral, and ivory. In the rioting and looting after the end of the war, the screen had apparently been stolen from the Shenyang Palace or Emperor Puyi's court. One day a Chinese man pulling a large cart stacked with goods showed up at the Shinkyo factory. "I copped these from the Shenyang Palace," he said. "They're all of the highest quality and worth a lot, but no one is willing to pay the price I'm asking. Would you be interested?" Father bought the screen at the asking price, thinking he would return it to the Chinese government, and the thief threw in a number of hanging scrolls for free.

As long as the Nationalist government was under Soviet control, it couldn't entirely be trusted. However, Lin Feng could be, so Father kept the screen in safekeeping until Lin's return. Lin was very pleased at this gesture, but said at the moment he didn't have the means of transporting it, and Father should keep it for the time being.

Mounting his horse, Lin once again said, "We will come back. We will come back. Goodbye. Goodbye and farewell."

Looking back any number of times, Lin headed up Xing-an Boulevard until he disappeared in the distance.

* * * *

The next morning there was not a single Eighth Route soldier left in Changchun.

The following month, on May 24, the regular Nationalist Army entered the city.

These troops were said to be an elite group that had fought in Burma and were furnished with the latest American weaponry.

Different from any other soldiers we had seen, they all wore brand-new uniforms. Their treatment of my father was also different.

Two or three days after the arrival of the Nationalists, when factory workers were just getting up, a group of soldiers came thundering into the factory in heavy boots. Almost immediately, as if they had it all planned out, every working area and every room was occupied by fifty or so armed soldiers.

"Don't move! Raise your hands!"

Everyone in the factory froze as they were; everyone raised their hands.

The officer who appeared to be in charge immediately began searching the premises, along with two other soldiers. They checked the pharmaceutical storehouse and were just about to start on the ether storehouse when Father cried out, "Don't go in there! That area contains ether. It's dangerous if not handled properly."

"Ah, so you're the main Communist collaborator here, is that it? Restrain him!"

Father's hands were tied behind his back.

"You've got weapons stashed here, right? Or you're hiding some Communist bandits. Search the place!"

"You can't do that! This is a pharmaceutical factory, with many dangerous chemicals. One false step and we'll all be blown sky-high, including you. If you are going to look around, at least see that all the fires are out. I won't cause any trouble—just untie me."

At this time there was hardly any space left for making medicine, and so a kiln had been set up in one of the ether storehouse's inner gardens.

The officer reluctantly freed Father. There were some fires that had to be put out, and others that had to be kept going. Taking care of each, Father showed them the ether storehouse. Again his hands were tied behind his back, and he was led off, prodded by a rifle, to who knew where.

The factory was now surrounded by about a hundred soldiers.

All of us children were sent off to a room upstairs, watched over by an armed guard. One hour passed, and then another. Then night came. Meanwhile, Mother and several other women were confined to the kitchen where they made rice balls and pancakes, and served coffee and tea for all the soldiers. The soldier guarding us children, dressed in an American-made uniform that was too big for him, the sleeves rolled up, was obviously enjoying the polished rice balls, his cheeks bulging out like a squirrel's. Even this soldier, who had been behaving as if he belonged to a superior race, enjoyed white rice as much as we did. It seemed so strange, the combination of arrogance and white rice. What do they usually eat, I wondered. Their skin glowed; their hair was glossy. Their rifles, uniforms, and belts were all brand new, perfectly clean. They were different from any soldiers I had ever seen before. They must be awfully rich, I thought. They must be awfully powerful.

When Father was taken away, he kept his head high and proud. He had resisted at first, but in the end was led off by these power-ful-looking soldiers. He might be beaten with a whip; he might be tortured by fire. In fact, maybe they had already killed him; maybe he was already dead. One after another, such ominous thoughts crossed my mind. But in the middle of the night Father was released and came home, and the stakeout on the factory was lifted. The factory workers admitted that they thought that father, or Dr. Okubo as they called him, was done for this time; some had worried how they were going to make a living without him.

Some of the neighbors had whispered among themselves: "Even the great Dr. Okubo won't be able to get out of this one. They'll kill him for sure."

However, contrary to such speculation, Father wasn't abused in any way, and in the end the pharmaceutical factory was restored to its status as the First Manufacturing Depot of Changchun City, with Father as leading technician. There was some confusion about what the new name of the company should be, but in the end it was decided to keep the original one. This happened only after the stake-out on the factory had been lifted and the heavy-handed Nationalist investigation completed.

"What a bunch of good-for-nothings," Father said. "They must have too much money, time, and manpower on their hands."

Father disliked the arrogance of the Nationalist soldiers. He much preferred the Eighth Route Army with its shabby uniforms but friendly faces. The Eighth's devotion to the people held something in common with Father's idealism. Covered in sweat and oil from work, Father stood with the Eighth against established authority.

Finally, the news that all Japanese residing in Changchun had been waiting for spread excitedly throughout the city.

This was in July 1946. The repatriation to Japan had begun.

Mother wanted to return to Japan as soon as possible. What with one army entering the city and then replaced by another, each change brought its own troubles, and each time the company name was altered. Mother had had more than enough. The problem was, the Nationalist government was not likely to let Father leave.

China still had an enormous number of drug addicts, and drug addiction could be the ruin of a nation. Whichever party came into power, Giftol played an important role. Moreover, it was also a source of income. Here the American-clad and -armed National-ist government unilaterally raised the price of Giftol and put it on a sliding scale. The Nationalists planned to make a profit from the requisitioned factory.

As a matter of course, Father was forbidden to leave the country, and his new status was registered in a formidable nomenclature consisting of as many as twenty-five Chinese characters. It essentially meant that the individual in question was to be detained in China under the supervision of the Changchun branch of the Chinese National People's government.

Changchun's Japanese residents were divided up into blocks

according to the town councils (*chokai* in Japanese) comprising the neighborhood associations (*tonarigumi*), and block by block Japanese began leaving the city and heading south at the rate of about 1,500 people a day. Then, just as it was the turn of the block that included Xing-an Boulevard, something unexpected happened. A woman staying with us came down with cholera. This person had evacuated with her family from Haerbin, which was under Communist control, thinking that it would be easier to repatriate from Changchun than northern Haerbin. The woman in question was immediately isolated, but unfortunately my sister-in-law contracted the disease. Thinking that she would like something cold to eat, we fed her chilled tofu, but that seemed to make her worse. In just a few hours she got as shriveled up as an old woman.

She had one last request: "Mother, please look after Takashi. Please look after Takashi." Lying on a stretcher, she used what seemed to be her last ounce of energy to ask Mother to take care of her son, who had just celebrated his birthday. Two days later she was dead.

We were not the only ones to suffer, however. Because of the outbreak of cholera the repatriation of the whole block containing Xing-an Boulevard was put off for one month.

Moreover, returnees were limited to what they could take with them, one rucksack per person. Anything that would not fit into a rucksack had to be sold, meaning that returnees had very few possessions. Also, an official notification was circulated stating that if a person was found to have jewelry or any other precious items, everyone in the block would be prevented from boarding the ship and forced to do manual labor as punishment. The amount of money that one could have on one's person was limited to a thousand yen. Owing to the outbreak of cholera, everyone in the block would somehow have to survive on what they had for another month.

A person representing the block came to see Father. "I expect you to take responsibility for this," he said.

"I'll do my level best," Father replied.

Father ended up providing one month's living expenses for everyone on the block.

On the other hand, my sisters and I became the objects of some harassment. "Because of you we won't be able to go back to Japan," other children said, and no longer welcomed us in their games.

As it turned out, our home was not the only source of cholera. All the camps where the refugees from Haerbin were housed eventually broke out in a mass infection, and all repatriation activities were halted for a month. Thus even if cholera had not broken out in our home, all Japanese in Changchun were fated to be delayed in their departure. Ignoring this point, however, Father continued to pay the living expenses of the people on Xing-an Boulevard until repatriation was resumed.

* * * * *

It was about this time that Changchun's Japanese Resident Association was renamed the Changchun City Japanese Resident Remedial Liaison Office. The bank books and securities that Father had at the end of the war, and still possessed, were all requisitioned by this Liaison Office. Real estate as well, and the site of the future factory at Dadonggou, were all appropriated. At the currency rate at the time of Japan's defeat, the monetary value was estimated to be about 20 million yen. Given that a fighter plane was said to cost 120,000 yen, this was a considerable amount of money. Aside from those of the Shinkyo Pharmaceutical Company, among the receipts in the Liaison Office were some that referred to companies we had never heard of before, such as a company involved in distribution of medicine in Manchuria, a company dealing with veterinary medicine, a company dealing in glass instruments and materials. Given the fact that below the company's name in each case was father's name, Takuji Okubo, could it be that he was managing all of them?

The names of the persons responsible for the receipts are given as Toshio Hirashima or Hiroshi Okudaira. I was told to take particular care of these receipts since Japan might be able to retrieve their value later as overseas investments. However, perhaps because the receipts were in the custody of Japanese Resident Associations in Changchun, Haerbin, Siping Jie, Qiqihaer, and Dalian, they apparently never made their way back to Japan.

During the repatriation all of the refugees staying with us finally left. Even Dr. Churuchuru Dondon departed, taking with him the urn containing the remains of his wife. The members of the Luyuan gang came to say their farewells to Father. Most of the factory workers also left, but some were detained and some decided of their own volition to stay. Those who decided to stay figured they would not be able to find work if they returned to Japan, and it was much safer to stay with Father, who had the protection of the Nationalist army. With this first repatriation from Changchun, the Japanese population dropped from 200,000 to 6,000.

With so many people now gone, their houses stood desolate and forlorn, only their nameplates showing that Japanese had once lived there.

"Rags! I buy rags!" The calls of Chinese dealers in secondhand clothing, meant for the ears of departing Japanese, were no longer heard. It was now approaching the end of October 1946.

In November the name of Father's company was changed from First Manufacturing Depot of Changchun City to Jilin Province Hygienic Supplies Depot.

In April 1947 I entered Changchun School as a first-year student at the elementary level. The school had been established on October 1, 1946, for the children of detained Japanese and had had elementary and intermediate divisions. The main school was on Longli Street, with two campuses on Anda Street and in Jiye. I went to the school on Anda Street, which was called the White Chrysanthemum Campus. With Datong Square behind me, I would walk down

Xing-an Boulevard to Xing-an Bridge and turn to the left there to find the school on the left side of the street. Entering the school, there was a hall paved with shiny stone. Immediately on the left was my classroom. Further down the hall on the left was a door leading outside. Going through it, you came up against a tall concrete wall. In the narrow passage between the wall and the school was a toilet for male students. The boys competed to see who could reach the highest on the wall, shouting out with glee as they directed their pee skyward.

My homeroom teacher was a tall, handsome man. When he raised an arm while standing on the podium, it seemed his hand would go right through the ceiling—he was that tall.

My memories of this class are enveloped in a purple cloud. During drawing class we were told to draw anything we wanted, so I drew a balloon flower. The teacher gave me an A+, and I was so proud that I showed it to my mother.

"What a beautiful flower," she said. "I really love the color purple. When I was still a schoolgirl, I and some friends formed a cheer-leading group called the Purple Squad and had a lot of fun. I some-times acted as the leader of the group."

Mother's eyes had a nostalgic look as she talked about the color purple. As it happened, in class there was a boy in the row to my left whose name was Purple. Behind him there was a girl whose name was also Purple. They were brother and sister. They both had tuberculosis and had whitish complexions—in fact, almost deathly pale—and they were both very skinny. Apparently because of the tu-berculosis the sister had to stay back a year. She rather proudly said that this was the second time for her to be in the first grade.

* * * * *

It happened one afternoon just after the rain had let up.

My second oldest sister and I had just left the school, along with a friend of hers. When we reached Xing-an Boulevard, we found it inundated in water. It was as if the street had become a muddy river, flowing on and on, as far as the eye could see. There were no cars in sight. Giggling and frolicking, we went out into the middle of the street, splashing along in our rain boots. Making patterns in the water, we started down the boulevard toward Datong Square. As our boots slid along the watery ground, they made multilayered waves. As we moved ahead, many little semicircular waves would be created by the tips of our boots, each wave attempting to catch up with the earlier ones, producing even bigger waves that continued to spread. The waves had us as their starting point and spread out behind us in an acute angle. When my waves got close to the waves of the other two, they would break up. All three of us wanted to get out in front of the others, and we slid our boots along the ground as fast as we could.

Since I was only in the first grade, I couldn't keep up. And if I fell just a little behind, the waves created by Sister and her friend would come and ruin mine. When my waves broke up, they made a little whirlpool, and in that whirlpool a little leaf appeared and swirled around and around. It must have fallen during the rainstorm. The leaf had a fine luster to it, still fresh and light green. When I stood still, the whirlpool would vanish, and the leaf would ride on one of the waves left by Sister and advance toward me.

Kerplosh! I stomped by boot down as hard as I could. The wave I made won, and the leaf sank beneath the surface, and then came up again, floating away. As I stood watching, the leaf got on a big wave created by Sister and her friend and once again came unsteadily toward me, rocking from side to side. Somehow I began to feel sorry for it.

No matter what was done to it, the leaf didn't fight back; it just rocked from side to side, going between the waves, advancing before them, then following after them, forever meandering.

How far would it go, rocking from side to side, that little leaf? I just hoped that no one would step on it, that no one would crush it. For the longest time I kept watching it, rocking and meandering between the waves.

Then all at a once I realized that I was all alone in the middle of that river.

I became deathly afraid, afraid that I would be left there forever, all by myself. This fear entered deep down into my heart, so deep and so ingrained that it would never leave, not ever.

Calling out Sister's name I began frantically running. She was far ahead of me, but I could hear her shouting something in the distance. And I could see her friend walking near the side of the road. The center of Xing-an Boulevard was for the passage of cars, either side of which was a road for carts and wagons, and outside that was a path for pedestrians. On either side of the cart path was a line of trees. This area was not paved, and here and there you could see where bomb shelters had been dug in the earth. The road itself was built up in the middle and so water had not accumulated there. But the sides of the road inclined downward, and so whenever it rained, there would be an immediate buildup of water. With a heavy rain, muddy water would flow into the bomb shelters until it was no longer possible to tell where the entrance was. Needless to say, it was a dangerous area to be walking in.

Almost every child had been warned of this more than once. Sister was apparently shouting out that her friend should be careful, but the friend paid no attention whatsoever. Even ordinarily this friend was a bit of a showoff, and she hated losing out to anyone. In the game with the waves she took the lead from the very beginning. But maybe she got tired of that and wanted to do something even more amazing. She became bolder and went splashing into the dangerous area.

It was then that it happened. I heard a faint "Ah!" sound, and she suddenly disappeared from sight.

Both Sister and I stopped in our tracks. We were unable to utter a word. Time and space seemed to have frozen in that instant.

What should we do? What could we do? We somehow had to save her. Call for help—that was it. We had to call for help.

We noticed a Nationalist soldier sitting on a small chair on the pedestrian pathway, eating. Judging from the way he was smirking in our direction, he had been watching us. We called out for all we were worth, the sound ripped from our throats.

"Help, please help! A friend has fallen into a bomb shelter!"

The soldier didn't even lay down his chopsticks. Instead he tipped the bowl he was eating from to show us what was inside.

Sister and I called out again hysterically. "Oh, hurry, hurry! Our friend has fallen into a bomb shelter!"

But the soldier didn't come. He just smirked at us and continued eating.

She'll die! She'll die for sure! Maybe she has sunk to the bottom of the shelter, dragged down by the heavy book pack on her back. Maybe that's what keeps her from coming up to the surface. Maybe she has gotten stuck under the ceiling of the shelter and can't float up to the entrance.

Just at that moment, our friend's umbrella floated up. It must have been filled with air.

We shouted her name. We shouted her name again and again. We shouted as loud as our lungs could bear.

There was no answer. Suddenly losing hope, we began to cry. Our continued shouting was swallowed up in tears.

It was then that the Nationalist soldier decided to help. He brought a long rakelike stick, which he dragged around inside the shelter. When he pulled her out, she was no longer breathing.

The soldier's face with its faint grin resembled that of Jiang Jieshi on the posters plastered throughout the city.

Around this time the Eighth Route Army had loosely encircled Changchun, and ordinary citizens were having trouble finding enough to eat. The Nationalist Army, on the other hand, was leading a life of ease thanks to American aid, and seemed to consider the common citizens' plight amusing. Any number of times I had seen Nationalist soldiers eating bowls of white rice topped with meat, and this out on the street as if to make a show of it. After the tragedy involving my sister's friend, I developed a hatred for the Nationalist Army and a disliking for Jiang Jieshi, who resembled the soldier who had refused to help until it was too late.

* * * * *

In the summer of 1947 the second repatriation of Changchun Japanese residents began. The railway as far as Shenyang had come under the control of the Eighth Route Army, so transportation would have to be done by army truck.

The Changchun repatriation was influenced by the request of various government agencies that a minimum number of foreign technicians be detained as a part of Nationalist policy. The plans for the second repatriation were set in place that spring, and the Nationalist government sent Chinese apprentices to the factory for technical training, with the idea that we would be repatriated after the transfer of technology had been completed. Almost all of the Japanese workers and technicians left the factory at this time to return to Japan.

The older glass craftsman who had barely escaped with his life from Xiajiutai was among those left behind. Largely bald, he was tough and wiry, a man of few words but whose face showed that he meant business. He had large scary eyes, one of which had turned white, maybe because he was always working in tremendous heat. When he was there, the atmosphere on the glass factory floor had a certain tension. He and my father, also bald, swarthy, and thin, would tour the factory in their long johns, peering into the red-hot crucibles. In profile, their faces were so serious, dripping in sweat, that not a single extraneous sound could be heard. The crucibles were makeshift things, holes dug in the ground five meters wide and three meters deep and lined with fire-resistant bricks. When the trainees were blowing the glass, bubbles would often appear in the process of serialization, causing the glass to burst. Wearing a pirate's headband as he rushed about the tension-filled factory floor to see that all was going well, Father looked for all the world like some kind of religious ascetic.

Eventually this old glass craftsman also left for Japan, leaving behind a man he had trained to take his place. At last, one and all, everyone was gone. The factory became a very lonely place, as if its spiritual fires had gone out. The Changchun School also vanished.

Now there were very few people out on Xing-an Boulevard, only the conspicuously dispirited and demoralized figures of Nationalist soldiers. The wall posters of the grinning Jiang Jieshi still stared down at us, but in some places the posters had become loose and torn, flapping in the autumn wind. Below one poster, I saw a dog that had lost its owner, its tail hanging down forlornly.

The sentries posted around the factory pulled their hands inside their much-too-long sleeves, coldly hunching their shoulders and sniffling their runny noses. Their American uniforms were, in the end, much too big.

In this deeply chilling atmosphere, a foreboding shadow was approaching Changchun. We had no idea of what was coming, no idea of what would soon befall us.

CHAPTER 2

Changchun: A City without Hope

In October 1947 the lights went out in Changchun. Gas was stopped. Water ceased flowing.

"Why, that's strange," said Father. "Maybe it's just a power failure. Or maybe Fengman Dam has been damaged, or has fallen into the hands of the Eighth Route Army."

"That means there is going to be more fighting here, then?" Mother asked, knitting her brows.

"Well, I don't know. The Commander said they would be coming back, for certain."

Father always referred to Lin Feng as the Commander.

However, the Eighth Route Army didn't come back. Gaining control of Fengman Dam, shutting off the electricity, gas, and water to Changchun, it had then surrounded the city and settled down for a prolonged siege.

This happened just as the factory was on the point of putting a new manufacturing system into operation, using the trainees sent by the Nationalist government. With its power cut off, the factory was virtually paralyzed, and the Chinese trainees and the two or three Japanese technicians at the factory stopped showing up for work. Moreover, the Nationalist government washed its hands of the factory. Until then, the Nationalists had sucked up all the factory's profits, leaving Father just enough to keep the factory going. From what he received, Father paid the salaries of the workers and the daily expenses of the family. From the moment the Nationalist government realized that the factory was not going to produce a profit, it cut off all relations, though it retained Father in his status as a detained technician.

Strictly speaking, since Father had been detained by a government agency that agency was obliged to guarantee his livelihood, whether his business was making a profit or not. Only that would make detainment worthwhile for the detainee. However, even though Father's source of income had been cut off, the Nationalist government did not offer him a penny in compensation, nor did it change his status.

Mother said, "Isn't it terrible! Just leaving us to fend for ourselves, and not even changing your status. If the electricity comes on, they'll be back in no time flat, siphoning off all the profit they can."

From the very beginning Mother had been against the idea of being detained. The fact is, she was pregnant. That's why she wanted to get away from the instability of life in Changchun and return to Japan. At the time Father apparently didn't know she was with child.

"They think that if they release me, I'll leave the city and join the Eighth Route Army. They want to make sure they still have access to Giftol."

Mother said, "No matter how hard it would have been, we should have returned to Japan when we had the chance. At the very least we should go to Nanjing like they promised."

During the second Changchun repatriation, when Father had been designated a compulsory detainee for the second time, the city mayor had pleaded with Father to stay on.

"We would really like you to stay on and continue manufacturing medicine. In a pinch I will see to it that you are taken to Nanjing by plane."

With that promise Mother was forced to give up her hopes of returning to Japan anytime soon.

"Let's wait a little longer," Father said. "The Eighth Route Army should be coming back pretty soon, and I promised the Commander I'd wait."

Father was expecting the Eighth Route Army to return to Changchun. He believed in Lin Feng.

But there was no movement on the army's part. Changchun became a gloomy, desolate desert, encircled by the Eighth Route Army, abandoned to what fate had in store for it, its sources of food cut off.

Still, at the beginning we managed to keep food on the table. It was Father's practice to maintain a stock of medicinal material that would last three years. That stock was still in the pharmaceutical storehouse. We could sell it off a little at a time; we could trade it for food.

At the time there were five Japanese families staying at the factory, including our own, twenty-three people in all. Among these people were those working at the factory and those using our facilities as a convenient place to stay. In any case, Father had to feed twenty-three mouths. We couldn't hope to continue living off medicinal stock forever. In order to earn an income Father tried various ways of making medicine without the proper manpower.

I wasn't exactly sure what he was making, but I saw him preparing small pills from lumps of creosote and other substances. Upstairs in the kitchen there was a line of vats that were apparently used to make bootleg alcohol. In exchange for pharmaceutical materials Father could procure some Chinese baijiu, and with a little tinkering he made drinks closely resembling Japanese sake and whiskey. For example, by soaking shavings from a cypress tree in baijiu he could produce the aroma of Japanese sake, and by adding black tea to baijiu he could produce the color of whiskey. The Nationalist Army was particularly fond of sake, and it wasn't suffering from a shortage of food. It turned out that instead of bartering medical materials for food, it was infinitely more advantageous to barter questionable sake. Father made the most of this cycle of trade.

The Nationalist Army was supplied with materiel by the United

States. Although Fengman Dam had been damaged, and the rail-roads around Changchun had all been made inoperable, there was still the air. The Nationalists could still be furnished with a rich amount of supplies by plane.

However, the ordinary citizens' supply routes for food had been completely severed. As Changchun had become increasingly urban-ized, agricultural products had increasingly come from outside the city. Sources within the city soon began to peter out. And with that, the prices shot up from one day to the next, and the value of cur-rency plunged.

Rumors began to circulate that people were dying of starvation.

Despite Father's valiant efforts, our daily life began to be af-fected. And with the approach of an early winter, heating became a problem.

Winters in Changchun are bone-chillingly cold. The tempera-ture can sink as low as minus 30°C. At the beginning we fed the boiler with wall panels and doors removed from the company houses and dorms vacated by departing Japanese. We tried conserving heat by shutting down the radiators in unused rooms, but no matter how tight we turned the valves on the radiators, that didn't compensate for the fact that five families were living in separate rooms. Finally Father suggested that all twenty-three people should live in one room. It was decided to make Father's room and Mother's room on the second floor into one space by removing the sliding partitions between them, and to build a Russian stove called a pechka. If the pechka were used not only for heating but also for cooking, it would prove doubly effective. However, one family, the Azumas, declined to move in with the others.

Mr. Azuma was Father's nephew. He had been in Korea during the war, but life there wasn't to his liking, so he came to Changchun to work in Father's factory. He was called up in an eleventh-hour con-scription just before the end of the war. He was stationed in Siping Jie (now Siping City) on the border between Jilin and Liaoning provinces when the war ended on August 15. He fell into the hands of the Soviet army and was being sent to Siberia as a forced laborer when his train passed through Changchun. He used that opportunity to escape and hide under another train until the one headed for Siberia had moved on. He then made his way to our house. Father thought highly of him and made him factory chief.

Father asked him straight-out, "Why don't you want to move in with the rest of us?"

"Well now, I'm sort of used to where I am," he replied.

"Don't talk nonsense. We all have to work together to overcome this crisis, right?"

"Well . . ."

"If you live off by yourself, that means using that much more fuel for heating. Now's the time to put our heads together and hold on until the Eighth Route Army comes. Let's give it all we have until then."

"Well now . . . living with you, Uncle, in the same room, that would be above my station, I think."

No matter what arguments Father presented, Mr. Azuma would counter with some implausible excuse. In the end, he remained where he was, in the company house behind the ether storehouse facing Xing-an Hutong.

Everyone but Father was perfectly aware of why Mr. Azuma was so adamant about not joining the others. But no, maybe Father knew better than anyone else.

Back when there were still many Japanese working at the factory, there were some who took advantage of Father's easygoing ways and filched medicine and material from stock and sold it to the Chinese, lining their own pockets. The biggest culprit of all in this respect was Mr. Azuma. Since he was factory chief, it was easy for him to cook the accounts for material and medicine. What he was doing amounted to petty theft, and was almost public knowledge, but he was Father's nephew and the factory chief, so no one informed on him. Still, everyone looked askance at his appalling behavior and, behind his back, referred to him as the "White Rat." "Rat" is Japanese slang for "thief," and since the faces of rats are not usually white, he came to be called the white-faced rat. Appropriately, Mr. Azuma had narrow slits for eyes and a pale complexion. Even though our sources of power were gone, even though the factory was facing a crucial moment, he still couldn't give up his old ways.

The first time I heard the words "white rat" was a little before the pechka was built.

I was in my brother's room, keeping warm at the brazier while playing with little Takashi, whose mother, my brother's wife, had died from cholera. The glass craftsman who had been enlisted to replace the old veteran came into the room. He was one of the few men still working in the factory.

Grinning, he gazed out into the inner garden and said, "Look, the White Rat is up to his old tricks."

"What—a white rat. You mean a mouse?" I had an image of a small white mouse.

"No, no. I mean a big white rat with a black head of hair. Want to see one?"

The glass craftsman motioned me over to the window. It was the same window where I had been shot in the arm by a stray bullet from the Eighth Route Army.

This room was my favorite place. From there I could see the beautiful setting sun; from there I could see the manifold colors of the sky, almost like looking through the eyehole of a kaleidoscope. It was this that brought me there. Yet there was another factor that drew me to that room, a much more dangerous one.

This room used to be my brother's, but he had been drafted in the last desperate conscription before the end of the war and was sent to Siping Jie, leaving the room empty. When the war ended it was occupied by a young woman with tubercular myositis. Though the room was officially off-limits, I popped in and out so often that the young woman became extraordinaryily fond of me. With the progression of her illness and her instinctive awareness of the limits of life, her affection became a bizarre obsession. Her desire to cling to life somehow became fixated on me. She doted on me and didn't want to let me go. Since I spent most of my time alone, I accepted her affection, though with some misgivings. Eventually she came to show me the wounds on her arms, and had me help in changing the dressing. Both arms bore lateral incisions filled with bloody pus.

When tuberculosis eventually spread to her lungs, Father had her admitted to what had formerly been the South Manchuria Railway Hospital. She died there just as I was starting elementary school. Before she passed away, however, she almost daily expressed a desire to see me shouldering my school book pack and asked that I be brought to the hospital. Mother was afraid of contagion and refused. But when the young woman said this would be her last earthly request, Mother finally gave in, and we met separated by a glass door, me with my book pack on my back.

When she saw me, she raised herself upright in bed and gazed fixedly at me, as if her life depended on it. After some moments she stretched out a trembling hand toward me and moved it through the air as if patting my head. Then, suddenly, she breathed out a deep sigh and burst into tears. Without taking her eyes off me, she continued to cry, tears running down her cheeks, seemingly forever. She died the next day.

With her passing, the room now became my brother's once again, and I found a good playmate in Takashi, his son. That's why I happened to be in the room when the glass maker came in. My brother was never very strong, and after being sent off to Siping Jie, his health deteriorated. That's the reason he had come back to Changchun and escaped being sent to Siberia. Thereafter he spend half his time in bed, the other half up and about.

Going to the window as directed by the glass craftsman, I peered out into the garden, only to see Uncle Azuma. He was energetically carrying boxes out of the pharmaceutical storehouse, while keeping an apprehensive eye on his surroundings. I thought he was really at work, and that the glass craftsman was referring facetiously to his quick movements when he called him a white rat.

"You're right," I said. "He does look like a lively little mouse."

"That's not it—don't be stupid. Don't you know anything?"

Thanks to this white rat, storehouse stock dwindled dramatically.

*****

With the coming of the new year in 1948, we began to hear the sound of firearms in the distance. Maybe the Eighth Route Army was coming. Maybe my old friend Zhao would be returning. We were all suddenly filled with expectation. However, the direction from which the sounds came remained basically the same, only the interval between them becoming shorter, reverberating far in the distance. Then, as the lunar New Year passed, the intervals became steadily longer, until the sounds finally vanished.

Sighs of disappointment came from every mouth.

"That wasn't just New Year's fireworks, I hope."

"Fireworks wouldn't go on for that long, would they?"

"Just when I was thinking that the electricity would come on again, that food would start coming in . . ."

There were even rumors that upper echelon Nationalist officers had escaped to Nanjing and Shanghai.

During this time the Eighth Route Army tightened its ring around Changchun, even making inroads into the city center, but then it suddenly came to a standstill. Changchun was once again abandoned to a cold, silent, dreary existence.

While the guns were reverberating, the feeling of apprehension was alleviated by the expectation that the Eighth Route Army would soon be coming. But once the guns had stopped, once we had lost the sense of hopeful expectation, all that was left was the terrible cold of Changchun, the terrible gloom.

Ice crystals were forming on the windows.

Here and there throughout the city, people began to die of starvation.

* * * * *

Little Takashi liked the pechka.

Maybe because my brother was not very strong himself, Takashi's growth was rather slow from the very beginning. He was slow to learn to speak and slow to take his first steps. Malnutrition seemed to have affected his legs, and he could walk only by holding onto something for support, although he was already two years old.

The pechka, sitting in the middle of the room, was soothingly warm, which Takashi liked. He would walk around it playing, patting its wall as he used it for support. I would sit in the back of the pechka, and Takashi would have fun sticking his head around the corner and shouting "Boo!"

Takashi and I got along particularly well after the pechka was built. Physically I wasn't very strong myself. Or maybe I should say, without my realizing it I had somehow grown weak. The wound on my right elbow from the gunshot wouldn't heal and was always oozing, and the palm of my left hand turned red, swelled up, and began to produce a dull pain.

It was about this time that I began to feel a general overall sluggishness. With the shortage of food and power, my condition worsened. My right elbow began oozing bloody pus, and there was a stabbing pain that seemed to come from deep inside my bones. The back of my left hand swelled up as tight as a drum, and one day the thin skin burst like a balloon. With an ordinary boil things would get better from this point on, with the affected area developing a scab. But that didn't happen this time, the wound refusing to heal over. The break in the skin was always full of blood and pus.

The wound in my arm looked exactly like that of the young woman's who had been so fond of me.

This realization filled me with dread. Had tuberculosis infected my right elbow? While healthy I had been stronger than the bacteria, but now they were becoming increasingly more powerful. My left elbow, the joint of my left arm, one after another various places began to swell up and turn red. I felt so sluggish and drained of energy that I spent most of my time sitting down. Takashi stuck by my side, always wandering around me.

One day Takashi began to act strangely.

Since the corners of the room tended to get cold, there were two or three braziers placed there. On this day I was leaning up against one of them, resting. Takashi came up and laid his hand on the edge of the brazier for support and laughed.

"Oh, Takashi," I said. I turned toward him and returned his laugh. Ordinarily he would next put his hand on my shoulder and then start walking tirelessly around the brazier, using it as a support. But not today. Today he lowered his head as if bowing to me and thrust it into the burning embers of the brazier. Some of the thin hair on his head crinkled up in the heat and burned in a small plume of smoke.

"Be careful! You'll burn yourself!" I cried out, but Takashi wasn't paying attention. He just raised his face and beamed at me. He even looked sort of proud, as if he'd done something wonderful. Then he started to do the same thing again.

"Takashi, stop that immediately," I shouted at him, but he just laughed and tried to do it again. When smoke rose from his burning hair, he lifted his head and laughed again. His small face was covered in wrinkles, his grin like that of a feeble old man. Even though he was laughing, the corners of his mouth didn't curl upward but sagged down.

A few days later he was no longer with us. His body was cremated on the iron plate over the crucible in the glass factory.

* * * * *

By now we had all become starved and emaciated. Our skin was deathly pale, almost transparent, and the veins stood out. Our noses were sharp and beak-like. Our eyes sunken, our bellies big and swollen.

The medical supplies in the pharmaceutical storehouse had dried up, completely depleted.

In the past the storehouse always held a lot *mizuame*, a type of corn syrup. *Mizuame* was a very profitable item for bartering and was actually quite nutritious, a valuable commodity. It was the first thing that the White Rat turned his attention to. When there was still *mizuame* available, there was also agar, which is one of the in-gredients used in making medicine. Mother would often make us a kind of transparent jelly called *kanten* by melting the *mizuame* and mixing it with agar. After the *mizuame* disappeared, she would sub-stitute artificial sweeteners like dulcin or saccharin, which were two of the substances produced by out-of-work pharmacists who had come to work at the factory after the end of the war.

Kanten just passed through the body without contributing much substance, but it did help the hunger pains. In time, however, there was no more *kanten*, not to mention lucrative dulcin and saccharin. Thus it happened that, in order of profitability, one thing after an-other disappeared into White Rat's pockets, and Father's bootleg-ging business also fell to ruin.

Moreover, since the Changchun airport had fallen into the hands of the Eighth Route Army, the Nationalist Army saw its sup-plies diminish. Even if Father's dubious alcohol had still been pos-sible, it wouldn't have been as rewarding as before. Almost every day supplies would be dropped by parachute, and when they hit the ground, the packages would almost invariably burst open. Since the Eighth Route Army had tightened the ring around the center of the city, the Nationalists planes couldn't approach the city's airspace. If they came in low for a parachute drop, they would most likely be shot down, discouraging them from attempting that feat very often.

As a result, much-too-heavy packages would be suspended from parachutes and sent down at terrific speeds, without finely calculating weight and velocity, only to break apart and scatter when they hit the ground. Moreover, since the packages were dropped from a great height, the target area was rarely hit with any precision. If one of these packages happened to fall on a person, death would be the inevitable result, and if they hit a house, they would go straight through the roof. Consequently, whenever we heard the sound of a plane approaching, tension filled the air.

Whenever a plane did come, Nationalist soldiers would listen for the sound of the descending parachutes and then rush to the landing spot to gather up rice and whatever else they could find, weapons in hand. Ordinary citizens could only look on enviously. If you made a false step, you might be shot. Sometimes the Nationalist soldiers would fight among themselves for the best pickings.

The Nationalist Army in Changchun was not uniform in its composition. There seemed to be differences in the chain of command as well as in ethnicity, and these rose to the surface when it came to a struggle over supplies.

There were particularly noticeable differences in the treatment and condition of the neatly clad and amply furnished New Seventh Army under Jiang Jieshi's direction and the Sixtieth Army that had come up from Yunnan Province. The latter was officially called the Sixtieth Army of the National Revolutionary Army. Eighty percent of its soldiers consisted of minorities such as the Yi and the Bai ethnic groups, who were Yunnan born and bred and known for their heroic efforts in toppling the Qing dynasty in Yunnan. However, after being transferred from southern Yunnan to northern Changchun, they were looked down upon and discriminated against by the New Seventh Army, leading to a great deal of frustration. Not being privy to the internal affairs of the military, none of us knew at the time that this would eventually lead to a revolt against Jiang Jieshi. However, what was clear even to an outsider was that the Sixtieth

Army soldiers were dressed in dirty uniforms, were somewhat shortish, and had round dark faces, whereas the arrogant New Seventh Army soldiers were a little taller and dressed in brand-new American uniforms.

What was also clear was that whenever the parachutes spilled their goods on the ground, there would be a fierce struggle between these two Nationalist parties for what could be had.

When the Nationalist soldiers had gathered up all the rice and food they could and had withdrawn, ordinary citizens, watching from a distance, would rush forward with a shout, scrabbling for a grain of rice or two; anything was better than nothing. One and all, everyone was desperate to prolong their life, if even for a single day. To that end, they were willing to do anything.

* * * * *

There were drug addicts even among the Nationalist soldiers, and they were eager to get their hands on some Giftol. There was some still left in the closet on the second floor. For a while this is what kept us alive.

Now and then a Nationalist soldier would bring some flat, round buns to barter. They were a kind of yellow bread made of corn flour and called *mantou*. Each *mantou* was divided up among twenty-two people, with each person getting a slice about five millimeters thick. Since the edges where the *mantou* had been cut tended to crumble and fall, Mother placed each piece on a slip of paper used for wrapping powdered medicine. We would be lying on the floor intently watching the needle of the scale as she weighed the pieces. Even a milligram-sized crumb could make the needle move. On which piece of paper would she put that crumb? That was the question that riveted our attention as we watched her fingers move.

Silk kimonos, damask sashes, fur coats, radios, record players, sewing machines—we sold them all, but the problem was that hardly anyone wanted clothes or household effects like that any-more. The food shortage in Changchun had reached such a critical juncture that a few grains of kaoliang were more precious than any household valuable.

However, going into the Inner City, things were different. The Inner City was an area that had originally been walled off to pro-tect it from roving bandits, whose inhabitants were now exclusively Chinese, a sort of Chinatown. It was located at the point where the central Datong Boulevard ran parallel to Xing-an Boulevard, with a north gate south of Sanma street, an east gate at Dongda Bridge, a south gate in the area including a mausoleum dedicated to the leg-endary Guan Yu, and the west gate abutting Datong Park. It had an entertainment district and a place called thieves' market, where stolen goods were openly sold. The market was considered too dan-gerous for children, but it was filled with an energy not to be seen on the main streets.

I had been to the Inner City, but only once.

Zhao, the Eighth Route soldier acting as a sentry at the factory, offered to take me in a horse-drawn cart. We went down a street that was only about one-fourth the width of Xing-an Boulevard. It was overflowing with people, and the horse could do nothing more than steadily plod through them. The busy shopping district continued on and on, with multicolored advertising banners hanging down on both sides.

The air was redolent with the smells of cooking oil, meat, and garlic, along with an odorous cloud combining the smells of kneaded wheat flour and musty old books. When someone said the man on the cart was an Eighth Route soldier, the way was immediately cleared, with some people looking up curiously at the odd combina-tion of a rifle-carrying soldier and a young girl in baggy work pants. Eighth Route soldiers were referred to as Communist bandits and feared by the local people, particularly the shopkeepers.

There were a great many open-air vendors on both sides of the street, as well as street performers and fortune tellers. They were all full of life, smiling cheerfully, as though they didn't have a care in the world.

Inner City Chinese seemed to possess a special vitality owing to some inherent life force. In the Inner City you could even procure kaoliang and soybeans, rarely seen in those days, though in pitifully small amounts.

Any work that needed to be carried out in the Inner City the White Rat was happy to do. He knew the place like the back of his hand. In fact, he was much more adept at "working" in the City than at working in the factory. He was taking a cut from any transactions he made, we knew that, but there wasn't much we could do about it. Aside from him and his family, the rest of us were nothing but skin and bones, unsteady on our feet. If something happened, there was no way we could protect ourselves. Our life force had been sucked up by the White Rat, sucked up to keep him and his family healthy and strong. We had no choice but to borrow his strength.

For all its infamous renown, the Inner City wasn't ready to give up its valuable food resources for just any trinket. In a pinch Mother relinquished her precious jewelry, but there was a limit to what she had. In the past the family had owned a great deal of valuable items, but they had been repeatedly confiscated by the Kanto Army as part of the war effort. Those who still possessed jewelry and other valuables were considered traitors to the country. After the end of the war, it became possible to buy things freely, but Father refused to let Mother buy any jewelry; he preferred to devote all his energy to helping refugees, saying that jewelry could be bought later.

"I told you over and over," Mother complained to Father. "In case of an emergency we should give each of the children a big diamond or a gold bar. And now, look what has happened. If I knew things were going to turn out like this, I would have been more persistent."

Thus, what Mother possessed soon disappeared.

Then the rumor started circulating that the Inner City now

had a "human market." It dealt in young girls of families whose breadwinner had starved to death and left behind his wife and daughters.

When there was nothing else to be had, we ate the broiled lees of kaoliang sake compacted into brick-like blocks. Sometimes we were able to obtain pig feed called *doubing*. This consisted of the strained lees of soybeans that had been compressed into the shape and size of a truck tire, several centimeters thick. It was rough and dry, containing a mixture of what seemed to be hay and straw. We ate this after broiling. It had a strange taste. We also ate the adzuki beans that were used as fillers in pillows. The beans had become oxidized and made you feel like vomiting. Still, it was better than nothing. We also ground into powder the buckwheat husks we had filled our pillows with and ate that.

By this time we were all horribly emaciated and deathly pale, our skin covered with dark wrinkles as if we had suddenly become very old. Our ribs stood out starkly like those of a skeleton in the desert, leaving our bloated stomachs bulging out below. Our arms and legs had become bony sticks that made a hard clacking sound when they bumped up against one another. There seemed to be nothing separating the skin and the bones. The skin became loose and slack, and if you pulled it with your fingers, it just hung there where you had let it go. It was said that you could judge the state of malnutrition by how long it took the skin to return to normal. We must have been at the most critical level, for unless you poked it with your finger, the skin never recovered.

Our skin also started to develop ulcers due to a vitamin deficiency. The flesh began to deteriorate, and even though you were still alive, the skin proceeded to die. These ulcers also appeared on our scalp. They weren't painful so much as itchy. It was hard to resist the temptation to scratch. When you did scratch, your hand would come away with a patch of hair a centimeter square, scalp and all. It was disgusting enough to see a lump of hairy skin sticking to the tip of one's fingers, but there was nothing you could do about it, just quietly watch as pieces of one's own body were peeled off.

As we grew weaker, next we were tormented by bugs. We were overwhelmed by hungry bedbugs and lice, which were intent on sucking up the last drops of our already pathetic supply of blood. Even after spending a whole day getting rid of the lice, the next morning they would be back, mainly on our scalps and underarms but also along the seams of our shirts, where they would form neat lines.

As for myself, I didn't know it was tuberculosis at the time, but in any event the bacteria seemed to have spread throughout my body. No one appeared to notice that my festering wound was tubercular. True, Father may have known, but even if he had, there were no sulfa drugs or anything else in the house. Buying antibiotics was out of the question, so there was really nothing to be done.

* * * * *

In May Mother gave birth to a boy. One year earlier no one had imagined that there would be a food shortage. Changchun was then in a fever of excitement about the second round of repatriations. Mother had insisted that we should be a part of that group, but the Nationalist government had refused permission.

At one point Mother's labor contractions were so weak that the midwife gave up hope, and Mother had prepared herself for the worst. She called us five children to her bedside and said her final farewells in a weak, hoarse voice, apologizing to Father for leaving him in the present state of affairs.

"What are you talking about?" Father scolded her. "Get a hold on yourself." He immediately rushed out and a short time later returned with a young doctor from White Chrysanthemum, a nearby village inhabited entirely by Japanese. Until just a year ago one of the men living there had been a manager at the then Shinkyo

Pharmaceuticals and another had served as accountant in the post-war period. So even now there were some people in the village that Father was on familiar terms with.

Taking one look at my convulsing mother, the doctor said, "Just hold on now. I'll put you at ease very quickly." Taking up a pair of forceps, he quickly delivered the baby and saved Mother's life.

The baby boy was awfully small and thin, and even though just born, he had fine, clear-cut features.

"When he grows up," Mother remarked with a smile, "he's likely to be very popular with the girls." She was particularly fond of him, the boy whose timely delivery had saved her life.

He was named Mayozo and given the nickname Ma-chan. The names of all the children were taken from the key words in a poem Father wrote when his first child was born.

> The merits of the Okubo family are towering, like Mount Fuji;
> Its glory sweet until the end of time.

It turned out that the principal words of the poem perfectly matched the number of children in the family. How Father could foresee this is beyond me, but he seemed to possess that kind of power.

With the approach of summer, budding plants broke through the winter-long crust of earth and ice. We could now get food to eat just by picking what we needed. Mother, cutting short her postpartum convalescence, rushed madly outside to return with armloads of fat-hen.

"Look at this," she cried out to Father. "Vegetables! We now have vegetables! Eat up, everybody, as much as you like!"

Mother boiled the fat-hen in rock salt, and it tasted very good, like spinach. It was decided that we children, since we had regained some of our strength, should follow Mother around in her foraging. We would go out the back gate on the left side of the ether storehouse and past where the company housing ended, and emerge in the Xing-an Hutong alley.

The Xing-an Hutong didn't have paved streets—they were just dirt roads—and it looked for all the world like an uncultivated field populated by shortish plants of various kinds. On either side of the main street was the company housing of the former Central Bank of Manchou, and below the housing's concrete wall grew a great many castor-oil plants. They were leftovers from the wartime period when people were forced to plant them because they could ostensibly be made into airplane fuel. Some plants there were poisonous, so we children concentrated on those that could be easily distinguished, such as fat-hen and two types of plantain called *obako* and *kobako*.

The wind was warm on our cheeks, and the sun shone gently down. Little plants were peeking out of the black earth, their sprouts dark-green. This little patch of earth was overflowing with life.

The heavens above, the earth below—as long as they endured, life would endure. No matter what powerful body encircled and strangled Changchun, it could not obliterate this life force or block the rays of the sun. The sun shown down equally on all living in this starving city—how gentle, how warm.

On the verge of starvation, the citizens of the city crawled out of their hovels to pick the emerging grasses. One and all, they were desperately hanging on to the last shred of life. In their desperation, they greedily snapped up the bounty of nature. Before long, there was nothing left.

With the other plants gone, we began picking the leaves of elm trees. Elm leaves are very slimy and stick to the sides of the mouth, but at the time we thought of them only as a means of prolonging life. If I looked up at a tree, I would feel dizzy. If I reached for a leaf, my arm would hurt. So I chose only the lowest hanging branches.

When the wind blew, the elm leaves would caress my cheeks. I would pick one leaf at a time and place it carefully on the palm of my hand. The young leaves had absorbed the rays of the sun; they were bright and shiny, swaying almost proudly in the air.

The young leaves seemed to be softly breathing, proud of their fresh young life. Did they realize what was happening in Changchun?

Nearby stood a Nationalist sentry, guarding a field that had been confiscated from an ordinary citizen. In the distance could be heard the sound of firearms.

* * * * *

Eventually, as soon as new leaves appeared, they would be picked and disappear. We ended up chewing the bark of the trees.

It takes time for nature to renew its riches. There was a gap between the time nature needed for renewal and the time the citizens of Changchun needed to prolong their lives. It wasn't long before this gap became unbridgeable. Even the mighty powers of Heaven, begetting all things, could not fill this gap in time.

Now there was nothing to eat. Our only choice was to conserve our energy by lying down and keeping quiet. Just like recumbent alligators we remained unmoving until the coming of night.

When night did come, Ma-chan would start crying as if he were afraid of something. There was very little kerosene left, but nevertheless Mother would occasionally light the lamp for him. The light not only made the room brighter, but it also cast a faint ray of hope into our hearts. The lamp was sitting on the ladder for the children's slide that had somehow escaped being burned as firewood, and its darkly flickering light somehow touched our hearts.

We were still breathing. We were still human beings. We were still alive. Why oh why did we have to go through all this?

People said that the Eighth Route Army was laying siege to the city, cutting off all supplies. But I didn't believe it, not for a minute. Zhao was part of the Eighth Route Army, and Zhao knew that I was here. He knew that I was waiting for him. He couldn't do anything like this. A malicious rumor spread by the Nationalists, that's what it was. Still, how long was it going to last? When would someone come to rescue us?

Even to speak, to utter a sound, required energy. But we needed something to show we were still alive. Who started it I am not sure, but we began to sing. More than a song, however, it might have been a cry for help.

> *The evening sky clears.*
> *The autumn wind blows.*
> *The moon casts its shadow.*
> *The crickets are chirping. . . .*

As we sang in broken voices, the flame of the lamp rose in plumes of twos and threes through our tears. Which one of us would still be alive tomorrow? Or would we all be dead by the time we finished singing?

Tomorrow may never come, but still we had to sing, or maybe that's precisely why we sang.

> *. . . Thinking of it now, so far away.*
> *The sky over our old home.*

Without singing, I thought, we could no longer call ourselves human.

When the kerosene was almost gone, the wick would sputter and verge on blinking out. The lamp would merge with the darkness, the intermittent periods of gloom growing longer and longer, until the flame appeared to have breathed its last.

"Oh no, don't go out. You can't go out. Don't . . ."

Holding my breath, I prayed to the lamp as if praying for my life.

Father suddenly said, "Just a little longer. Let's give it our best, OK?"

I could see Father in profile as he stared into the light, his face wavering in the dimness. The shadow of the slide shimmered large on the ceiling, and then with the last flicker of light, it disappeared into the dark.

* * * * *

There was a well in the inner garden where we got our water. One day, my older brother, who had ruined his health while in the army and then had lost his wife, his son, and his will to live, suddenly said he would like to be put in charge of carrying water from the well to the house. In a time like this, he didn't feel right doing nothing, he said; in fact, it made him feel depressed. "If that's the case . . . ," Mother thought, and she decided to let him try it for a while. But apparently that's where things went wrong.

Shortly afterward he told Mother, "I'm having some trouble with my stomach. I hate to ask you, but could you take over carrying the water?"

He had somehow ruined his remaining health before drawing much water at all. When Mother went to finish the job, she found that water from his bucket had splashed on the ground in a zigzag pattern.

"He must hardly have been able to stand, poor thing," Mother said. "There was no need for him to push himself so hard."

Mother had an indescribably painful look on her face. She had no food for him. The only thing she could do was to give him some of newborn Ma-chan's gruel. Being malnourished herself, Mother had no milk, so she was raising Ma-chan on gruel.

The gruel was made of the kaoliang that my Big Sister had managed to get hold of. One day, when she was out picking plants at Xing-an Hutong, a Japanese woman passed by, saw my sister, took a liking to her and suggested that she drop by her home someday. She was living with a Nationalist soldier and wanted to have his child, but so far had been unable to conceive. She wanted to have a cute little girl like my sister, and asked Sister to spend some time with her.

Sister's features resembled those of a classical Japanese doll. Her eyes were rather large, her nose clearly defined without being too prominent, and her lips red and firm. When she danced at the culture festival of the White Chrysanthemum School, wearing a red dapple-dyed long-sleeved kimono, she looked for all the world like a real doll, lovely in every respect. Sister would sometimes go to the home of the Japanese woman and be fed there, occasionally bringing home some kaoliang. It was this kaoliang that Ma-chan was raised on.

Mother encouraged Brother to try some gruel, but he said he didn't want any.

"How about the grains of kaoliang that are left after the gruel has been sifted?" She asked.

"No, I don't want any," he replied.

Saying that his stomach was bothering him, he started to doze off. Mother thought that he would feel better after a nap, and she took the slide out into the hall to break it up into firewood. Suddenly Brother shouted out: "Bring me a thermometer, I say! Bring me a thermometer!"

When given the thermometer, he crazily shouted out again. "No, not this! A thermometer, I say. My temperature is going way up. I can't measure it without a thermometer."

His voice was huge, surprisingly so for someone in such frail condition. It was July, with no worries about heating, so everyone had returned to their own rooms. Brother's room was on the second floor, the first on the right as you went up the stairs. This room was the nearest to the first floor, and his voice clearly reverberated downstairs. Father happened to be in the first floor drawing room, conducting some important business with officials from the Nationalist government. He was presenting an idea for making bread out of the pig feed called *doubing*, which consisted of strained soybean lees. The Nationalist officials were typically arrogant and self-important, but somehow Father had to get them to support his project. In any case, he didn't want to create a bad impression. This attitude was rather untypical of Father, but he wanted at any cost to avoid any deaths by starvation. He rushed upstairs and chastised Brother: "Can't you keep the noise down! You're not a child, for heaven's sake. Get a grip on yourself." So saying, Father rushed again back downstairs. When he had finished his business and went upstairs again, Brother's pupils were dilated.

"Isao, what are you doing? Brace up!"

Calling out his name, Father held Brother's head in his arm, but there was no response.

"You can't do this, you hear me? You can't die before me.... Isao, listen. I'm telling you. You can't go first. Do you understand? You can't die before me."

Mother brought a spoonful of gruel up to Brother's mouth. "Isao, try some of this," she said. He swallowed it, making a gulping sound.

He was still alive.

Father immediately bared Brother's chest and listened for a heartbeat. But swallowing that spoonful of gruel proved Brother's last act in life. Father refused to give up, straddling his son and continuing to massage his chest, a technique I hadn't realized he knew. But Brother didn't respond.

"A tragedy, what a tragedy! I scolded you because I didn't want any more of you starving to death. Who would think those would be the last words you would hear out of my mouth? What a terrible father you must have thought me. Forgive me, Isao. Forgive me."

Father put his arms around his son and cried. This was the first time I had ever heard Father shout out in anger, the first time to see him cry.

Brother was buried in the ether storehouse. It was July 13, 1948. Not long after, Father fell ill.

* * * * *

Looking down on Xing-an Boulevard from the second story window, what one saw was a tableau of death. Though it was the height of summer, all the luscious trees lining the street had been stripped of their leaves. This deathly boulevard stretched out into the distance, and people who had fallen at the foot of its trees were abandoned there. A small child of two or three was crying loudly, some dogs circling it from a distance. Dogs had taken to eating the bodies of children who had just died. Corpses could be seen almost everywhere. Children who had lost their parents were often pushed out into the street, calling for their mother and father. They were easy targets for starving dogs, which had reverted to their feral state and acquired a taste for human flesh.

We had a dog of our own, a little brown thing named Pochi. One day a Chinese man appeared and asked if we would sell the dog. We knew what he meant. Amid all the starvation in Changchun, the dogs alone were plump and fat.

It was then that it was suggested that if the dog was going to be sold, we might as well eat it ourselves. The speaker was the White Rat.

Mother had actually seen Pochi eating a human baby. One day she saw Pochi coming out of the no-longer-used drawing room on the first floor, licking its red mouth. Having a premonition that something was not right, she went quietly into the drawing room and saw, beside the sofa, the heads of two or three babies that Pochi had eaten. One of the heads was still bleeding, and the carpet around it was spattered with blood.

On the wall of the drawing room was a large poster showing a sword slashing through the words "Groundless Rumor." The poster had been put up on the orders of the Nationalist government as a warning against rumors spread by "Communist bandits."

The spattered blood had reached as far as that poster. It was clear proof that the baby's heart was still beating when it was killed. After that, Mother always felt something sinister about Pochi. She was afraid the day might come when Pochi would attack Ma-chan. Pochi wasn't allowed upstairs, but the look in its eyes was somehow different. There was no telling what it might do.

Mother finally agreed to White Rat's proposal. My oldest sister tried to protect the dog, crying and screaming, and she was the only one who wouldn't touch the meat or even eat the soup. Big Sister was thirteen at the time, an indispensable member of the family, always helping Mother in any way possible. From that time forward, however, the smile that was always on her face disappeared; she became uncommunicative and difficult to deal with.

* * * * *

Father had grown so skinny that it was a miracle he was still alive. Unusual for him, he began to complain, perhaps because of his general weakness.

"If only the Horse Administration Bureau had returned that money . . . ," he would say.

Father had loaned money to the Horse Administration Bureau of the Agricultural Reform Department and the Manzhouguo Equestrian Association when they were experiencing financial difficulties, but of this, 4 million yen had never been returned. This was at a time when a fighter plane cost about 120,000 yen. The amount he lent was huge, equivalent to thirty fighters. It was meant to stabilize the finances of a whole country, Manzhouguo, so it was understandable that such an enormous amount would be needed. Of course, it was probably far less than what Father spent on helping refugees. Still, it was unprecedented for him to complain about something of that nature.

"What are you talking about?" Mother attempted to console him, with a pinch of sarcasm. "That's not like you at all. Even if the loan was repaid, you'd spend it all on people in trouble, like you always do. In any case, there wouldn't be anything left for us."

"Ha, ha, ha. You're probably right," he replied good-naturedly.

Father seemed to have returned to his usual self. His laugh, however, was not the hearty laugh of days gone by. It was weak, wheezy and raspy. His face resembled that of a newborn chick. His eye sockets were sunken deep, his eyes bulging out, covered by dark, thin eyelids through which you could clearly see the movement of his eyeballs.

One day Mr. M. from the Horse Administration Bureau came visiting. "It looks like the President's time has come," he whispered to Mother, referring to Father's condition.

When the Soviets had invaded, Mr. M. had worked as an interpreter among other things, and he had decided not to take part in the second repatriation. Even if he went back, he said, there wouldn't be any work, and if he could be of any help to Father by staying, he preferred to stay. He had studied agriculture, and his family was composed of his wife, one daughter, and two sons. In the immediate postwar period his wife would often sing Silcher's "Lorelei" in a beautiful voice.

One day Mr. M. suddenly took to his bed. "I'm having trouble with my stomach," he said.

That was the same thing that Brother had complained of, and the way he had of dropping off to sleep was similar. We all had a premonition of impending disaster, and our worries proved correct.

While Mr. M.'s wife had come to report to Mother that her husband had gotten worse, Mr. M. in fact passed away. A few days later, the youngest son also died. This was near the end of August.

Mother began making preparations for Father's funeral by collecting the proper clothing for the deceased and checking the whereabouts of the cyanide that would seal the fate of the rest of the family after Father's death.

Mother then heard something disturbing from White Rat. "Changchun is just about done for," he told her.

"What? You mean the Eighth Route Army is coming?" She took this to mean that Changchun was surrendering, and there was a lilt to her voice. Everyone was waiting for that day, the day the Eighth Route Army would enter the city.

"No, just the opposite. You shouldn't be shocked, but a human flesh market has gone up in the Inner City. A human flesh market! They're selling human flesh cut up to sell by the piece! I may be cut up and sold myself. I still have some flesh on my bones. Ha, ha."

In the distance there was the sound of firearms. The shooting seemed to have become more frequent in recent days. It may have been a trick of the mind, but it appeared to be coming closer.

"The Eighth Route Army will be entering the city pretty soon," said White Rat, who was our informant on matters concerning the city. "That's the rumor, at least."

"What? Is that true?" Father, who had been lying in bed like a mummy, suddenly sat up. "OK then. Take this and sell it." He pulled out a heavy, specially made Waltham watch on a chain. Each link in the chain was about a centimeter in diameter and consisted of pure gold. Not knowing how long the siege would continue, Father had saved this watch for the day when the Eighth Route Army would enter the city, the last of the family heirlooms.

Of course, there was still the imperial screen that belonged to the Empress Dowager Cixi, six panels embellished with precious stones. But he had promised the screen to Lin Feng, and a promise was a promise. Father had concealed it in a dark corner of Mother's room, out of the sight of the White Rat. Its value was immense, on the level of a national treasure. If he sold it to the Nationalists, it would bring in a considerable amount of money, enough to keep us in food for a while. Still Father didn't sell it, but kept it for Lin Feng, whose return was completely uncertain. Refusing to break a promise until the very end was so typical of Father.

"OK? I'm leaving this in your hands," he told White Rat. "With this we should be able to survive a little longer. You understand? Our fate depends on this. I'm counting on you."

Father took White Rat's hand in his own and left the fate of the family in his care. Everyone tried to forget White Rat's past behavior, attempted to trust him, but no one was completely successful. Since it was dangerous to send him off alone to the Inner City with its human flesh markets, it was decided to have a young glass craftsman accompany him. We all gathered in one room and awaited their return. We would finally have something to eat. Father wouldn't have to die. With Father alive and well, we could somehow survive. Ma-chan, who was barely holding up, would pull through.

We waited, but the only one to come back was the glass craftsman.

He had been told, "I can do this on my own. After all, I'm known in the Inner City. No one is going to kill me, but nobody knows you. With you along, it will just invite trouble."

That's why he had come back alone, the young craftsman said. An uneasy premonition filled the room. Maybe, just maybe . . . doubts arose in every mind, but they were soon rejected as being impossible. Of course, he would take something off the top; that was to be expected. It was his percentage for getting the job done.

Night came and White Rat returned, but, unbelievably, he was empty-handed. As soon as he entered the room, he rushed to Father's bedside and burst into tears.

"Oh, Uncle! I'm so ashamed. I was robbed. They took the watch."

He sat formally before Father leaning slightly forward, his left hand on his knee, his right clenched into a fist that he used to wipe his eyes, continuing to cry out in a loud voice. That voice rang hollow in everyone's ears. Without it, however, his fake tears would be entirely unconvincing.

"That's going too far, isn't it?" said Mother. She was crying real tears.

Even the young glass worker, who had never opposed White Rat before, put in, "Going too far by half!"

"Who is the robber in this case?" someone said.

No one could keep quiet any longer. How long did he plan on sucking our blood?

Father had never said anything about White Rat's past behavior, but now he spoke up. "You, what a pitiful excuse for a man you are. I have waited long and patiently for a change of heart, but who knew you were rotten to the core? A hopeless case."

I realized then for the first time that Father had known about White Rat's activities all along but had kept quiet.

Perhaps a bit shocked, White Rat suddenly stopped crying. He removed his fist from his eyes and looked up. There was not a sign of a single tear.

"Oh, so that's how it is?" he said. "You don't trust me either, Uncle, do you. I completely understand." With these parting words, he gave Father's bedding a kick and rushed out of the room.

As we watched his departing energetic figure, we were overcome by a feeling of hopelessness.

* * * * *

"Let's leave Changchun," said Father as he stood up, using his pillow as a prop, in the full realization that he had lost the ace up his sleeve.

Lin Feng, secretary to the Changchun City Committee of the Communist Party, had said that he would definitely return. "Please wait for that day," he had said when he departed. And Father had waited, but now his limit had been reached.

Father now looked like a skeleton wrapped in a shroud of intense determination, not just a simple mummy. Within that shroud only his heart seemed to be moving. During the last year his hair had turned perfectly white, hanging down to his shoulders. Every time he opened his mouth, his long beard would sway as far down as his chest. Below his white eyebrows his eyes emitted an extraordinary glitter. It was like looking on a ghastly being from another world.

When he tried to stand up to leave for the city, there was no one brave enough to try to stop him. He would visit city hall, he said, to have his status as a compulsory detainee revoked.

As it happened, early in this year, 1948, Father received a letter of appreciation from Jilin Province in acknowledgment of his invention, manufacture, and sale of Giftol. Almost immediately afterward, orders arrived from the Hygiene Department of the Nationalist government in Nanjing, informing him that Giftol had been officially adopted there and requiring him to move to that city. In accordance with these orders, the mayor of Changchun immediately flew to Nanjing to make preliminary preparations for Father's factory and his reception there. In the meantime, however, the Eighth Route Army had grown rapidly in strength and power, and the Nationalist forces in the Northeast found themselves in a critical situation. As a result the mayor of Changchun was unable to return to the city.

"The mayor managed to get as far as Jinzhou, but it was too dangerous to come any closer to Changchun, so he had no choice but to return to Nanjing. That's where he is now."

In later years Mother recalled what Father had said then, but she didn't remember what month it was. The Changchun airport fell into the hands of the Eighth Route Army in May, so it must have been around then. But why was the mayor, who was supposed to be held up in Nanjing, now back in Changchun? Had he come in a military airplane or had he parachuted in?

"Are you really Dr. Okubo?" asked the mayor when he saw the totally transformed figure of my father.

When the mayor was satisfied with Father's identity, he asked him, "But why did you hold out for so long, to this extreme?"

Father told him that promises had been made, and he felt the need to honor them. The mayor then offered a considerable amount of money as a relocation fee as well as provisions of rice, kaoliang, and soybeans, not to mention walnuts, pine nuts, and other edibles that constituted part of a soldier's emergency rations. It was an unexpected windfall. With part of this money Father bought a large cart, and the rest of the money and food he divided equally among the other families.

White Rat, realizing that Father still had his uses, tried to ingratiate himself with Mother and Father. One thing he suggested was that since the factory could still bring in this much money and food, we should hold on to it and stay in the city until the Eighth Route Army came.

However, Father thought differently. "No, that won't work," he said. "The mayor provided the relocation money because I agreed to leave Changchun, and so if I don't, I will have deceived him. And he may have intended it as a final farewell. I don't want to turn into that kind of person.

"And when will the Eighth Route Army enter the city, I'm not sure anymore. And what will we do if they don't come soon? It would be better to use this money and food to build up our strength and then escape from the city while we can. Swindlers and extortionists are already beginning to hover around. Who knows what they have in store for us?"

In fact, the news of the relocation money had quickly reached the ears of the Chinese populace, appearing in a mimeographed newspaper. They had their own view of the matter.

"We're as hard off as you are. Are you planning to keep it all for yourself?"

"Share some of it with us!"

"If you don't, you'll regret it."

Almost every day Chinese would come with threats. There was murder in their eyes. There was no telling when we might be killed.

Just at this time we learned that Japanese residents were planning on escaping the city en masse. We decided to join this group. The fateful day would be three days later, at 6:00 in the morning, September 20.

Once the decision was made, we needed to build up our strength.

For the first time in ages we ate kaoliang rice. We ate rice broth, gruel, and rice in that order, increasing the amount only a little at a time. If a person on the verge of starvation suddenly overeats, she can ruin her stomach and die or, in the most extreme case, break out in a cold sweat and die of shock. Father was strict in seeing that we followed this regime.

"OK then. Let's build up our strength and go to the liberated zone where we can eat delicious rice cakes covered with sweet bean paste," Father said. "You hear? It's delicious rice cakes! It's the liberated zone!"

A liberated zone was an area that had been occupied by the People's Liberation Army (the new name of the combined Eighth Route Army and other Communist forces). "Liberation" meant freeing the people from the oppressive Nationalist government. From this time on the Revolutionary War was also known as the War of Liberation.

Sweet rice cakes! The liberation zone!

Hearing Father's words, our thoughts flew off to the liberation zone. Father himself had begun to look a little more like a normal human being. Mother feverishly busied herself preparing for the escape and in making food to take along. We hadn't had any white rice since Ma-chan was born, so Mother immediately set about making some strong rice broth for him. But he refused to touch it.

Mother asked Father to look after Ma-chan while she continued her preparations. "Poor thing, he must be surprised at such rich food," she said. "If you don't mind, just give him a little at a time until he gets used to it."

In the evening of September 19 Father called out to Mother: "Ma-chan, he's acting a little funny."

Ma-chan's beautiful, limpid eyes had lost their luster, and simply stared out into space. His tiny lips had lost their color and were trembling uncontrollably.

Calling his name, Mother pulled out her withered breast and

tried to insert the nipple into his mouth, but his lips were already cold.

White Rat's wife, who had rushed in, said, "Let me try," and attempted to put her nipple in Ma-chan's mouth. She had given birth to a boy around the same time as Mother. Her full white breasts were overflowing with an unimaginable amount of milk.

When the nipple entered his mouth, Ma-chan's expressionless face suddenly became contorted, and he pushed the nipple out with his tongue.

That was to be the last movement he made in this life.

Father washed Ma-chan and made him presentable.

Looking at the poor little body, which was nothing more than stick-like limbs attached to a skull and bloated belly, Father said by way of apology, "In conditions like this, it was too much to ask you to keep on living, wasn't it."

He was buried under the window of the company house facing Xing-an Hutong. This was the closest patch of earth; the inner garden was paved in concrete.

When Father had come downstairs, he had held Ma-chan in his arms. He said to Mother, "Here he is. Don't you want to see him for one last time?"

Ma-chan was sleeping quietly in Father's arms, it seemed. He was dressed in the crested kimono that had been made to celebrate the one hundredth day following the birth of his three-year-old brother, Chiyoji.

Later Mother recalled her thoughts on that day.

"I wanted to be there when he was buried, but I still had five other children to look after. I couldn't let them die. It was my duty to protect them. These five lives would be leaving the city tomorrow, and I couldn't stop preparing for that departure. Ma-chan was sleeping peacefully in Father's arms, breathing quietly, it seemed. I didn't want to watch as he was covered with earth. Covered with earth, he wouldn't be able to breathe. I didn't want to see Ma-chan unable to breathe. I wasn't sure what would happen to me if I did. Ma-chan would always be sleeping peacefully in Father's arms, forever and ever. That's the way I wanted to remember him."

This is what she kept telling herself, she said, and why she continued to work without letup, preparing for the day to come.

* * * * *

Around 6:00 in the morning, on September 20, 1948, we left the Shinkyo factory, the place of my birth, with high hopes in our hearts, not knowing that a living hell awaited us. We cut across Baishan Park, Mudan Park, Shuntian Park, walking on and on toward the south side of the city. About the time we passed in front of the Japanese Resident Association, we merged with another group of refugees, and out of the blue Father was asked to act as the leader of the group.

"I'm sorry," Father said, "but I'm really not up to it. I don't have the energy."

"It's only a nominal position," he was told.

"It may be merely nominal, but responsibility comes with it. As you can see, I am not physically up to the task. You'll have to forgive me this once."

"You shouldn't take it so seriously," Father was told. "The group has to have a leader, merely for formality's sake. Just as far as Qiazi, the military checkpoint. Please, if you would."

Pressed in this way, and feeling that precious time was being wasted, Father finally acquiesced.

The route for citizens of Changchun hoping to escape the city was strictly defined. On the southwest side of the city, on Hongxi Street, was a military checkpoint or Qiazi—a narrow route of egress guarded by a sentry—that we had to pass through. We learned later that there were checkpoints on all four sides of the city, but at this time the Nationalist government gave strict orders to use the southern Hongxi route. It probably led to the port in Huludao, Liaoning Province, which a million Japanese passed through during the repatriations. Huludao was located southwest of Changchun.

All exits other than those stipulated by the Nationalist government were encircled by barbed wire, and it was said that anyone trying to cross this wire would be shot.

Even though we had two or three days' provisions, there was no change in the fact that we were basically skin and bones. Simply walking required tremendous effort. On top of that, there were now more than ten festering spots on my body, some having appeared on my legs. The pustules on my feet hadn't burst yet, and were very painful. But I didn't complain. To have open wounds covering my arms, to have these painful wounds perpetually exuding bloody pus, to have difficulty breathing—all this constituted who I was. Just as I accepted my existence as a given, I accepted these other things as a given. The person who had innocently loved the red glass bead of the sun, who believed that an unlimited future existed on the far side of that bead, that person no longer existed.

And yet there was something out there. There had to be something out there. What it was I didn't know, but at some place deep in my heart, there was a warm light pointing toward something, to a far-off unlimited future. It was that light that kept me going, that kept me walking.

The liberated zone.

I wasn't sure what that meant, but somehow it became synonymous with Father's "delicious rice cakes," and I imagined it must be a kind of paradise that overflowed with food. Different from Changchun, which had been stripped of every blade of grass, the liberated zone must be rich in verdant foliage and resplendent in blooming flowers, the sun shining down on small birds flitting to and fro. The decorated streetcar that ran down Xing-an Boulevard during the Shinkyo Shrine festival might be there. The paper flowers that decorated the front of the streetcar—pale pink, blue, and yellow—looked exactly like the cream ornamentation on the marvelously decorated cake we used to buy at the catty-corner Osaka-ya, which gave me so much pleasure.

Let's hurry, hurry to the liberated zone. Surely there must be something there. What I had been searching for must surely be there. So thinking, I continued to walk.

By the time we reached Qiazi, the sky had already begun to turn red. It had taken us a whole day to cover the ground that a pair of healthy legs could have covered in an hour or two.

"So the Eighth Route Army has come this close, has it?" said Father, surprised at how tight the encirclement had become.

"If I had known it was this close, I would have brought the down quilt futon, even if I had to carry it myself," Mother said regretfully. We had just started up the slope near Anmian Boulevard.

Suddenly White Rat shouted at Mother and Father. "It's because your damn stuff is so heavy, that's what is wrong." And he started tossing our things off the cart, one after the other. Since Shinkyo Pharmaceuticals was being left behind, Father was no longer the president of the company and of no use to him, White Rat realized. As soon as we left the confines of the factory, his attitude had abruptly changed, and now he was speaking in the rudest language.

"Hey, you! Can't you keep pace, can't you push a little harder?"

The first time Mother heard this, she couldn't help looking back to see what was wrong, she said later. She couldn't believe that this was directed at her and her husband. But there was no one behind her but Father, the only person White Rat could be yelling at. When she fully realized that they were indeed the objects of White Rat's bellowing, Mother recalled an old poem.

Fallen in luck,
Your sleeves wet with tears,
You first know the heart of man.

So this was the meaning of that poem, she thought, the words striking home.

* * * * *

Descending the slope, there in front of us was Qiazi. It consisted of a wood fence tied together with barbed wire. The scene we saw on both sides of the entrance to this fenced area was absolutely astounding: it was a row of open-air stalls. They were selling boiled edamame, corn *mantou*, and, most surprisingly, Japanese white *manju* buns. It was completely unbelievable, like something you might encounter in a dream.

On the way from Shinkyo Pharmaceuticals I had seen with my own eyes any number of people who had died of starvation along the wayside. They were particularly numerous in parks and fields. Even on Xing-an Boulevard there were daily stories of who had died and where. Then how, in the same city of Changchun, was it possible for this scene to actually exist?

I suddenly recalled a story Mother had told me.

Just down the street from Shinkyo Pharmaceuticals was a general store. When the Japanese owners were repatriated and left the store empty, a Chinese family moved in and began selling provisions and various items needed for daily life. Mother would often take clothing and furniture to the store and trade them for a little food. Since Mother never brought money, but always some object, one day the puzzled matron at the store asked Mother a question.

"Where do you people keep your valuables hidden?"

At first Mother wasn't sure what she meant. "We don't have valuables hidden anywhere," she said.

"There's no need to lie," the matron replied, refusing to believe what Mother said. "You were always so rich. You must have a lot of money hidden somewhere. You're keeping it for the very last, I suppose."

"No, we don't have anything at all. We used it all for people in need."

"Oh, so it's really true. I heard rumors to that effect, but to think it's really true . . . If it is true, you must be the biggest fools around. We Chinese, we've been fighting on this land for thousands of years. And every time we ordinary people get sucked in. Who is going to win and who lose, we don't know. We always have to figure out which side we're going to be on, in order to survive, you know. And some of us don't take sides at all, but do like we are doing now."

As she spoke, the matron pointed to the sole of one of her cloth shoes. She said that when they had the money, they would buy gold bars and sew them into their shoes.

"You have to be ready to do this much if you're going to survive in China," she went on. "You Japanese don't know how to lose a war, that's what I think. You've never lost a war until now, right? You've never been caught up in a war on your own land, right? In China, those who don't know the proper way to lose a war end up dead. People like you have to learn to use this," and she pointed to her head.

For some reason this story remained etched in my mind. Even though still a child, I somehow understood what the matron was saying.

While Father had become a mummy, and the rest of us little better, White Rat was the picture of health, grown fat from the ill-gotten goods he had stolen from Father, and his family was not starving. While White Rat's way of doing things was undoubtedly different from what the Chinese had practiced for thousands of years, still he had the strength to survive. Looked at in this way, I had mixed feelings.

Was White Rat's way really the right way? No doubt about it, in some respects Father was honest to a fault and too straightforward. But this didn't come from weak sentimentality. It came from strong principles, almost a religious belief, from something essential at the core of his being. This was something that even a child could understand. Which way would I choose when I grow up, I wondered. I wasn't sure, but at least I could say that I liked Father's way better. Coming to this conclusion, I felt a sense of relief.

When Mother spoke of the survival skills that the Chinese had demonstrated over thousands of years, was she referring to something like these otherworldly booths? No, I doubted it. Maybe the food sold at the booths had been provided by the Nationalist government. Although everyone attempting to escape the city was prepared to abandon their homes, many of them brought with them their most precious valuables, scanty as they were. Maybe it was this that the booths were aiming at.

No, it was just a smoke screen. It was a screen thrown up to keep refugees from becoming aware of the sight that awaited them on the other side of the barbed-wire fence. Since the beginning of August the Nationalist government had been trying to get as many people as possible to leave the city. It hoped to prevent food riots. In fact, the leader of the Nationalist government, Jiang Jieshi, had issued orders to that effect to the Nationalist Army in Changchun.

"What could all this possibly mean?" Mother said. "So many booths . . . Now I'm glad I brought along the remainder of the relocation money, not knowing what might happen." She reached for her purse.

"I don't know how much this will buy, but I have a few other things I can barter as well. Let's negotiate with them and see what we can get. Come on."

We rushed forward and gathered around one of the booths. It was hard to believe.

Looking at the things lined up on a shelf, Mother said, "Well, let's see," and started to open her purse.

Suddenly an older woman grabbed Mother by the arm. "Just a second! You plan on leaving the city without saying a word?" It was the midwife who had helped out at Ma-chan's birth.

"You haven't forgotten, have you—the money you promised me back then? You still owe me, you know. Since you're so rich I thought you would pay up sooner or later, but I never thought you would run off like this. I found you just in time. Now give me what you owe me."

The words tumbled out of her mouth, her features ferocious. She wiggled her fingers in front of Mother's purse. We had explained to the young doctor who had successfully delivered Ma-chan that we had no money and had given him my long-sleeved kimono instead, as a token of our appreciation. The midwife had found the delivery beyond her skills and had given up and left. Apparently we hadn't paid her for her services or presented her with any token gift.

"I appreciate your help then," Mother said. "Unfortunately, the little boy died yesterday." Holding out her purse, Mother continued, "I'm not sure if this is enough, but it's all I have."

"Is that so?" the woman said, her shrill voice suddenly becoming more subdued. But then, as if to say that the two events were unconnected, she snatched the purse from Mother's hand.

"Will you be staying in the city?" Mother asked politely.

"Yeah, I'm not moving from here. As long as there are people, there will be babies. The work of a midwife never dries up." Leaving these words hanging in the air, she hurried off.

"I'm so sorry," Mother said to us. "I should never have said I'd buy you something. I really wanted to, though. Forgive me. But just through this gate is the liberated zone. We'll be able to eat white rice and all kinds of things. You can hold out a little longer, can't you? Just a little longer."

"Uh-huh," we said; we could.

All we had to do was to go through the gate. The liberated zone was just on the other side. That's why there were so many booths here, because the liberated zone was so nearby. It was hard to imagine just how wonderful the liberated zone must be. There was no need to buy anything now. We just had to cross the fence.

The area around the fence gate was swarming with refugees. That's where the Nationalist checkpoint was, where the soldiers inspected your belongings. "Inspect" might not be the right word since the soldiers were principally concerned with whether you were carrying weapons or not. After that, everyone was invariably given permission to pass through. This permission consisted of being told to move quickly along and not loiter. However, there was one strict condition: "Once you had passed through the gate, there was absolutely no coming back."

The line of refugees didn't flow smoothly: some people were reflecting on the condition of no return, some were taking time parting with family and friends, others were still bartering at the booths. Nationalist soldiers urged the wave of people on, prodding them with their bayonets. Before the refugees realized it, the path they were walking down was lined with barbed wire on both sides.

We didn't need to be prodded; we just wanted out. There was no question of our going back.

The setting sun was beautiful as it reflected off the fence.

On the other side, the light was very bright, as if inviting us to come in. I no longer cared if there was a strange man called Mao Zedong in my red glass bead. Zhao was probably waiting for me there. My heart was beating with anticipation as I crossed to the other side of the fence.

* * * * *

A big empty field. Not a single blade of grass. It is strangely quiet.

Then there is suddenly the sound of flapping wings. A single voice cries out "Ah—" as a crow flies up from among our group of refugees, then disappears noisily into the setting sunlight.

Aside from our group, there is not a soul to be seen. We walk silently and cautiously forward, making sure of each step.

Something is odd, though. Our whole bodies become eyes and ears, searching for what is wrong.

Then from the front of the line, there is a sudden commotion and cries of "Ooh—." My body begins to tremble as a swarm of flies rises up from the tumult ahead. A swarm so thick that the air turns dark.

In Changchun there is only one thing that attracts so many flies.

"This can't be! This can't possibly be! A mistake! It has to be a mistake."

But it wasn't.

Bony skulls with festering skin, staring eyeballs, mouths wide as if laughing, teeth bared, flies swarming and buzzing.

And it continued: flattened desiccated chests turned black, green bloated decomposing bellies. The green stomachs were spotted with white mold, sometimes bursting and spilling out on the ground.

The flies were swarming around the bloated bellies. The arms and legs had no flesh, were dried and blackened like the flattened chests, sticking out of the bodies like sticks, offering nothing for the flies.

It was the first time in my life that I'd seen a decomposing body up close. I felt vomit coming up in my mouth; the skin on my face seemed to contract and shrivel. I began to feel lightheaded, and the only thing that kept me from falling was Father's arm.

Yes, Father. Father was there.

I would stay close to Father. With Father there, I was safe. Unsteadily I kept walking. But the more we walked, the more bodies there were.

Turning to the right, there was a kind of woods with a smattering of trees. From the right side of the woods there appeared a few soldiers.

They were Nationalist soldiers. What could this mean? This was the liberated zone, wasn't it? But the soldiers were wearing the

Nationalist uniforms so often seen in the city. Our belongings had been inspected when we came through the gate, but now they said they needed to inspect them again. "Inspection," however, was only a pretext. They were looking for plunder. Among the things they took this time was Father's leather bag, in which he kept all his important papers: research results, documents issued by the government, and even the diary he kept following Japan's defeat. They must have thought these papers had monetary value, something that was worth looting refugees for.

Going through the woods, we again met with more soldiers. This time they were from the Eighth Route Army. They wore the same uniform as Zhao, the young soldier who had stayed at our house, with a red star on their caps. They too wanted to inspect our belongings. As they went through our things, one of them asked in Japanese, "How is Changchun?" I could tell from his accent that he was Korean. Koreans are very good at Japanese, but they often have trouble with voiced consonants.

"People are dying because of the food shortage. Our group of nineteen left Changchun to escape starvation," Father answered.

"Huh! Move on then, that way," the soldier responded.

We moved on in the direction indicated, but that didn't stop these Eighth Route soldiers from again taking off the cart anything that appeared to have value.

The number of bodies increased, and we often stumbled on arms and legs sticking out into the path, almost falling. Their stomachs must have become so bloated that they exploded, for their intestines were splattered over the ground.

Lying face down, a small baby, almost nothing but head, had its hand on its mother's breast, both of them black and mummified.

Some bodies were nothing but bleached bones, some were in the process of putrefying, others seemed to have just then fallen to the ground and died. They were scattered here and there, or piled on top of one another, all left to lie where they had fallen, abandoned and discarded.

Most of them were wearing no clothes, probably stripped off. Their bloated stomachs were uniformly green, but as the setting sun grew darker, they took on a purplish tinge, heightening the horror.

* * * * *

Before we knew it we had arrived at a spot where many refugees had gathered. They were sitting and lying on straw mats and futon spread on the ground. The sun had already gone down, leaving a dim afterglow. We could see their glittering eyes turned toward us, but that was all, like wolves watching in the night.

By the light of the moon we found a place that seemed to have few bodies, spread our futon on the ground, and quickly sat down. To the left behind us were the walls of houses fallen into ruin.

When I lay down, there was a sharp pain in my back. My ears were ringing. I shivered from the cold, my legs trembling.

Where were we? The Eighth Route Army was here, but so were the Nationalists. Wasn't this supposed to be the liberated zone? Where had we come?

Looking up, the sky was full of cold stars. I felt unbearably tired, and I closed my eyes. This was the first time in my life I'd slept out of doors.

* * * * *

In the middle of the night I woke to an eerie rumbling sound that seemed to come from the earth itself. Or was it the sound produced by human voices? "Whoa, whoa, whoa!"

It seemed to be coming closer, rippling the air. It seemed to be crawling over the surface of the land, an agonized cry from the center of the earth.

My hair stood on end. My heart began to beat wildly, pounding in my ears. I tried to cry out, but there was no sound. I sat up, saw that Father was also awake. I rushed over and clung to him.

"There, there," he said. "So it woke you up too. This isn't the liberated zone yet. I'm so sorry."

Father rubbed my back, and the warmth of his hand seem to put me at ease. That and the exhaustion of the day soon sent me to sleep again, still clinging to Father.

* * * * *

When I woke the next morning, I was in for a shock. Just above my head there was a human hand emerging from the ground. I scrambled to my feet and looked around me. The panorama of endless crowds of refugees overwhelmed my senses.

Glittering eyes like wild animals, forlorn faces, vacant unfocused features, the sounds of painful breathing. The black crowds of people seemed to go on forever into the distance. Where could this number of people have come from, and how?

The gaps between the different groups were filled with bodies. Suddenly scared, I squatted down on the futon. I felt something round beneath it, and when Mother turned back the edge of the futon, she found a skull half-buried in the earth.

To my left was a man who was lying with his bedcovers neatly pulled up to his chin, but who never woke up. He was dead.

A little further over was a man staring straight ahead and gnawing on something: his leather belt.

Behind us and to the left were several concrete walls with embedded red bricks, fallen into ruin. Next to them was a tree with its bark stripped off, showing the white wood underneath. Beneath these trees were refugees sucking on the trees' bark.

"Father, where are we?" I asked.

"This is the no-man's land between the Eighth Route and Nationalist armies: Qiazi. It seems to be enclosed by two fences. That over there is the exit to the liberated zone."

Looking to the right, I could see an exit in a barbed-wire fence just like the one we had passed through last evening, which was perpendicular to a railroad line. A big gate had been built into the fence.

"Father," I asked, "won't they open that gate?"

Suddenly from the group on our right, a voice called out, "No, they won't." It was a middle-aged Japanese woman.

"That gate," she said, "is only opened once a week, or at worst once a month. It was last opened just four or five days ago. Just when I had gone over by the tracks to pick some grass."

The woman pointed to the right, where a small hill could be seen.

"Unluckily, I apparently ate some poisonous grass, the kind with thorny berries. And for a while I felt a little dizzy, while the gate was open, you see. When I hurried back, it was too late."

Now that she mentioned it, there wasn't a blade of grass anywhere nearby. But if you went to the tracks and kept going to the right, there were apparently places where grass still grew. Of course, on the other side of the barbed wire, in the liberated zone, the vegetation was lush. But if you stuck your hand through the fence and tried to pick some, you risked being shot by Eighth Route soldiers, it was said.

As the sun rose high in the sky, we got thirsty, but there wasn't a drop of water left in our canteens. There was a well near the crumbling walls with embedded red bricks, and a long line of people waited their turn to get some water. Japanese, however, being the enemy, weren't allowed to join the line. Mother and Big Sister took a tea kettle and tried to line up, but as soon as it was discovered they were Japanese—probably from their clothes—they were yelled at ferociously and turned away. The only thing we could do was to skim the water that had collected in hollows, transfer it to a pot, boil it over a fire made with twigs and bits of bed sheet, and drink that ever so carefully, practically licking it. Our undernourished bodies were close to complete dehydration, and without water death could not be far off.

It had rained two or three days ago, but it was still hard to say if what had collected in the hollows was actually rain water. Sometimes there was water that had collected in the space between dead bodies. Toilets, of course, were nonexistent. Just as Mother was worrying about these things, the middle-aged woman next to us spoke up again.

"The water from the well is no different," she said. "Any number of people have fallen into that well. Just as they are drawing up the water, the bucket gets too heavy for them—being so weak—and starts to go down again. But they hate to give up, almost having the water in hand, so they keep trying, finally falling into the well. And then some people, just as they are leaning over the well to pull up the bucket, are pushed from behind and fall in. But it's hard to say 'Don't push' in a situation like this. Everyone is desperate."

How long had this person been here? She seemed to know an awful lot about Qiazi. How was she providing herself with food?

Then, all of a sudden, there was the sound of rifle fire off toward the right. It was coming from the place along the railroad tracks where the middle-aged woman said she picked weeds. A group of refugees came rushing back, screaming at the top of their lungs. Some were bleeding from their heads, others had been shot in the leg. One woman was carrying a small baby, her breast bared, her long thin hair trailing behind her. There was blood oozing from her chest. It seemed that the Eighth Route Army and Nationalists had exchanged fire over the fence.

When the gunfire stopped, Qiazi became eerily quiet. Everyone was holding their breath, watching warily for any movement by the Eighth Route Army.

Three armed Korean soldiers from the Eighth Route Army entered from the gate on their side—apparently ready to shoot anyone who made a suspicious move. Pointing their guns at the refugees, they moved their eyes warily over us. Father and Mother wrapped us children in their arms, as if that would provide protection. The

Soviet soldiers had already taught us to be sensitive to quick changes in the direction in which a rifle was pointed. We kept as still as possible, even controlling our breathing so as not to be heard. The soldiers walked watchfully around the refugees and then disappeared into their gate. As the last soldier vanished, there was a universal sigh of relief.

"That often happens, firefights like this," whispered the middle-aged woman, waiting for her chance to speak. "Over there," she said, indicating the area to the right of the tracks with her jutting jaw, "the fences of the Eighth Route Army and Nationalists are just too close, you see."

After the tension had let up, a buzz of activity ran through the area, and people began preparing to eat whatever food they had. Mother opened a cloth bag containing powder made of roasted kaoliang, and placed a little on the palms of our hands. In my bandaged left hand, which had regained some of its movement, I held a piece of paper describing the efficacy of Giftol rather than limp tissue paper, where Mother placed the powder. Licking it a little at a time, I felt my body begin to relax.

Still there was one thing that bothered me: I had to urinate. I had been holding it back since I woke that morning. I was almost seven years old at the time, old enough to be embarrassed to lower my trousers where people could see. I was afraid to leave our futon, but I asked Mother to watch after me as I went to the crumbled walls behind us and to the left, threading my way between the dead bodies. There was a narrow opening between the walls of two houses, and peering into the crevice, I saw no one there. Finding a place where there were few bodies, I squatted down to finish my business. Shortly I felt something hard touching against my backside. Surprised, I look to see. It was a human hand, its fingers like dried twigs, sticking out of the ground.

Instinctively I jumped forward, only to be faced by a pair of wide-open glaring eyes. Apparently the urine had washed the earth off the face of a shallowly buried body. It seemed to be new. There was still skin on the skull, all wrinkled from the moist soil. The folds of its skin and its mouth were packed with soil.

I felt the blood drain from my body. There was a leaden ball in the pit of my stomach. Vomit rushed into my mouth. A chill ran over my skin. Drops of cold sweat fell from my nose.

In all of Qiazi was there no place that was not occupied by buried bodies?

Grabbing on to the wall, supporting myself with trembling hands, I finally managed to stand up. The wall was about chest height, and I leaned against it to keep from falling. Everything before my eyes had gone dark, and I closed them, waiting for them to return to normal. My lips trembled, my breathing was broken, cold sweat enveloped my body. Finally I opened my eyes, and then I gasped.

Just below me was a woman on the ground, a baby at her breast, its face smeared red, licking with its tiny tongue the blood that oozed from her chest.

It must be the woman I had seen earlier running with her baby after the exchange of gunfire. The starving baby had taken its mother's warm blood to be her milk.

Desperate to get away from there as soon as I could, I pressed against the wall again with both arms to get to my feet. When I raised my eyes, I saw something that froze me in place.

In one corner of the walled area there was a man chewing intently on a long, thick bone. The man was staring greedily down at the body of a woman on the ground in front of him, noisily gnawing without stop.

The man was wearing ragged black clothing, frayed around the shoulders. Sitting on the ground, his extended left leg was bare below the knee. He was wearing no shoes. His face, framed by long hair and a beard, was surprisingly full, and his eyes gleamed like our dog Pochi's after eating the babies.

If the man caught sight of me, I might be killed and eaten. As this thought raced through my mind, I jumped away from the wall as if propelled by a powerful force. As I threaded back through the bodies, I couldn't help thinking that I was stepping on human remains. I hated for my feet to touch the ground.

Just as I returned to the family futon, the shadows of newcomers appeared in the distance.

Then what should happen? The ground around us, near and far, seemed to swell and rise up. People who had been lying down were now getting to their feet, each holding a stick or a piece of wood. Letting out a low animal-like growl, this black mass immediately surrounded the new arrivals. The growling changed to tumultuous shouting, and then, like a receding wave, the black mass return quietly to their usual places.

In the silence that followed, a silence seeming to signify that all had returned to normal, the newcomers were left standing dumbfounded, stripped of all their possessions. Some were lying on the ground. Some of the women wore the distinctive Japanese work trousers called *monpe*. The black mass quickly settled back in their usual spots, wolfing down the food they had just taken. There was one man, grasping food in both hands and eating out of one, who was rushing madly to get back to his family and share his loot. Someone among the other refugees apparently noticed his uneaten food, and one of them began to chase after him. The man realized his predicament and tried to stuff the remaining food into his mouth, but it was too late. He was already encircled by a wall of people.

Among the refugees, there was one who was crunching the small bones from a funeral urn taken from a Japanese. Then there was another, his mouth turned white, licking the pulverized powder from the urn.

When we entered Qiazi, Father had been carrying Ma-chan's urn, wrapped in white cloth, hanging from his neck. If we had met with the same type of looting, would poor little Ma-chan's bones have met with the same fate? Would we have been clubbed and beaten? Even if we hadn't, we might have been trampled to death.

A horrified look on her face, Mother said to Father, "How lucky, not to have that happen to us!"

"It *is* strange," the middle-aged woman spoke up from the side. "Looting like that happens several times a day, without fail. Why you escaped it, I really don't know. It's strange. You must have good karma."

"It's because Father was here to protect us, that's why," Mother proclaimed.

"No," said Father. "It was the gods protecting us. Maybe Ma-chan paid the price for all of us."

Then a man sitting on the other side of the middle-aged woman spoke up in a deep voice, looking in our direction. "All you talk about is being robbed. But before long you'll be doing it yourself."

He had a long beard, high cheekbones, sharp eyes, and from the fact that he was sitting with the middle-aged woman's group, he must be Japanese.

"And it won't be only looting. There's something even more interesting awaiting you," he said, almost spitting the words out with a weird laugh, turning his back on us.

The man had missed his chance to leave Qiazi, the middle-aged woman whispered.

"Something more interesting . . ."

Blood-curdling words! But then the eyes of the man gnawing on a bone between the walls crossed by mind. That bone, was it, after all. . . . ?

I wanted it to stop. I wanted all this to stop. But there was no one who could stop it.

There were people dragging bodies across the ground. Here and there the refugees created circles, their dark backs forming a wall. Whatever was happening inside the circle was hidden from sight.

A slender plume of smoke rose here, another plume there. All reaching up high into the sky.

The man next to us turned in our direction, his eyes glittering knowingly, as if to say, "Now you understand?"

* * * * *

Until now I had refused to believe that the Eighth Route Army had purposely cut off supplies to Changchun. It was nothing but a rumor, I kept telling myself, a baseless rumor spread by the Nationalists. But what about this scene before my eyes . . . ? Wasn't it the Eighth Army that was keeping the gate shut?

Zhao had told me that the Eighth Army was fighting for the people. And when I asked who "the people" were, he had said, "It's everybody living in China. Your father, too, who's making medicine for China. You're all our comrades. Both you and your father are part of the people."

That's what Zhao had told me. If that was true, why were you now killing the people, I wanted to ask? By keeping the gate closed, you were killing many, many people every day, dying before your eyes. And including those in the city, there were countless more. Was it right, killing people in this cruel and heartless way?

I still couldn't believe it was really the Eighth Route Army behind this tragedy.

Father was always saying that Eighth Route soldiers were good people, so I asked him, "Are those soldiers really from the Eighth Route Army?"

"It's the Eighth Route Army, all right. Made up of Korean soldiers."

"Then why don't they open the gate for us?"

Father grunted a reply and then fell silent, staring gravely at the gate leading out of Qiazi.

Just shortly before, Father had apparently taken the cloth Lin Feng had signed and gone to request permission to leave the area from one of the Korean soldiers at the gate. After all, he had been made group leader, even if it was only nominally, and even though he had accepted the position reluctantly. He had told them that the position was beyond his present capabilities, but still he couldn't help but feel responsible. Lin Feng's departing words had been, "If you are ever in one of the liberated areas and have any trouble, please show this. Anyone should be happy to help you out."

Father had shown the piece of cloth and asked that all Japanese be released. He had a list of the people in the Japanese group. He placed all his hopes on the piece of cloth bearing Lin's signature. But the Korean soldier he approached refused to hear him out, shouting, "Release all the Japanese? Don't be absurd. You think we can forget thirty-six years of Japanese exploitation so easily?" Rule under the Empire of Japan had begat a deep hatred of Japan among the Korean people. Making the leader of the group a Japanese had produced the opposite of the hoped-for results.

If Father hadn't been asked to serve as group leader, he could simply have asked that his family be released. In that case, the Eighth Route Army soldier may have put more credence in Lin Feng's signature and let us go. But Father's request that all Japanese be released only fed the soldier's loathing of Japan. The weight of thirty-six years of colonization proved paramount, and Lin Feng's name was useless. That seems to have been what happened. Even if being group leader was only a "nominal position," Father was still, in fact, group leader. He couldn't bring himself to ask that his family receive special treatment. In this case, Father's upright character produced unfortunate results.

The sun began to sink, taking on a red tinge and suddenly swelling in size.

The evening sun I saw on Xing-an Boulevard only became the setting sun when it had transformed itself into a red glass bead. This was the first time to see the sun's movements on a flat, endless plain. Here, where there was no place to hide, no means of protection, the descent of the swelling sun was a ghastly sight, an object of horror.

When the bright-red sun reached the hill on the other side of the fence, Qiazi suddenly caught fire, flaring up in ravenous flames. My beloved setting sun was now emitting rays of terror, beams of horror. It was as if this horrific light foretold the coming of some terrible rite that would see the destruction of all Qiazi in an ocean of scarlet flames.

The living who were dying, the dead who spent their days with the living, all who straddled the border of life and death—all were illuminated in red, all writhing in agony.

The bodies of the dead, reflected in red, appeared to have living blood still flowing under their skin. At any moment, it seemed, they might come back to life.

I had always thought that if I didn't give up, if I persevered, something good would happen, something good would eventually happen. I waited patiently for that something. But there was no hope here in Qiazi. There was nothing I could say to myself to salve my mind. I lacked the energy to even give up hope. I just wanted to become oblivious to it all, to become unfeeling, unthinking.

The setting sun was no longer my red glass bead.

Zhao was a liar.

What was all that talk about the Red Flag?

What did he mean by the blood of the people?

How did he explain Qiazi, now dyed in red?

You said I should think of the Red Flag as being dyed with your blood as well as mine. That we were comrades.

Impossible!

That flag doesn't stand for people who murder others like this. I don't want to be the comrade of people who do this kind of thing.

I tried to turn my eyes away from the setting sun. Then, out of the ball of fire, I saw Pochi running toward me. Panting, wagging his tail, he came running toward me.

Without thinking I called out his name.

In that instant Pochi's face merged with the huge ball that was the sun. His mouth and eyes were blank holes, flaring with bloody flames.

*****

The sun set quickly in autumn. Once it fell below the hill, it was as if a curtain had been suddenly drawn between the world of light and the world of dark, plunging Qiazi into gloom. At night a chilling autumn wind had begun to blow. People spoke in whispers.

Our eyes, accustomed to the golden sun, lost their ability to see in this enveloping jet-black world, enticing us into its gloom.

While it was light, the moving figures of fellow refugees linked us tenuously to life, even in this surreal setting. But flung out into the darkness, people no longer visible, the dead bodies that were so recently dyed red now appeared black in the lingering light, giving rise to the chilling premonition that something terrible was about to happen.

Even the slightest movement in the air was frightening.

The dead might rise up, their cheeks flaming red; they might emerge from the earth, their grasping fingers dyed scarlet.

Moving figures couldn't be seen, and the unmoving seemed to move. It was a world of apparitions, where positive and negative were reversed. To protect us from these phantasms Mother and Father wrapped their arms around us. We snuggled up as close as we could.

In time my eyes became accustomed to the dark. Looking up, I was overcome by the feeling that I might be sucked down into the bottomless pit of the earth. Looking to one side, I saw an eerie bluish-white light that would soon reveal a hand emerging from the ground, inviting me to join it.

How long would these nights continue?

Is this where we would breathe our last?

The earth itself was scary. The earth was where bodies were buried, where bodies were abandoned in plain sight. And we, who had to sleep sandwiched between these bodies, who had to sleep on top of them, could we really call ourselves human?

Was life really worth living like this?

Is this how we should meet our end?

I felt my spine go cold. What if yesterday's rumbling should come again? I trembled at the thought. I trembled and couldn't sleep. I clung to Father even more closely, without moving a muscle, intently listening.

In the quiet of the night I could hear my heart thumping against the earth. What if something more terrible should happen, what if the earth should start rumbling again, would my heart then just give up and cease to beat? Just to sleep, that's all I wanted. O Mother Earth, just let me fall quietly to sleep. If there was a god, I just wanted to ask to be allowed to sleep . . . just for a moment, to be protected from this heartless night.

But god wasn't listening.

The trembling of the earth began in the quiet. Ripples of sound shuddered the night, and moaning crawled over the earth. The agonized sounds came from all directions, converged into a wave and broke, "Whoa, whoa, whoa!" Qiazi shook and reverberated.

The ground began to rumble. It was as if the dead were rising up from the restless earth. As if a deep desire for vengeance were welling to the surface, the dead restive in their sleep.

Fear gripped my heart; fear blocked my throat. Mad, at this rate I would go entirely mad.

It was then that Father's body gave a jerk.

"Kyaa!"

I clasped Father more tightly. I thought a body lying on top of us had moved. My blood froze.

"There, there, don't worry. It's just the voices of the spirits of the dead. Let's pray together. That's a good girl now. Just let go of me for a minute. There's someplace I have to go."

"No, no, no!"

My voice came out as a screech. I had never gone against Father's wishes, but this time I absolutely refused to give in. Father finally agreed to let me go with him. So we set off, me clinging to his arm.

From where we were sleeping we walked toward the gate leading into Qiazi and turned to the left. Ahead was a two-story building whose walls were still standing. Going between this building and the gate to the liberated zone, Father turned to the left and kept walking.

The air was tense with a feeling of impending disaster.

In the dim distant I saw a pale-blue hill. The closer we came to it, the greater became the rumbling of the earth. In the space between me and the hill I could sense a feeling of repudiation and rejection building up. The hill grew larger before us. The feeling of exclusion mounted ever higher.

Then, standing before the hill, looking up, the whole thing exploded in my eyes.

It was a mountain of corpses.

Each body stood out perfectly defined under the light coming from the liberated zone and the moon.

Half-open glassy eyes, thin straggly hair, legs thrust into the air, hands starkly grasping at nothing.

Then a hand moved, a dead hand. Here and there on the surface of the pale hill, the hands of the supposedly dead were vaguely moving.

The angry red setting sun, which had foretold this festival of the dead, which had warned that it would decimate by fire all and everything that was Qiazi, had also pumped living blood into the pale bodies of the dead.

The reversible world of apparitions had come alive before my very eyes.

My nerves, like a thin thread pulled beyond endurance, suddenly snapped. What had been connecting me and the feeling of fear suddenly collapsed, the circuit broken. What was left was a huge, white, empty hollow. In that space something made a clanking noise and spun fruitlessly around. One of the gears of my heart had broken.

Next to my bewildered figure was Father reciting a prayer for the dead.

When we are invited to the other world,
Let God's merciful heart remain the same.
Let the soul be happy and unharmed.
Let it be protected and blessed.
When our life on this earth comes to an end,
And we depart for God's abode,
Let us be welcomed warmly, forever as now.

* * * * *

Father's sonorous voice, raised on high, resonated throughout the night. It was hard to tell how his frail and emaciated body could produce such a deep, powerful sound.

The moon was shining brightly in the heavens; the earth was filled with the solemn sound of Father's prayer for the spirits of the dead. His prayer enveloped the waves of moans, enveloped the rumbling earth, enveloped the mountain of bodies.

"Please help us! Please help us!"

Exhausted, Father fell crying to his knees before the hill, his hands placed on the ground, his body trembling. His white hair, falling to his shoulders, glinted in the moonlight.

The movement of the moaning bodies on the hill, unable to relinquish their time on this earth, suddenly stopped. Father's prayers, it seemed, had reached the souls of the forlorn spirits.

Once again Qiazi fell into silence.

But in that silence there was one seven-year-old soul who had been stripped of all feelings of fear, who had been reduced to a hollow shell.

I was having a hallucination. My father before me, as well as the mountain of dead bodies, had become mere objects, mere things, growing smaller and smaller until they turned into nothing but tiny points, and then vanished from my field of vision. What was left in my eyesight was a vacuum, a moral vacuum, and in that instant my ears stopped working, and the world of sound also disappeared. Everything became enveloped in glass, with me enclosed inside.

This hallucination lasted only a few seconds, I imagine, but the world it created lasted for a number of years, coming to visit and torture me now and then. It fashioned a certain path in my life from which I was not allowed to wander.

* * * * *

The next morning two Eighth Route soldiers came out of the side door next to the big gate and began gathering up corpses with something resembling a large rake. They were probably going to add them to the mountain of bodies. They were relaxed, taking their time, as if working in their own backyard. This was quite different from the time they had come with threatening rifles. Taking advantage of this change in mood, one of the Japanese group approached the soldiers and began to talk. After a while the Japanese came back, his face full of good cheer. He reported to Father that permission for him and his family to leave had been granted.

"When I showed him my identity card," the man said, "the soldier said that permission had come through and apologized for detaining me."

It had been decided, in order to assure fairness of treatment, that no one leaving Changchun should take along an identity card. The fact that this Japanese man had one with him was thus an infraction of the rules. This card probably identified him as a technician or an expert of some sort who was useful to the Communist government. Learning that this man and his family, about ten people in all, would be leaving Qiazi, those to be left behind subjected him to a good deal of abuse.

"Just you and your family, how fair is that?"

"Traitor! Turncoat!"

As this was going on, White Rat, who was standing behind us, clicked his tongue in disapproval.

"To my way of thinking," he said, "he's done nothing wrong. Quite the opposite. No matter what you're called, no matter what's said about you, the right to life comes first. It's alright to be as honest as a saint, like Uncle here, as long as you're not just an honest fool."

White Rat glanced over at Father with a look of contempt and continued.

"And who decided you shouldn't carry an ID, anyway? Whoever it was is probably a fool, but whoever follows such a trivial rule is a fool too. 'Duty,' 'the right path in life,' even going so far as to feel indebted to the mayor . . . That's why I said we should stay in Changchun. Compared to this, the city would have been far better, right? You have to formulate a strategy, like him; otherwise you don't have a chance."

Back off to our right, newcomers were being looted again.

"The other choice is . . . ," White Rat said, giving Father a mocking glance. "Are you eating human flesh, Uncle?"

Having said that much, White Rat put his hands behind his head and flopped down on the futon. Then he went on sulkily, "If only we had some evidence concerning Shinkyo Pharmaceuticals . . ."

"But Uncle being Uncle, I don't suppose he has anything," White Rat said, looking grumpily up at the sky. "There's no way he could have brought some proof along, no way."

Then looking sideways over at Father, he asked him, "Do you have anything, Uncle, anything at all?"

Father kept his mouth firmly shut, gazing at some point in the distance. As if in answer to White Rat's question, Father glanced over at him once and then resumed his staring.

Mother quietly followed up on White Rat's question. "You haven't brought anything with you, have you?" she asked.

Father's first word was, "Well . . ."

Perhaps detecting the indecision in Father's face, White Rat jumped up and practically kneeled at Father's feet.

"What? You have something, Uncle? What is it?"

White Rat desperately tried to pull the words out of Father's mouth.

"Well, as a matter of fact . . ."

"What could it possibly be, Uncle? Did you perchance bring something along with you?" White Rat's way of addressing Father had suddenly become more polite.

Mother also leaned forward in Father's direction.

"Well, as a matter of fact, I broke the rules too."

"Really? That's wonderful. I knew I could count on you. So what is it?"

"Don't talk so loud, you hear! The fact is I have the patents to Giftol."

Mother tried to confirm what he said. "But when we came here, you lost your leather bag with your important papers, isn't that right?"

"Well, the patents, I had them wrapped around my waist."

"My goodness, around your waist. You wrapped the patents around your waist. When it comes down to it, you foresee everything. How typical." Mother's face suddenly brightened up.

"But Uncle, if someone finds out about it, what then?"

"This is my lifework. I couldn't leave them in Changchun, and I can't let anyone take them from me now, no matter who. It is my lifework."

"Uncle, oh Uncle. That's so like you. Nerves of steel, I say. Fantastic! OK then, I'll just take the patents and go and negotiate, that's what I'll do." White Rat was in fine spirits as he thrust out his hand.

"Now just a second. That's not why I brought the patents with me. Of course, I didn't foresee this situation, but in any case to use them in this way . . . to abandon my countrymen."

"Come on, Uncle. Are you sticking to that old tune?"

"In one way or another I've been appointed group leader. That man, all he needed to do was inform me that he had gotten permission and then leave. But who am I supposed to get permission from? That's what taking responsibility means. And yet, you know, I can't just lie and say that everyone in the group is an employee of Shinkyo Pharmaceuticals. They have their own list they can check. In the end, what this piece of paper means for us . . ."

White Rat's eyes glittered as Father pulled out a sheet of paper—a certificate signed by the mayor of Changchun listing all the employees of Shinkyo Pharmaceutical Company and related individuals who would be evacuating the city. When Father called upon the mayor to offer his resignation as a detained worker, the mayor had provided him with this certificate, naming him the leading technician of the Jilin Province Hygienic Supplies Depot and at the same time revoking his status as a detained specialist. The document was signed by the mayor himself, specifying Father as the president of Shinkyo Pharmaceutical Company. His detention revoked, Father was returned to his original status as a private individual.

Father pointed to where White Rat's name was listed and said, "Without this certificate your status can't be verified. The only name given on the patents is mine. You can't easily pull the wool over the Eighth Route Army's eyes, as you well know."

"Well, Uncle. This is really something."

For a change White Rat looked very solemn. His fate depended entirely on what Father decided to do, a thought that had certainly crossed his mind.

"I'll tell you what, Uncle," he said. "You're not really fit to move, so I'll just take this document and the patents along with me and see what I can do."

Father had exhausted himself with last night's praying, and he couldn't move from the futon.

"No, just hold on a second," Father said.

"You still can't make up your mind, Uncle?"

White Rat then turned to Mother and asked for her help. "Auntie, can't you persuade him?"

"I fully understand how you feel," Mother told Father. "You have a strong sense of duty and responsibility, I know that. Yet you were told it was only a nominal position, and even after you said you weren't capable of fulfilling the duties of group leader, they forced it on you anyway. If you stay in Qiazi out of responsibility and end up dying with all the rest, who is going to thank you for that? And what about our children? They'll die too, for no good reason, every one of them. That may satisfy your sense of duty, but what about your responsibility to the children? I would like you to think about that."

"That's right, Uncle. We've got to get out of here and quick, or we'll all die. Isn't that right, Auntie?"

"Yes, there's something to that. Homare and Chiyoji already seem beyond help. And you yourself, the head of the family, can't last. . . ."

"That so true, Uncle. We have to do it while you're still alive. Otherwise, the nineteen lives associated with Shinkyo Pharmaceutical Company will all be lost. Don't think you're saving your own life but the lives of eighteen people, and just hand over the patents. What do you say, Uncle? If we all die here, every single one of us, then the patents will have been wasted, right? Saving eighteen lives is better than not saving anyone at all, don't you think?"

"There is something to that," Mother said, speaking to Father. "No matter what people say of us, we should give priority to the children. They say that necessity knows no law, and I guess this is one of those situations."

Mother having sided with White Rat, Father pulled aside his kimono to bare his belly as if he was preparing to commit hara-kiri, and pulled out the patents.

"Oh, thank you, Uncle. Thank you."

The patents—for Japan, England, and the State of Manzhou-guo—had been tightly tied around his waist in a narrow cloth bag.

"This is great!" said White Rat. "This practically guarantees our way out." He all but tore the patents and the mayor's certificate out of Father's hands and made to rush off to the gate leading to the liberation zone.

"Hold on there," Father stopped him.

"Now listen. I want you to try once again to see if these documents can get all of the Japanese released. Can you do that?"

"Yeah, well. If that's the way you want it," White Rat replied.

"OK. If you'll do that . . . I'm counting on you."

White Rat flew off in the direction of the gate.

"I just hope everyone can be released," Father said wistfully.

"That would be so nice if it were true," Mother added.

Feelings of apprehension, hope, and guilt filled the air. Each person with their own individual thoughts watched White Rat head off.

After a while Father said, "Why is he taking so long? I should have gone myself. I'll just go and take a look."

Just as Father was trying to rise from the futon with the help of his cane, White Rat came back, light of step.

"Well, Uncle, it seems we will all be able to leave," he said.

"Everybody?" asked Father.

"No, not everybody. They say that's impossible."

"You negotiated that point, right?"

"Of course. Trust me. But if it's just the Shinkyo group, they'll think about it. They wanted to keep the patents and the mayor's certificate until tomorrow, so I left the papers with them. They want to examine them closely."

"What? You gave them the patents?"

"Yeah, but there's nothing to worry about. The possibilities look good, but they need some time to study the patents."

"But to leave the patents in their hands . . ."

"They say they'll have an answer by tomorrow morning."

"Tomorrow morning? I just hope they return everything, that's all."

* * * * *

It rained that night, a violent downpour. At first everyone was happy since rain was the safest drinking water, and Mother and Big Sister put out pots and kettles to catch as much as they could. But before long it started coming down in torrents. We opened umbrellas and turned up the edges of the futon, but the rain was so heavy that we and the futon were soon drenched. About the time the night sky began to turn white, the rain stopped, and in the morning mist we could see that the downpour had brought many shallowly buried bodies to the surface. By then, of course, they were as familiar to us as sticks and stones.

Throughout the night Father continued to agonize. Would the patents be returned? Would permission to leave be given? If it was given, would it be right for only the Shinkyo group to leave? All night long these questions continued to torment him.

However, the sight revealed by the rain prodded him to come to a decision.

Just at that moment we saw three Korean Eighth Route soldiers come out the gate and head toward us. One of them shouted, "Hey, Shinkyo Pharmaceutical group. Step forward."

A commotion arose from the gathered Japanese. The shortest of the three soldiers, a bayoneted rifle slung from his shoulder, was holding one hand high in the air and flourishing two or three sheets of paper. One of them was surely a patent; the red British seal was visible.

"Oh, the patents! Thank you, heavenly gods. Thank you," Father mumbled.

That's when Father irrevocably made up his mind.

The soldier stopped in front of him. "Are you Shinkyo Pharmaceuticals?"

"Yes, that is me." Father stood up, leaning on his cane.

"Leave immediately," the soldier told him.

"Yes, sir," Father replied, military fashion. And then, looking around at the group, he said, "Shinkyo Pharmaceuticals, make ready to depart."

Mixed in with feelings of apprehension, there was a strong sense of relief.

The soldier then handed the patents to Father, saying, "I'm returning these to you. You should count your blessings."

"I'm truly appreciative."

But there was one patent missing. That for the State of Manzhouguo.

"Excuse me, but the patent for Manzhouguo . . ."

"What the . . . ? Just say that again!" the soldier shouted, pointing his rifle at Father. "There is no such country as Manzhouguo," and he jabbed Father's chest with the tip of his bayonet.

Father was unable to respond. He quietly tucked away the English and Japanese patents.

The Korean soldier pulled back his rifle, his lips twisted in triumph over the hated Japanese.

Father had us get ready and then asked the fifty-some Japanese in the group to sit in a circle, we nineteen in the center.

"I am afraid it's true, as you have undoubtedly heard. And I can offer no excuse," he began.

He placed his hands on the ground in front of him and bowed in apology.

"I fully realize that what I have done is wrong. I hope you can find it in your hearts to forgive me."

As expected, there was a roar of protest from the remaining Japanese.

"How can that be?"

"Yesterday it was that other guy! Today it's the group leader!"

"You're going to betray us, is that it? You think you can be for-given for that?"

"A dirty rat, that's what you are!"

"And you, the leader of the group!"

"How can you call yourself a leader?"

Even though Father was only leader in name, being leader is what it came down to.

"I can offer no excuse. Somehow forgive me."

Without any other way of expressing himself, Father divided up our remaining food and gave half to the Japanese who were to be left behind. We had no way of knowing what awaited us on the other side of the gate; we didn't know what to believe any longer. We had to keep some of the food for ourselves, for whatever lay in wait for us in the unknown world beyond the gate.

* * * * *

At the gate each name was checked and each person's relation to the group confirmed. An Eighth Route Army soldier read the names from the status list provided by the mayor of Changchun and called out each name. No one doubted that if you were a part of Father's group, you would be let through the gate.

As a final confirmation, one soldier called out, "So everyone here is a member of Shinkyo Pharmaceuticals?"

"No mistake about it," replied Father, glancing down the line we had formed. "Every person here was a colleague at Shinkyo Pharma-ceuticals or a family member."

"OK. Move out!" The big gate opened.

And then . . .

"All halt!" A different soldier appeared from the side and stopped the line with his bayonet.

The whole line came to an abrupt halt and drew back. The

soldier's gun was pointing straight at us, but then he swung it to one side and pointed it at Mrs. M., the widow of the man who had died in Changchun.

What could this mean?

"You can't leave," he told her with a Korean accent. "Your children either."

Using his bayonet he separated Mrs. M. and her children from the group. The soldier was apparently higher in rank than the three who had given us permission to leave, who now silently listened to his orders.

"What? Why are you doing this?" asked Father, visibly upset.

"Widows are not technicians," he was told.

All the blood had drained from Mrs. M.'s face.

"What could you mean by that?" asked Father. "Her husband was an outstanding technician and contributed much to the company. She is the same as a company employee. No, the same as one of my family. It is my responsibility to protect the bereaved families of employees."

Convinced that he should be able to take anyone with him who was associated with Shinkyo, Father desperately fought back.

"If you are going to release my family, please let the widow and her children accompany us. It is the same thing, isn't it?"

Mother also pleaded with the soldier. "Please . . . They are the same as family." And White Rat added a few words of support.

The soldier began to lose patience. "Are you going to leave or not?"

Up to this point the soldier had been fairly calm, but now he roared out, "Not leaving? That's fine with me." He laid a hand on the open gate as if to say he would close it if Father didn't do as he was told.

"What the . . . ," Father said, fixing his irate eyes on the soldier. No matter what, he couldn't leave the widow behind in Qiazi.

Suddenly Father prostrated himself before the soldier.

"I beg of you. . . . Just this one time."

"Can't take no for an answer, can you." And the soldier kicked Father in the face.

Weak as he was, Father fell back facing upward, his knees doubled under him. Mother rushed to his side, "Are you alright, dear?" and helped him sit up.

"Which is it to be? Are you leaving or staying?" The soldier prodded Father's cheek with the butt of his gun.

Assisted by Mother, Father crawled unsteadily to where Mrs. M. was standing, placed his hands on the ground, and raised his eyes. His face, broken out in a heavy sweat, had lost all color.

"Please forgive me," he said almost inaudibly. His head was hanging down, his shoulders trembling.

Mother also kneeled down with her hands on the ground and begged forgiveness. "Please find it in your heart to forgive us," she said, crying openly.

Mrs. M. stood stock-still, her face as pale as paper. She clasped her children's hands in her own, slumping slightly forward, her lips trembling.

We collected all the food we had, every last bit, and gave it to her, including the cotton clothing that the Chinese liked and other things useful in bartering. But still she just stood there, her arms dangling at her side, staring into space. Her crying children took the bag of clothing and goods that was slipping from her hands.

"Get a move on!" shouted one of the soldiers, encouraging us with his bayonet.

As we went through the gate, the voice of Mrs. M.'s fourteen-year-old daughter, Taeko, followed after us. "Please, don't leave us here. . . . Don't leave us behind!"

Her beseeching cries were cut off by crossed bayonets. Eventually her hysterical pleas changed to screams of abuse. "Traitors! Turncoats!"

Hearing these screams at our back, hearing them but still moving on, we sixteen people gradually drew further and further away from Qiazi.

* * * * *

None of us had the courage to look back. Father, who was just managing with his cane, would occasionally stop and place his hands together in prayer. The tips of his fingers were trembling.

Without speaking a word, we trudged on—for how long it was hard to say.

Reaching the top of a slope, Father broke the silence. Speaking to Mother, he said, "That's Changchun there, where Ma-chan is buried. We should say goodbye." He started to say something more, but he couldn't bring himself to utter the words, so he closed his mouth tightly, his lips pressed in a straight line.

Looking back, we could see the city in the distance. Slate-colored, surrounded by barbed wire, it had been shelled into ruins.

All at once, speaking to Father, Mother cried out, "Ma-chan . . . Ma-chan is . . . He's . . ."

She who had not shed a tear when Ma-chan died, she who had gritted her teeth and continued to prepare to leave Changchun, suddenly broke out into tears, as if a dam had burst. Twisting her body in a contorted shape, she continued to call, "Ma-chan, Ma-chan," facing far-off Changchun.

If let be, it seemed that she would stand on that slope crying out her son's name until there was not a breath left in her body.

But here we were, outside Changchun. We had escaped. Until this moment, as she later recalled, Mother's only thought had been to protect her remaining children and husband. But now, realizing that they had actually managed to leave Changchun behind them, she felt the stress and strain that had accumulated in her body drain away, and the realization that Ma-chan was truly dead struck her full force.

Finally Father placed his hand on her shoulder and said, "Shall we go now, huh? Shall we go?"

We started down the slope, leaving the despairing city of Changchun behind us.

Author's father, Takuji Okubo, in his last years.

Author's mother (age 29) shortly after arriving in Manzhouguo, with her oldest daughter (1 year old).

Traveler's certificate of
author's mother.

Giftol package.

Japanese patent for Giftol.

British patent for Giftol.

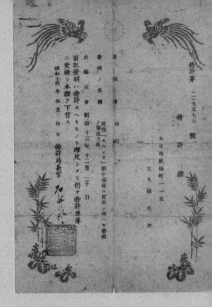

Masako's gift of *chiyogami*.

The Hyakunin Isshu cards made of discarded cardboard.

CHAPTER 3

The Free Earth

Not long after leaving Qiazi we were given some gruel to eat. The Eighth Route Army, officially called the People's Liberation Army since September 1948, had set up emergency kitchens for refugees. The gruel consisted of kaoliang and a little Chinese cabbage. To our emaciated bodies, which had had little to eat for so long, the warmth of the gruel was a godsend.

These same soldiers had watched silently as countless common citizens starved to death on the other side of the fence, but now they were feeding us. Why? The reason was that this was "the liberated zone."

Mao Zedong had given orders to the effect that the people should be made aware of who was providing them with food, for the people would then adhere to that side. This was a basic principle of the Communist Party. It didn't matter how many people died to demonstrate its validity. It didn't matter how many lives had to be sacrificed to drive the logic of this lesson home. It was many years later that I realized this.

We walked on and on in the direction indicated, without knowing why or wherefore. The earth was soft and spongy, undependable and hard to get a grip on, like sliding over snow.

My soul was suffused with a vacuous white light. Looking up through that light, I could see the clear but indistinct sky of the liberated zone. As far as the eye could see were fields of kaoliang, their heavy ears hanging lusciously down as if they had not a care in the world.

Jiefang qu. The liberated zone.

Was this really the longed-for liberated zone? The place where we could eat sweet rice cakes?

Like a funeral procession winding its way through some rustic setting, we sixteen plodded on, our footsteps heavy and unsteady. We followed in the tracks of the cart that led the group, our eyes directed ahead but focused on nothing in particular. Our bodies leaned forward, as if our shoulders were bearing some heavy burden, and our feet were continually on the verge of stumbling. No one spoke a word.

The dying we had witnessed. The life we had seen. The death we had been forced to accept. The parting with friends.

The price of freedom had been too high. Our hearts were much heavier than our feet.

* * * * *

It was then that I . . .

At first I didn't know what was happening. It was as if something had suddenly snapped. As if the string to a kite had broken, sending my body floating up into the air. I no longer felt I was walking on solid ground; the earth no longer responded to the tread of my feet. I planted my feet on the ground, but the ground didn't answer.

Even the rich fields of kaoliang, even the familiar sky overhead, now appeared to be remote detached worlds. It was as though I was walking in a painting.

* * * * *

The dirt road through the kaoliang fields continued unchanging to the horizon. The only things that stood out were a few open-air booths set up to service refugees. Below the booths' sooty red banners were rows of steamed *wowotou* buns made of corn flour and long twisted, deep-fried candy, a type of *mahua*. Lying on the ground near the booths were the emaciated bodies of the dead. No one made an effort to remove them. The proprietors of the booths stood around casually gazing up at the sky, as if to say the bodies were not their concern.

When Father finally spoke up, he said, "That's what happens when you gorge yourself. I know you must be hungry, but let's control ourselves a little longer. You understand?"

These people had not died of starvation so much as the shock of eating. When human beings have suffered a long time from a lack of food, the only thing they want before dying is to eat to their full. They are willing to trade whatever they have for something to eat, even the clothes off their backs. Once they have come by some food, they stuff it down without a second thought. But their malnourished bodies can take only so much. They go into shock and die while still eating, or succumb to dehydration from indigestion.

There were bodies even in the liberation zone. There were bodies next to booths selling food.

This seemed to be an ominous sign, a sign that even here danger lurked ahead. To escape that danger, we picked up our pace. We moved rapidly ahead as if pursued by some evil spirit. If we didn't hurry, we'd be overtaken by the God of Death.

Just as we were approaching Mengjiatun, there was a sign in the road indicating the direction to be taken by refugees from Qiazi. The road curved off to the right. From here we were to proceed to a camp in Liujiatun. It was there that our subsequent movements would be decided.

Here was the land of freedom, the free earth, but we weren't allowed to move about as we pleased. Apparently to keep an eye on us, Eighth Route sentries were posted here and there.

To reach Liujiatun we had to walk about double the distance we had covered so far. From this point on the road was bad, consisting of slippery clay, mucky from the previous night's rain. The sun had gone completely down. It was decided to spend the night there out in the open.

Looking back the way we had come, we could see the night sky in the direction of Changchun suddenly flare up. Listening carefully, we could hear the faint sound of firearms, probably the two sides skirmishing.

* * * * *

The next morning we set out at sunrise. We were all hungry, and it showed in the tottering way we walked. We hadn't had a bite to eat since the previous morning, when we had been given the kaoliang gruel at a sentry post shortly after leaving Qiazi.

Along the country road we were moving down were occasional farmhouses, smoke rising from their chimneys as the morning meal was prepared. Hoping to get food in exchange, Mother took some clothing and knocked on the door of one of the houses. An elderly woman appeared at the door, and realizing that we were Japanese, she treated us very kindly.

Looking at Mother and the other women of our group, she said, "Oh, you poor women. You're having a hard time, I see."

Moved by our pathetic figures, she briskly produced some water for us to drink. When Mother handed her the clothing she had brought to barter, the woman received them with outstretched hands, almost reverently, as if they were sacred objects. She repeatedly thanked Mother: "*Xiexie, xiexie.*" She rubbed the cloth against her cheek a number of times, apparently to show how much she valued it. Then she disappeared into the house, returning a short time later with all the freshly made *wowotou* bread they had.

While it was true that some Chinese loathed the Japanese, there were also some who still possessed kindly feelings toward us, even in our present state. Particularly in Changchun, the opening of the railroad and the building of electric power stations had contributed much to the lives of ordinary citizens. And there were no instances of massive slaughter. Thus, even after Japan's defeat, there were some Chinese who still treated Japanese with kindness. This elderly woman may have been one of these people, or it could be that she knew the good life that Japanese had once led and couldn't help but pity their present state.

Having fully satisfied our thirst with the first fresh water in ages, eating bits of *wowotou* a little at a time, we concentrated on putting some distance between us and the God of Death. Without reaching Liujiatun, the connection with Changchun wasn't fully broken. Our worst fear was that we would be taken back to Qiazi.

At noontime we visited other farmhouses to barter for food. The farmers were all very kind, happy to put together something for us to eat. However, if a soldier should appear nearby, they would immediately stop, as if they had been detected doing something wrong. They would wave their hands at us to shoo us away and disappear quickly into the house, shutting the door.

At this time the Eighth Route Army was not fully accepted or trusted. The Communists were known to kill landowners, and were fearfully referred to as "Communist bandits." Among the farmers the Nationalists were more trusted. This was related to the rumor that the Eighth Route soldiers "shared" women, and thus their appearance was always a source of apprehension.

While Eighth Route soldiers were undoubtedly not all cut from the same mold, the soldiers that our group of refugees met along the way were not always "friends of the people."

On the pretext of an "inspection," they would often stop us in the middle of the road and go through our things, pocketing whatever struck their eye. Father had the crematory box wrapped in a white cloth hanging from his neck, containing the bones of his daughter-in-law and her son Takashi as well as strands of hair of my older brother and Ma-chan. The sentries invariably thought that anything deserving of such careful handling must be valuable, and without fail they would have us open the box. When they discovered it contained bones and hair, they would recoil in horror and permit us to pass without further ado. They had an intense dislike of cremated remains, apparently having no such custom themselves.

It was almost evening when we reached Liujiatun. Without the permission of the refugee administration office there, we couldn't go any further. Perhaps for that reason, there was an unusually large number of sentries posted in the area. We were taken into custody by one of the sentries and led to a certain house.

From its appearance it must have once been a farmhouse, but now it had become a derelict ruin. Going in, we found ourselves in a room with an earthen floor. To one side of the entrance was a plank-floored room about thirty centimeters higher than the earthen one. The planks, however, only a few centimeters wide, weren't fitted neatly together, but placed so that there was a gap of several centimeters between each of them.

The Eighth Route soldier told us to go into the plank-floored room and rest. He spoke in Chinese, which meant that he was probably not Korean: if he were Korean, he would have spoken in Japanese. We went up into the room, watching that we didn't step into one of the gaps between the planks, and cautiously sat down.

Just as Father was lowering his body to the flimsy floor, the soldier said, "No, not you. You come with me." Apparently Father was going to be questioned at the Eighth Route sentry post at the refugee administration office. Taking a deep breath, Father pushed himself up with all the strength left in his arms. It seemed to be his last ounce of energy. Leaning heavily on his cane, he slowly moved his feet forward one step at a time and left.

All the soldiers at the sentry post were also Chinese, Father later told us. He was first asked how he had escaped Changchun. If he answered that it was because he was a technician, he might be detained again. If possible, he would like to be designated an ordinary refugee. As such he could get a *lutiao*, a kind of traveler's certificate or pass, which would serve to identify him as an ordinary refugee and allow him to go further south to Shenyang. Shenyang led to the port of Huludao, a common departure point for Japanese being repatriated.

At this point Father was completely drained of energy. He was no longer confident that he could lead our numerous troop across the Chinese continent to safety. Still, he wanted to return to Japan, and that's what caused him to hesitate. Logically speaking, there was no way that the gates of Qiazi would have opened for an ordinary refugee. If they decided that he had avoided the blockade in some devious way, he might be considered a spy or some other heinous character, resulting in him being returned to Qiazi. Outright prevarication—saying that he was nothing but an ordinary refugee—might be a dangerous ploy.

Feeling that he had no choice, Father stated that he was the inventor of Giftol, a treatment to cure drug addicts, and explained that when he had shown his patents at Qiazi, he had been let through the gate. He showed them the patents that were tied around his waist. The soldiers were convinced of the truth of what Father said, and decided on the spot to detain him as an employee of the Eighth Route Army. He was told to leave for Jilin the following morning.

From Changchun to Jilin was 111 kilometers. By train it probably wouldn't take long. However, at this point in time not only was Changchun under a food blockade but all the railways around the city had been destroyed by the Nationalists to prevent people from escaping. How long it would take to get to a train station that was still functioning, nobody knew. Still, there was a sense of relief in having a clear destination, a designated goal, and a definite direction to our movements.

As soon as Father returned to the derelict farmhouse, he said, "OK, everybody, we're off to Jilin!"

His voice was very cheerful. His intention was probably not only to give us hope but to keep up his own spirits. However, belying his cheerfulness, he suddenly collapsed.

Having successfully completed the first stage of the escape from Changchun, having moreover established a means of survival in the next stage, Father had fulfilled his responsibilities. But that effort and the sense of relief that came with it had drained every ounce of energy from his body, even the ability to stand on his feet. Until now he had been living by sheer willpower.

Mother and Big Sister helped Father, ashen-faced, to his feet and took him to the plank-floor room. If we lost Father, we would be losing the main pillar of our existence. Even in the liberated zone it was Father who provided the chief support for the family. Without him the family could not exist.

Father was fifty-eight at the time, but his white head of hair and long beard gave him the appearance of someone over ninety. His head looked like a mere skull, with nothing of a living human about it. The thought that he was not long for this world crossed every mind.

But he was still alive. "Sorry about this," he said, the words emerging hoarsely from his bluish lips, much to our relief.

Just at that moment, quite unexpectedly, a soldier appeared with a big pot of kaoliang gruel and some stir-fried soybeans. We happily accepted this godsend as a sign that Father's life was not yet at an end.

The next morning we were awoken by bright sunlight shining directly down on us. There was a gaping hole in the roof, and the sun's rays were coming through it in multiple shafts and falling on our faces. Birds were singing, and light was even coming from beneath the floor, with the morning mist rising from between the planks.

The mist from the floor was rising straight up, reflecting the light coming through the roof. The slanting rays of the sun set off the mist in mysterious wavering patterns. We could hear the musical sounds of the earth's creation. We all listened attentively.

That morning the Eighth Route soldiers provided us with the same food we had had the previous night.

*****

Then the long journey to Jilin began.

Supporting the weight of his body on his cane, Father walked slowly ahead, one deliberate step at a time, occasionally stopping to raise his hands in prayer. Whether he was apologizing for leaving Taeko and the others behind in Qiazi, or whether he was thanking the gods for giving him the strength to walk, it was hard to tell, but the pace was extremely slow. It turned out that this pace was just right for me.

I had reached the limit of my strength. Maggots had infested the wound in my arm, and they would sometimes crawl out into the open, dragging bloody pus after them. They attracted hordes of large flies, but I had neither the strength nor the will to fend them off.

It was as though I was wandering through a desolate wasteland, unsure of where to place my next step.

I was scared of the ground. Scared of what was buried under it. Scared of what was lying on it. Scared to touch the ground with my feet.

In fact, however, I had largely lost the ability to feel real fear. Between my feet and the earth was a fluffy cloud. It was by walking on that cloud that I was able to avoid touching the earth with my feet. This desolate wasteland, lit by a wan white light, was the reverse side of the world inhabited by the leering, laughing dead. That was the world I now occupied.

What kept me from being engulfed by that world? It was probably the solitary thought that I had to keep walking. It was that thought, nothing else.

Why did I have to keep walking? Where were we going? Such thoughts were beyond my powers of reasoning.

The only thing I knew was that to walk meant to live. Keeping my eyes on the feet of the adults in front of me, watching pebbles being kicked up by the cart, I walked on and on, without thinking. What kept my seven-year-old body walking was the idea, the will, that I had to keep moving. All living things, no matter how small and insignificant, have a will, and it was this that somehow kept my riddled heart and pain-racked body from breaking asunder.

* * * * *

How long did we walk, and where, I have no clear memory. Only certain scenes remain in my mind.

When the sun went down and the night dew rolled in, we spread our futon on the ground.

The night air made the ground and grass wet.

The smell of the wet ground and grass filled the late autumn air.

At night the vast plains surrounding us grew relentlessly cold.

The time must have been near the end of September. The smells of the plains contained hints of the fast-approaching winter so typical of the north.

The insects had grown quiet, the plains shrouded in silence. The faint ringing in my ears reverberated in the darkness, seeming to echo in the night. We slept covered solely by the smells of the night air. It was in this deathlike hush that we finally found sleep.

We began walking every morning at sunrise. The white morning mist flowed over the ground. It came wavering out of the earth and mounted to the heavens, creating celestial music.

As if drawn on by the tones of this music, I kept wandering over this vacuous wasteland. The earth would disappear in the morning mist, and the mist would cling coldly to my legs. A fog would rise as thick as paint on a canvas, and light up my heart in a faint glow.

* * * * *

Along the way the number of farmhouses finally dwindled and disappeared, and in any case we no longer had anything to barter, or to eat for that matter. On both sides of the road were occasional fields of eggplant. The plants were laden with fruit, shining in the morning mist. All we had to do was reach out to pick some, the eggplants being that close. There was no one around, so we just had to be careful not to be caught by the soldier who was accompanying the group. Before long, hands were reaching into the fields. The skin of the eggplants had a juicy, firm texture, and one bite suffused the mouth with a fresh, pure flavor.

That night we arrived at a hamlet and were put up at what appeared to be a guardhouse. The room consisted of a simple earthen floor, but it had a roof, a blessed thing. There was also a naked light bulb. Below the bulb was a cooking area, and one of the soldiers began preparing something to eat, busily cutting a big, oval winter melon called a *xihulu*. Chinese like to stir-fry this melon with a pinch of mustard, producing a nice sweet-sour taste. Was he doing this for us? The sweet and sour smell tickled our throats. However, the delicious smell was the only thing remaining when he left the room, taking the frypan with him.

Apparently the room we were in was the kitchen. After all, the earthen floor was wet, unsuitable for sleeping. The soldiers were stationed somewhere else, where they did their eating. They were probably going to serve us refugees with kaoliang gruel again. That's how it had been at the sentry post before. But this was the kitchen, and they weren't making the gruel here, so maybe that meant we weren't going to get any. Maybe they only made the *xihulu* here, and they prepared the other food in a separate kitchen. That might be where they would be making the gruel, which would be brought in any minute now.

We waited expectantly for the gruel. The night got progressively colder, but still it didn't come. We finally grew tired of watching the door through which the gruel should appear, falling asleep with the taste of disappointment in our mouths.

Nonetheless, the next morning we continued to hope, only once again to be disappointed.

Going outside, we found a well with a pump. At least we could have some water. The accompanying soldier watched us noncommittally, and then, as if he remembered an errand, he left.

Next to the well was a box filled with garbage, apparently the leftover piths of the melons the soldiers ate last night. Taking advantage of the soldier's absence, Mother went through the garbage. She found the piths and their fluffy fibers. They still smelled absolutely fresh. Recalling how delicious the eggplant tasted yesterday morning, we stuffed our mouths with the melons' pithy flesh. It tasted very much like an unripe watermelon. To an empty stomach it tasted just fine.

But the fact is that I no longer felt hunger pangs. Pain and hunger were now only dull sensations. I didn't feel afraid or apprehensive; I didn't feel happy or sad. In fact, I felt nothing at all, not even resignation, not even that I no longer cared. Difficulty in breathing and dizziness were my constant companions, but they were hardly worth special notice. Consciousness itself seemed on the verge of collapse.

For the body, pain and suffering are signals of danger, protective measures for the preservation of life. For people suffering from malnutrition, their response to outside stimuli is blunted, even if they don't fall into mental aberration like myself. This indicates that the ability of the body to protect itself has grown weaker. However, when pain and suffering reach an extreme and the body becomes desensitized to pain, this in itself can also be a means of protection from danger. In this case, the danger is psychological breakdown.

When pain and suffering exceed human limits, desensitization to outer stimuli—a loss of contact with reality—is a means of fending off mental derangement. On the other hand, mental derangement can also be a means of avoiding suffering and escaping death. Which of these two applied to me?

Perhaps half of me had become mentally deranged in order to avoid death. The other half had become insensitive to the outer world in order to avoid derangement. If physical suffering continued indefinitely, desensitization would no longer be a means of preserving life, but would be a path leading to death.

Was this the mechanism the heavens had provided for the maintenance of life and death?

Around noon on the day we had rifled through the garbage box, all at once I was assailed by a terrible headache, vomiting, and stomach pains. I squatted on the ground and stayed there, unable to get up. At the same time everyone else came down with violent diarrhea. If people suffering from malnutrition get diarrhea, the inevitable result is death. I had seen this happen many times.

In a voice devoid of all life Father asked Mother, "What was that? What was that we ate this morning?"

"Only melon pith," Mother answered.

"Melon pith? Why, that's a laxative."

"My goodness! What have I done?"

"Well, that's a relief. It's good to know it's only the melon. It's different from ordinary diarrhea. Just like taking a laxative. It'll go away pretty soon."

However, things didn't work out so simply. The affect of the melon was like priming a pump, drawing all the water out of our bodies, leaving us completely dehydrated.

But I wasn't afraid at all. Everyone had fallen to the ground, unmoving. So there was no way I would be separated from Father. That's why I wasn't scared.

Until now what had kept me walking was undoubtedly the almost obsessive thought that I couldn't be separated from Father and the others: that if I was, I'd be overtaken by the God of Death. But now the will to live was slowly being eroded by the comforting notion that there was no need to run from the God of Death—we were already walking hand in hand with him. The thin thread that connected me with life began to fray. I began to float in the air, to wander a vacuous spiritual wasteland.

All pain and suffering fled my body. There were no signals of danger, no attempts at self-protection. The comforts of Death beckoned me. I closed my eyes and felt my blood drain away.

I don't know how long I remained that way. I opened my eyes when I felt something rubbing against my cheek. It was a dried, yellowish shepherd's purse. The wind had come up and apparently blown it against my cheek.

Next to the shepherd's purse was a thistle with a single flower in bloom. Its leaves spread wide, the late-blooming thistle was thrusting itself up toward the heavens. The sun was still high in the sky, and the thistle's purple petals shone lustrous and translucent against the autumn sun. It was as if a deep-purple current of water was flowing within the sparkling petals and out to the white pollen at the petal tips.

Unconsciously my hand reached out toward the thistle, only to be pricked by one of its thorny leaves.

It was then that it happened. A bolt of lightning shot through my body. The pain from the thorn had knocked on the door of my heart. Perhaps it was a combination of the beauty of the flower and the pain of the prick, but in that instant my emotions were reborn and my senses resurrected. At the same time my whole body was assailed by excruciating pain.

What was I doing here? What was this urge to vomit, this pain in my stomach, this difficulty in breathing? My lips were preternaturally dry, my hands trembled, my legs cramped.

Was this how I was going to end my life? What an ignominious way to die! To fall by the wayside, to rot, to be transformed into bleached bones.

But this was no concern of the thistle, which would continue to bloom season after season. How many deaths had it seen, how many people convulsed in the throes of death?

These desolate plains might be completely inundated with ignominious deaths, but the thistle would never die, would continue proudly on, year after year, for ever and ever. As long as this earth endured, the thistle would not die.

Its roots in the good earth, never dying, the beauty of the thistle . . . Its sturdy leaves, the pure flow of purple . . .

I wanted to become a thistle. I wanted to be a thistle.

If I buried my feet in the earth, could I become a thistle? If that were possible, I would happily bury my whole body from the waist down. I could cleanse myself of ignominious death.

I would return to the earth. I would return to the earth and become a thistle, living and blooming forever. Once again Death was beckoning me. The thistle was attempting to pull me down into the earth.

It was dark. It was cold. My body began to grow frigid, its heat seeping away. In the dark earth there was a colorful flow of purple; within it pollen was floating, pale and damp.

Then I heard a sound.

From somewhere there came the sound of a voice. Was it the voices of the pollen singing? No, it was someone calling me back to life. What could the voice be saying? I couldn't make out the words.

"Mr. Boss. Mrs. Boss . . . Mr. Boss. Mrs. Boss!"

"Mr. Boss"?—then my eyes opened. There was someone standing in front of me, shouting loudly.

The person who had called me back from the dead was Xiaoli. We used to call him "Snot-nosed Xiaoli," a young Chinese boy who worked in the basement boiler room at Shinkyo. He was an orphan, and Father had looked after him like a son. When he was small, he always had green mucus running from his nose; thus the nickname Snot-nosed Xiaoli.

"It's you, Mr. Boss, isn't it? It's you, Mrs. Boss. What's happened? Is everyone alright?"

"Oh! Is that you Xiaoli? You're still alive and well?" said Father.

Continuing to repeat "Mr. Boss," Xiaoli clung to Father's side, crying. In his two hands he grasped one of Father's and repeatedly pumped it in the air, overjoyed.

"So it's you, is it, Xiaoli?" said Father. "A sight for sore eyes, I'd say."

As Father rubbed his head, Xiaoli remained by his side, continuing to cry. To Xiaoli, Father was the same as a real father.

He had joined the Eighth Route Army and was now a medic, he said. He was carrying a rifle and sporting a white armband. He was wearing a baggy uniform, his hands peeking out from its sleeves.

"So you're a medic now," Father said appreciatively. "You've come up in the world, haven't you? You've come up in the world."

Xiaoli's familiar small eyes sparkled with pleasure. His body seemed to be dancing inside his overlarge, dirty, greenish uniform. He had a lot of medicine with him, and bringing some lukewarm water from a nearby farmhouse, he had us take an antidiarrheal.

Close to where Father was sitting was some charred wood, and he was apparently trying to build a fire and make charcoal. He also wanted to find some medicinal cranesbill, but he couldn't move. The charcoal he wanted to make into a potion for its digestive effects, it seemed.

I am not sure where he got it, but Xiaoli soon brought us some hot gruel. We took our time eating it, one slow mouthful after another.

Before long, the trembling and spasms ceased. Our bodies began to get warmer. For the time being it seemed we had escaped the world of death, though we were still unable to stand up. Xiaoli's ministrations continued until nightfall. He then put us on a cart and took us to the shed of a nearby farmhouse. Covered in warm straw, we were able to sleep soundly that night.

The next morning Xiaoli brought us not only more hot gruel but white *mantou* as well. It had been quite a while since our stomachs felt so satisfied. The diarrhea also stopped.

"You've saved us, Xiaoli," Father said. "We owe you our lives."

Father took Xiaoli's hand in his own and bowed deeply. Xiaoli looked extremely pleased. He had finally been able to repay Father for all his past kindnesses, something he had always wanted to do. He was a very happy man, he said, able to return some of what he had received. He seemed proud of the fact that he had been able to help Father and to save our lives. He had a sparkle in his eye and moved briskly about. As the time approached for us to part, he handed us some twisted candy and *mantou*, which he had apparently bought at an open-air booth, as well as sweet potato candy seasoned in miso and some other things; for the road, he said.

Xiaoli seemed to find it hard to leave Father. He kept wondering if there wasn't something more he could do, and decided to go along with the group for a while. He had Father and the weaker children ride in the cart. While pulling the cart, he repeatedly asked the accompanying soldier to look after Father.

"I owe this man more than I can put in words," he told the soldier. "He is just like a father to me. He always took good care of Chinese and Koreans. Now it is our turn to take good care of him. Please treat him kindly."

The soldier nodded dubiously, looking seriously into Father's face.

Still, it was a wonder—to meet up with Xiaoli in this endless plain, at this particular moment, at this particular place.

It is not something that can be explained by calling it a miracle. Surely it reflects some kind of heavenly intent. It has something to do, I can't help thinking, with the good works performed by Father, who never thought of himself or of personal gain. A miracle of this nature can't be created by human hands. Who could imagine Xiaoli suddenly appearing, a medic and bearing medicine? Maybe it was his experience at the factory that eventually made him a medic. If we had not encountered Xiaoli at that particular time, there is no doubt that we would all have fallen victim to the desolate wasteland.

It makes one feel a profound reverence for the convoluted workings of fate, surpassing human understanding.

Just as the sun was tipping toward the west, Xiaoli bid his final farewells and headed back down the path he had come. He had to return to the corps and couldn't accompany us any further. Thanks to him, the soldier accompanying us became less reserved and distant, changing his attitude toward us entirely. Since Xiaoli himself was part of the Eighth Route Army, he was someone to be trusted. The soldier was particularly kind to Father. And he even let us ride on the cart, which was now empty of things to barter, and pulled the cart himself, just like Xiaoli.

Earlier, not long after we had left the camp in Liujiatun, Father had fallen to the ground, unable to walk any further. The cart was being pulled by the young glass craftsman and White Rat. The accompanying soldier ordered them to put Father on the cart. What the Eighth Army wanted was Father; everyone else was nothing but unwanted baggage. White Rat showed his displeasure, but an order had to be followed. On the other hand, he swore vehemently at Father.

If Father had not been there, White Rat reasoned, the group could have been recognized as ordinary refugees, who could then have proceeded south to Shenyang and Huludao, then returned to Japan. Father was necessary until they got out of Qiazi, but once out, he was simply a thorn in White Rat's side. White Rat's continual swearing and cursing seemed to know no end; in fact, it was extended to Mother and us children.

"What the hell are you good-for-nothings doing?"

"Auntie there! Push harder, ya hear me?"

And to Father, "Who do you think's givin' you a ride, for god's sake?"

Father's pallid face was drenched in a cold sweat. There might have been a mixture of tears.

Finally Father said in a trembling voice, "Enough. That's enough." Dragging his body, he got off the cart, Mother and Big Sister helping him down. He began to walk with their support.

If only we had met up with Xiaoli a little earlier, this kind of thing could have been avoided.

We sometimes crossed paths with Eighth Army horse-drawn wagons piled high with Chinese cabbages, potatoes, and other things. Our soldier parleyed with the driver of the wagon, who was sitting casually on a heap of cabbages and yielding a whip, and shared with us the potatoes and cabbage he'd acquired. We peeled off the cabbage leaves one at a time and ate it as it was, boiling the potatoes, dirt and all. The box of matches Father had put in his pocket when we left Changchun was put to good use.

* * * * *

Eventually there were no more farmhouses and no more fields. Then one day we found ourselves standing on a rocky riverbank. Exactly how it came about I'm not sure, but we had been joined by several other groups of refugees. I have no recollection of when or where this happened. In any case, since the railroad tracks around Changchun had been destroyed, refugees from the city heading for Jilin had no choice but to walk to the nearest station where trains were still running. Whether these refugees were actually from Changchun, people who had somehow escaped the city and who were now headed for Jilin, I couldn't tell. What we had to do was cross this river, following the other refugees in front of us. That, if nothing else, was clear. I don't remember the name of the river.

In the vast desolate plain, with no visible landmarks, there was suddenly this river, its banks strewn with boulders. Its water flowed in muddy swirls, splashing up against the rocks, sending off glints of reflected sunlight. It was midday.

The group in front of us started to cross the river. They were pushing a large cart piled with goods, up to at least a meter and a half high. Some women and children were squatting uneasily on the top. One woman was sitting with one knee raised, cradling a baby. The body of the cart wasn't a framed box but just a platform.

Just as the cart reached the middle of the river, it suddenly lurched. One of the back wheels had apparently gotten caught between two rocks and come off. The cart tipped precipitously toward the rear. The two poles on the front of the cart used for pushing shot up into the air.

Letting out screams of despair, the women and children clung desperately to the platform. But its sharp slant was beyond their strength.

The load on the cart, tied down with ropes, broke loose and disintegrated. The women and children were dragged into the river along with the things on the platform. The swirling waters swept them away, the men who pulled the cart attempting to rescue them.

But the river was too swift. Soon only the raised arms of the struggling women and children could be seen through the waves, finally only their hands. Then they too disappeared in the muddy waters.

It was like watching a movie in slow motion, the desperately struggling women and children. Once more a white light suffused my mind, and once again I found myself wandering in a desolate landscape. The pure beauty of the thistle that had once revived me was a thing of the past. If I hadn't been so enthralled by this moment of fear, if instead I had been capable of describing it clearly, surely it would not have become so deeply imbedded in my mind. The fear of that moment never took conscious form, but sank deep, deep down into my subconscious.

This experience was subtly connected to the one I had had in

1947 when I was a first-year student at Changchun School. As I have already described, it was early summer, just after a heavy rain, and Big Sister, a friend of hers, and I were returning home from school. Xing-an Boulevard was inundated with water, and I had had the frightening experience of being left alone on the deluged street. I had been mesmerized by an emerald-green leaf floating on the wavelets left by the boots of my sister and her friend. That experience and the present one somehow became unconsciously linked in my mind, in time making me petrified of swirling water. While this riverside scene would eventually vanish from memory for a time, I would later become tormented by dreams of swirling waters, and this experience, buried in my subconscious, would come to play a crucial role.

The river was flowing toward the northwest. We were headed toward the northeast, the direction of the railroad tracks. To go upstream would be an arduous undertaking. But we didn't want to repeat the experience of the preceding group. While we were mulling over which course to take, the soldier crossed the river and was beckoning to us from the other side. It was then that I noticed Father standing facing the river, his hands placed together in prayer, his head bowed, his eyes closed.

His prayer finished, he raised his head and shouted out, "OK, everyone. We're going upstream." There was a look of determination on his face that wouldn't brook dissent. Reluctantly the soldier came back across the river. Further up the river there was bound to be a shallow, less dangerous crossing. The problem was that the further upstream we went, the further we would get from the railroad.

Finding a likely place, Father shouted out again, "Alright, we're crossing here." We crossed over, safely reaching the opposite bank.

* * * * *

Usually we stopped for the night when the sun went down, but this night we kept walking, apparently with the idea that the railroad couldn't be far off. The vast plain was suffused with the smell of dew-wet grass and the scents of the earth. Winter was fast approaching. The sharp night air embraced us.

The dark, gloomy plain stretched out without end. The icy night was steeped in a pitch-black silence, devouring all light, all hope, life itself. The earth merged with primeval chaos, leaving one soul empty and alone, at death's door.

O Heaven, O Earth, devour me! Take me into that pitch-black night. Take me into the fathomless dark.

I couldn't walk. The rocklike determination that had driven me before was no longer there. My will to walk now consisted of a small speck in the dark, a speck that was being devoured by the night, on the brink of disappearing.

But then . . . that speck started to emit a light. That speck, the focus of all my being, began to blink. Was it some kind of heavenly light? The light grew bigger and bigger. It came closer and closer.

What was it . . . that light?

It wasn't an illusion. It was the train station, the train station standing alone in the middle of the vast plain. It was the station! I could see the station!

The purpose of my being, the reason for my existence, was there in that station. I could see it. The life that had been on the verge of being devoured was there, shining, in the station's light. God was listening, after all.

As if drawn by a powerful magnet, I hurried toward the light to become part of the life there.

In front of the station were a number of people warming themselves by a bonfire. Some had their arms crossed with their hands in the opposing sleeves; some were sitting around the fire, stamping their feet to ward off the cold; some were squatting in front of the fire toasting *doubing*. *Doubing* was pig feed made of strained soybean lees that had been compressed into the shape and size of a truck tire, several centimeters thick. Toasting it made it softer. The people at the fire motioned for us to come closer, to warm ourselves and have some *doubing*. Famished and cold, we happily gathered around the fire.

Mother lowered Chiyoji from her back and tried to feed him bits of *doubing*. But he shook his head in refusal, seeming to shrink within himself from the cold. When Mother wrapped him in a blanket, his body looked pathetically small, as if it were all head. His whole being was trembling. Hoping to warm him up, Mother took him nearer the fire and tried to force some *doubing* into his mouth. That triggered a violent fit of vomiting, and when the fit ended, his head drooped forward, all strength gone from his neck.

Would this damage his brain? Was he not long for this life?

The train came into the station a little before dawn. It had come from Jilin in the west and now would be turning around and heading back the way it had come. It couldn't travel any further east because all the tracks around Changchun had been destroyed. No one remembers the name of this station, just that it was a quiet, rustic building set off by itself in the vast plains. By this time we had sold the cart and didn't have any luggage worthy of the name.

What happened on the train from there to Jilin Station, for some reason I have no recollection at all.

* * * * *

As soon as we reached Jilin, Father was taken off to the Public Security Office.

Leaving the dim train platform, the rest of us emerged into a three-side station square that was dazzlingly bright. It was almost like having the reflected light from a mirror shone suddenly in one's face. For a moment the light was so glaring that I couldn't see anything at all.

We decided to wait for Father in the station square, sitting on what pitiful things we had, leaning against the station building walls.

Light shone brightly through the open sides of the square, the sky clear and blue. Liberation songs were playing over a loudspeaker in an upbeat tempo.

Food stalls lined the walls of the station building. Their eaves were adorned with biscuits the size of ping-pong balls strung together like a pearl necklace. Below them were heaps of deep-fried *mahua* and pure-white buns. The stalls' straw posts were pierced with skewered clusters of candied red hawthorn fruit called *tanghulu*. The contrast between the red of the hawthorn and the white of the buns was exquisitely beautiful.

There were also stalls selling grilled meat, as well as those with a spread of colorful hard candy. The people passing in front of them were all in perfect health, quite the opposite of being famished, chatting pleasantly, a spring in their step. Their mouths were full of candied hawthorn and white buns. We could almost taste the sweet-sour flavor of the glazed candy from where we were.

Thinking that this scene might be too much for us children, Mother tried to block our view with her body. On Mother's back, Chiyoji's skull-like head flopped backward, his chin pointing up. His lids were weakly open, his eyes unfocused and uncoordinated, no longer possessing a human gleam, much like translucent glass beads. His pallid lips were rounded into a circle as if he were trying to say, "Oh." He was no longer conscious, seeming to have little life left in his body.

Father finally came back, this time without an accompanying soldier. We thought that we would now be able to find a place to settle down, but we were wrong. Father told us that the medical authorities had ordered him to proceed immediately to Yanji, which was further east, near the Korean border. There were a great number of Japanese in Yanji, and Japanese doctors as well. He could have his son treated there. The question was, we thought, would Chiyoji last that long?

Aside from Father, Chiyoji was the last surviving male member of the family. My older brother had died of starvation, as had his son

Takashi and my youngest brother Ma-chan. In cases of starvation, males seem to be the first to succumb. If Chiyoji were to die here, that would mean the end of the male line. And what would Father's and Mother's feelings be, having come this far?

On the train on the way to Yanji, Father and Mother kept praying until we arrived. Father took Chiyoji from Mother and held him tenderly in the warmth of his arms for what might prove to be the last time, continuing to pray. Chiyoji had reached the point where he refused water.

The train was crowded, immersed in lively Chinese voices. The seats were all facing forward, and some people were sitting in the aisle between them. Vendors stepped over these people, balancing themselves against the sway of the train, selling slices of flat, white steamed sweets much like Japanese *karukan*, which they placed on a board hanging from their neck. They also had a knife for cutting the buns, hanging on a string. Mother removed the vest she was wearing and traded it for some sweet bun. This vest was one she had knitted for Big Brother, and she had carried it with her since Changchun as a remembrance.

* * * * *

When we arrived at Yanji Station, there was a horse-drawn cart waiting for us, as if prearranged. Father got hurriedly on the cart and took Chiyoji to a hospital. White Rat went with him.

The rest of us waited on the train platform for Father's return. Just as it began to get dark, White Rat came back.

Chiyoji's life had been saved. The hospital was a People's Hospital run by Japanese, and they had given Chiyoji a blood transfusion. Father had taken him to a construction company dormitory where we would be living, and was waiting for us there. Getting in the cart that White Rat had arrived in, we set off for the dormitory, which was occupied entirely by Japanese.

The living space assigned to us was a smallish room, six mats in size. Father was sitting alone under a dim light bulb holding Chiyoji. Father's eyes no longer shone with their usual strength; his shoulders were stooped; his long, dirty beard was entangled in the white hair falling to his shoulders. Father was a large man, but he looked very small.

Suddenly there was the sound of feet running up and down the hallway, and then the sound of voices.

"Refugees have arrived!"

"Refugees from Changchun have come!"

"Our countrymen, our comrades . . . !"

Almost simultaneously several heads appeared in the doorway of our room. An older woman came in with a big, round container of *chirashi-zushi*. A young man, standing behind the kneeling woman and peeking over her shoulder, held the container out and said, "It's our lunch meal, but we haven't touched it yet." He was holding a camping pot used by soldiers on bivouac.

"Thank you so much," Mother said, bowing in the polite fashion as she was wont to do. "Thank you so very much." She had tears in her eyes.

"My, my, what a condition you're in. You must have had a hard time of it. Well, the bath is ready. Take off your clothes and get in. I'll sterilize them in boiling water."

The woman's voice was followed by others.

"Changchun is the worst of them all, I hear."

"But you're with friends now. There's nothing more to worry about."

The people in the dorm brought in more food to eat, along with words of encouragement. But their voices gradually started to fade away. It was like a silent movie: their mouths were moving but there was no sound, no sound from their laughing mouths.

Then their smiling faces began to flicker uncertainly. The silent world started going round and round. The light from the bulb began to waver and then flicker out. The one thing that kept me steady, the one thing that gave me existence, slipped out of my body.

This was the last stop on our escape from Changchun. There was no need to walk anymore. I could now die in peace.

I no longer needed to fear being left alone. I no longer needed to face death on the rotting plains. There was nothing that tied me to the world of the living. My immediate destination was a desolate wasteland, an unhinged, deranged world. Just as I was crossing the line into those worlds, I lost all consciousness.

CHAPTER 4

Liberated Yanji

The population of Yanji, located near the Chinese-Korean border, was seventy or eighty percent Korean, with the remaining twenty or thirty percent being Chinese and a smattering of Japanese. During the era of the State of Manzhouguo, it was known as Jiandao and served as the capital of Jiandao Province. The dominant forces in the city were the Kanto Army, the State of Manzhouguo bureaucracy, and the local Chinese landowners. The ethnic Koreans were caught between the Chinese and the Japanese. With Japan's defeat, rioting erupted throughout the city, and government officials and landowners were summarily executed by people's courts.

Due perhaps to Yanji's proximity to the Soviet border, Communist "bandits" were common in the area, and even before Japan's defeat the city was notorious for its civil disorder. The influence of Kim Il-sung, "the tiger of Changbai," was also felt along the border with northern Korea as well as among the ethnic Koreans of Yanji.

Given the city's mixed population, Yanji has always been a unique entity in China, difficult for the central government to control from afar. Today this general area is designated the Yanbian Korean Autonomous Prefecture, having self-governing powers. In the postwar period it never fell under the sway of the Nationalist Party, or Guomindang, but after a period of Russian occupation it aligned itself with the Chinese Communists.

To the north of Yanji there are two historical sites that bear witness to the tragic end of Japanese prisoners of war: the remains of the 28th and 646th internment camps.

When we arrived in Yanji, the immediate postwar chaos and the rule of the people's courts had died down, and in their place a brainwashing campaign was in full swing.

The physician who give Chiyoji a blood transfusion at the People's Hospital was a certain Dr. Noda. Chiyoji's blood was type A, which didn't match that of the doctor, who had planned to transfuse his own blood; moreover, Dr. Noda, a thin, pale man, had tuberculosis. There was, however, a healthy-looking young man there who offered to donate his blood. Actually, Dr. Noda admitted that he was astonished that Chiyoji was still breathing. Postwar, the doctor had treated many refugees, but never had he seen one survive who was this debilitated, this dehydrated, and possibly suffering from brain fever.

Whether it was due to Father's and Mother's fervent prayers, or whether it was just a matter of Chiyoji's will to live, he stubbornly continued to breathe.

The Yanji Public Security Office, occupying the offices of the former Japanese Military Police Corps, directed Father to establish a pharmaceutical factory. Although Yanji possessed pharmacies, it apparently had no pharmaceutical manufacturing plant. Work was immediately begun on transforming a pharmacy called Yanji Pharmaceutical Company into a facility for making medicine. It would operate under the jurisdiction of the Yanbian Specialist Office and the Yanbian Teachers School (absorbed by Yanbian University in 1949), and was officially named the Pharmaceutical Factory Attached to the Yanbian Higher Teachers School of Yanji City, Jilin Province.

At first the factory was only a small facility run by Father and an assistant from the Teachers School. Over time, however, assisted by later economic reform, it would prosper and become the largest pharmaceutical manufacturing factory in the Yanbian region, re-named the First Manufacturing Depot of Yanbian. Its nucleus was Father's creation.

My two older sisters and my younger sister began to attend the Yanji Japanese Resident Principal Elementary School, the younger a first-year student and the two older fourth-year and sixth-year students. This was about October 1948, and most Japanese residents had repatriated to Japan. Still, there were enough remaining to form a school of sorts, albeit small in size. With the acquisition of a moderate income and a commensurate amount of food on the table, my sisters had put flesh on their bones and escaped the clutches of malnutrition. Chiyoji also recovered his health in a remarkably short time. As for myself, I continued to remain in a state of semi-consciousness.

Yanji was located in a basin surrounded by mountains on three sides. In the south, beyond Yanji Station on the city's fringes, was a mountain that resembled a hat placed on the ground, appropriately called Hat Mountain. In the north was a towering prominence called Candle Mountain, and abutting it on the east was Mount Mopan. Further to the east was the formidable presence of Mount Maan. When winter came to Yanji, circumscribed by these peaks, gloomy snow-laden clouds would hang over the city, and snow would pile high.

To get through the winter the first thing that needed to be done was to gather firewood for the *ondol*. *Ondol* refers to a system of under-floor heating in which the wooden flooring is raised thirty or forty centimeters above the ground, and a firebox near the entrance stile sends heated air under the floor, which is covered with impervious oiled paper. There must have been a layer of reinforced earth under this slippery, shiny paper, for grainy bits of gravel would appear here and there that had apparently made their way through the paper. In Changchun the principal means of heating had been radiators, but here it was the Korean *ondol*.

Seeing her daughters off to school, Mother's daily routine consisted of going out with the now healthy Chiyoji in hand and looking for firewood. But that was not all. There were other things she looked for, apparently discarded by Japanese soldiers: mess kits, empty tin cans, nails, and pieces of wire—anything that could be put to use. The empty cans served as plates and tea bowls, the mess kits as pots. Small pieces of wood could be carved to make chopsticks. More sturdy pieces were wired and nailed together to form the frame for a *kotatsu*, a short-legged table that is covered by a blanket to help keep the feet warm. Using the only remaining futon, the whole family slept with their feet under the *kotatsu*.

Out on these daily excursions, three-year-old Chiyoji would let out a triumphant cry whenever he found something interesting. "I found one, I found one," he would shout, proudly showing his discovery to Mother.

This sense of discovery went back to Shinkyo Pharmaceutical days when Father was working on cystine. To see whether deposits had formed or not, Father would hold a bundle of ampoules together, turn them upside down, and check them under a spotlight. Since cystine doesn't dissolve easily in water, it was difficult to obtain a sample without deposits. Chiyoji, who was only one then, would copy what Father was doing. He would take one ampoule, turn it upside down, hold it up to the sunlight and then shout out, "None, none." Watching him, Mother and Father couldn't help smiling to themselves, seeing in him what he might become in the future.

Out on these daily excursions, whenever Chiyoji shouted with joy that he'd found something, particularly something shiny, Mother would place her hands together as if in prayer and say to herself, "Sorry, Chiyoji, for putting you through this experience."

It is said that what is learned in the cradle is carried to the grave, and it is true that Chiyoji, who would later become a Doctor of Medicine and a Doctor of Pharmacy, didn't lose the habit of picking up things until he was a young man.

* * * * *

Among the Japanese residents of Yanji, "study groups" were held three nights a week, the purpose of which was to brainwash the participants, to cleanse them of their Japanese way of thinking by replacing it with Communist ideology. Those who could not be reformed were said to be "bad elements," that is, bad influences, and were repeatedly targeted until they had been thoroughly reformed. Anyone who changed sides, from the side being reformed to the side doing the reforming, could elevate their status, and many were eager to do just that. The more abusive the reformer's language, the more progressive they would appear. As a result, in order to maintain one's relative position, new targets were always in demand.

All Japanese had to take part in these study groups, not excepting Father, Mother, and White Rat. Clever in the ways of the world, White Rat was quick to fathom the relationship between reformer and reformed, and it didn't take him long to come to the conclusion that if he targeted Father as an exploitive capitalist, it would be to his benefit. He quickly resolved to make Father his target.

His first example of Father's heinous behavior was the incident that occurred just after leaving Liujiatun, when Father had been given a ride on the cart after collapsing on the road. White Rat cleverly manipulated this truth, going around and spreading the rumor.

"Though we are the same human beings, he sat on the cart as if king of the world, using me like a beast of burden. This, more than anything, shows the slave-like existence I led under him."

It is true that for a few hours White Rat had pulled the cart bearing Father. He was ordered to do so by the Eighth Route soldiers, so he had no choice. Why was he ordered to do so? Because there was a palpable difference in physical strength between the two men. How did that difference come about? How did White Rat come to bear that nickname?

More than anything, White Rat knew Father's character. He

knew that Father wouldn't reveal the truth of the matter or try to defend himself. He knew that Father wouldn't respond in kind, that he would find that below his dignity—that that was Father's weakness. Taking advantage of this, White Rat escalated his vituperation.

Father was saddened by the fact that his nephew had turned out to be this kind of person, and that he had failed to influence his character for the better. He looked upon it as a personal failure, apologizing and praying to god for his shortcomings.

* * * * *

As it turned out, White Rat took Father's faith in god and turned it against him. In societies based on a materialist ideology such as China, believers in a spiritual basis to life are considered counter-revolutionary, dangerous social elements. This is especially true of anyone with a deep religious faith. Here White Rat found good material for launching a personal attack.

Unfortunately, when it came to religion, Father was unwilling to concede a step. He didn't believe that life could be neatly divided into the spiritual and the material, given the very existence of human beings, the fact that human beings have conscious awareness, the fact that human beings have life and death, the number of things under the sun that are inexplicable to the human intellect. Even using the materialist methods of science, the more we know, the further the realms of the unknown seem to expand. Everything seems to have as its purpose the furthering of life. What could possibly be wrong, Father thought, with this type of thinking? To offer one's devout prayers to this power, to thank god for one's minuscule life, to share god's blessings with one's fellow beings. God's will resides in these lives, in their convoluted relationships. In the end, Father's religion consisted of forgetting the self and devoting one's life to the welfare of others. It was not, however, a type of philanthropy or charity. It was his philosophy of being, without which he could not exist.

The life of individuals can be extrapolated to mean the life of a people. If you don't selflessly help the individuals who are suffering before your very eyes, if that is not your basic stance, how can you be of service to the people? Service to the people can't just be so many words; it has to result in action. And that action has to be done without thought of oneself. That is precisely why it is not bad to pray to god and to thank god. This is the argument Father presented when attacked for his beliefs.

But the more Father rebutted criticism, the more vehement it became.

"Class warfare! Your way of thinking completely ignores class warfare!"

The newly brainwashed also joined in the attack, and White Rat took advantage of that.

At this point in time not only had Father become advanced in years, but he suffered from severe malnutrition and hemorrhoids. Without a cane it was impossible for him to walk. For Father the cane served the same purpose as crutches for the disabled.

It was this cane that White Rat decided to focus on. He asserted that the cane was a bourgeois symbol, a badge of the exploitive class. The fact that Father still used a cane was a sign that he harbored bourgeois thinking, proof that he had not divested himself of his bourgeois mentality. He himself, White Rat said, was a proletarian and didn't possess a cane. Thus, sprinkling his speech with plausible-sounding revolutionary terminology, he tried to make his case.

In a proletarian society, in a liberated zone, the workers are the highest social class. Those who had been impoverished in the past, those who had formerly been abused, were now to be treated as heroes. So, if you loudly proclaimed, "I was once a common laborer, treated like a slave, and this is the person who abused me," almost invariably this assertion would be accepted as the truth. This was the type of accusation that took place in the people's courts.

In a people's court the accused would have his hands tied behind him and be made to stand on a dais, whereupon someone would begin shouting out the accused's alleged crimes. The crowd surrounding the dais would let out a roar, sometimes mounting the stage and hitting and kicking the accused, or stoning him; in the worst cases the beatings were carried out with clubs. A verdict would then be given, and the Eighth Route Army would carry out the sentence, though often the accused had already died due to internal bleeding or shock.

Usually the use of force was not allowed in people's courts, so this description may not hold true for every case. However, it does seem that there were many instances in which violence erupted from long-suppressed anger and oppression, abetted by mob psychology.

Self-protection also played a role. As the crowd was taking turns berating and abusing the defendant, anyone seen as lacking in enthusiasm would themselves be accused of being a "bad element" or anti-progressive force, and might have to take their turn on the dais. This is what filled people with fear. This is what led some people to apologize to the accused in their hearts while publicly castigating and physically abusing them.

There were any number of cases in which Japanese businessmen were executed as villainous capitalists simply for being Japanese. And often the people who denounced them were Japanese themselves. By shamelessly denouncing others these people could have their own dubious deeds overlooked and be accepted as upright members of the community. Since Japanese were easy targets for censure, the best means of protecting themselves was to strike first, to denounce others before being denounced themselves.

While the study groups didn't have judicial power like the people's courts, their basic nature was the same. They took the form of ostensibly free, unrestrained self-criticism as their formal modus operandi, but the real goal was simply to force the accused to confess to whatever they were accused of. Once targeted in this way, the social damage to the accused was enormous—ostracism by the local community. In the end, the safest course was to denounce before being denounced.

White Rat's strategy was a success, and he began to extend it to Mother and Big Sister.

Following the defeat of Japan, Japanese refugees flowed into Changchun to be confined in internment camps, where countless died. Japanese residents of the city also saw the number of deaths increase. Most of the deceased in the camps were simply buried as they fell, but the resident population was relatively better off, and scraping together what money they could, they cremated their loved ones. Cremation was not only a sign of respect for the departed, but also, by keeping the cremated remains close at hand, a show of affection, an indication by the living that the dead would accompany them throughout the rest of their lives. On the other hand, if the dead were buried, they would leave the hands of their family, return to the earth, and become physically estranged. This explains why those who could afford cremation were objects of envy.

When Takashi, my nephew and son of my older brother, died of starvation, we didn't have enough money for a proper cremation, but we were able to build a fire under the crucible in the glass factory, where he was cremated. Thus, of all the people who died during that time, this was an unusual case. His bones still remain a permanent part of the family.

White Rat took this incident and turned it on its head.

At the time neither China nor Korea had the custom of cremation. It was this that White Rat manipulated to his advantage.

In Father's pharmaceutical factory in Yanji, there were a good number of Korean and Chinese working in the plant. White Rat began spreading the rumor among them that Mother was a vicious, heartless woman. Big Brother was not her son, White Rat explained, but the son of Father's first wife, and therefore his son, Takashi, was unrelated to Mother by blood. That's why, White Rat claimed, she hated Takashi. Mother wasn't satisfied with starving him to death, but threw his body into the glass factory crucible for incineration. This was White Rat's explanation of why Takashi had been cremated.

This occurred just about the time that Mother had started working in the newly established factory in Yanji, sealing ampoules. If the Chinese and Korean workers believed White Rat's groundless rumors, the factory could hardly continue to operate. Among Japanese residents the cremation should have been viewed in a positive light, but as often happened, good intentions were ignored and insidious rumors asserting "bad influence" spread.

At the time Mother had only one article of clothing left, the *monpe* work pants she had fashioned from a silk crepe kimono. All the rest had gone for food. When she went outside to sweep the sidewalk in front of the factory, a local middle-aged housewife would often ridicule her for her *monpe*.

"My goodness, crepe *monpe*! The wife of a factory owner certainly is different. Crepe, the embodiment of the bourgeois! Once a bourgeois, always a bourgeois, I guess. Quite different from us proletariat."

Mother wanted dearly to wear cotton, but the family simply didn't have the money. Since the Chinese were only interested in cotton as a means of exchange, Mother had given all the cotton clothing she had brought with her when leaving Changchun to the widow Mrs. M. as we departed Qiazi, hoping they would be useful in bartering. That explains why Mother didn't have a single article of cotton clothing. But this type of argument wasn't convincing to the newly brainwashed. Surprisingly, this self-styled proletariat woman was in the habit of saying, "I can't die until I see that all those Russkis have gotten their due." One could only imagine that in the postwar chaos she herself or perhaps a daughter had been raped by Soviet soldiers—that something terrible had happened.

Russki, of course, was a derogatory reference to the citizens of the Soviet Union, the granddaddy of all proletariat states. In liberated zones, Marx, Lenin, and Stalin were revered as the greatest of the great, and yet this woman, who considered herself a proletariat and who had belittled Mother for her bourgeois clothes, had referred to Russians as Russkis. While her feelings can be understood, there does seem to be a contradiction here. Perhaps this indicates the extent to which her brain had been successfully washed.

In the case of children, however, the situation was different. Their brains were like clean blackboards; there was nothing to erase or wash away. Out of the blue, these innocent minds were filled with strident Communist ideology. They had no defense against it, no immunization. They believed it, simply and fiercely.

One day Big Sister had a class on materialism. The teacher said that anyone who still believed there was a god should raise their hand.

In our household there had always been morning and evening prayers, in which we children took part along with Mother and Father. The idea that there was no god had never occurred to us.

Big Sister smartly raised her hand, the only one to do so. What followed was a rain of criticism.

"What, you think there is a god?"

"Where is this god then? Show him to us."

"If there is a god, what does he look like? Describe him"

"Antirevolutionary! Reactionary!"

The teacher told her to reflect on her erroneous ways, to "criticize" herself. Big Sister became flustered and unsure what to think. After all, she had just come from blockaded Changchun, occupied by the Nationalist Army, and was now thrust into a school dominated by Communist socialism.

That night, as we sat down to eat, Father began to recite the usual pre-meal prayer. It consisted of a recitation of Shinto precepts that Father deeply believed in. This had been the custom in our household for as long as we could remember. It was one of the beliefs of this religious creed that moral principles should be taught in daily life.

"Food is a gift for the life of man from the heavenly gods. Whatever we eat, whatever we drink, we should not forget to be thankful."

Just as Father finished reciting these lines, Big Sister, her face flushed bright red, burst out in tears and shouted, "Stop, oh stop! If you don't stop, I'll go outside till you do."

Holding her hands over her ears, she rushed out of the room. Mother hurried after her, and found her trying unsuccessfully to stifle her tears. What Big Sister had been suppressing all day long had gushed through to the surface.

This happened just as White Rat was spreading the word that Father was a reactionary. In the eye of this storm of brainwashing, there was little that the family could do.

To Big Sister Mother suggested that she think of the prayer's "heavenly gods" as meaning "glorious rice farmers," and Father agreed not to utter this phrase. A compromise of sorts was reached. On the other hand, the storm created by White Rat showed no signs of letting up. It was at this juncture that a witness to Father's honest, principled way of life appeared.

This witness was none other than Mr. Pak, the principal of the night school for Koreans in Changchun, who happened to be at the meeting held to censure Father. Mr. Pak remembered Father well. He raised his hand and asked to speak.

"You've got it all wrong," he said. "I know this man, Dr. Okubo. It is true that he was the president of a pharmaceutical factory in Changchun, but he treated Chinese and Korean workers very well. In particular, he had the young Koreans attend night school, telling them to study hard so that no one could look down on them. I was the principal of that school. To make up for the lost time Dr. Okubo worked in front of the hot kilns until 3:00 in the morning. The missus made the Korean students rice balls, some food to take with them. There is no one to whom we owe a greater debt. We Koreans couldn't be more thankful. The man who is attacking him, this Azuma, is full of nonsense, I say."

There was a stir among the crowd.

The Koreans were the dominant force here. The Japanese were freshly brainwashed outsiders; they couldn't gainsay what Mr. Pak had just said.

Mr. Pak's testimony was eminently credible and undeniably persuasive. It rescued Father from ignominy and made him an accepted member of the community once more.

In Yanji around this time the phrase "red radish" enjoyed a certain vogue. It referred to a radish that was red on the outside (that is, seemingly Communist) but white (unaligned) on the inside. Yanji was rich in radish fields, and this phrase became a sarcastic way of referring to thinly disguised opportunists.

The red radish group also gave birth to another word, *tenchan*, which was a belittling reference to the Japanese emperor. Whether a person could utter this word or not became a litmus test for one's commitment to Communism.

Father was against the unprincipled use of such words as *tenchan*, and against their pathetic employment as a means of self-defense. This, of course, was one of the reasons he was accused of being a counter-revolutionary, an accusation from which, fortunately, Mr. Pak was able to acquit him.

Times might change, but Father and Mr. Pak remained in agreement about the right path for a human to take in life.

For the red radishes of this time the word of the Koreans was the final word, deserving of the greatest deference. The extent to which Japanese debased themselves in order to protect their interests, to transform themselves to suit the situation, was truly pitiful.

Special envoy George Marshall, who advocated the One Million Repatriation, the return of all Japanese to Japan, was concerned that the longer Japanese stayed in China, the greater the chances of them becoming thoroughly brainwashed, and that Japan might become a Communist state. His concern was not far-fetched.

CHAPTER 5

Alive Again

As the family was struggling to survive the maelstrom of life in Yanji, I myself was sleepwalking through a wasteland. I apparently had some consciousness, but I was unaware of that fact. All mental activity had ceased. I lived in a stupor, meandering in a world of my own. Once the adamantine will to keep walking slipped from my body, I was reduced to an empty shell.

After Chiyoji received a transfusion and showed signs of recovery, Father carried me to the People's Hospital on his back. I apparently weighed only as much as a two- or three-year-old.

Just to the west of the construction dorm was the Buehatong River, and the hospital was situated between the two. Fortunately, it was only a short walk from the dorm to the hospital. Upon seeing me, Dr. Noda's first thought was that I was beyond help. On my medical record he wrote "tuberculosis of the entire body." My whole body had become infected. There was little that could be done, it seemed. Still, the doctor gave me nutrient and vitamin injections, and Mother poured liquid food of some sort down my throat. Somehow I managed to hold on to life.

Just once, while lying in our room at the dorm, I became conscious of my surroundings.

It was bright outside; no one was in the room. On the wall was a shelf. On the shelf was a glass jar about twenty centimeters in diameter and fifteen centimeters high. Tadpoles were swimming in the jar among some green algae. One of them, perhaps making the transition to adulthood, leaped up. Just below the shelf was the *ondol*. The leaping frog fell outside the jar, straight down onto the *ondol*. It must have been cold outside since the *ondol* was still being used. The tadpole fell directly onto the *ondol* firebox, sizzled, and burned. Vomit rose in my throat, and I felt sick to my stomach. Immediately I slipped quietly back into the comfortable world of semi-consciousness.

I am not sure how long I meandered between the world of the living and the world of the dead. When I finally opened my eyes, I saw Mother giving Chiyoji a bath out in the yard. It was broad daylight.

"Oh! Homare is up, everyone," Father shouted. "Thanks be, oh, thanks be to God!" He pressed his hands together in prayer and bowed deeply.

I was sitting up in bed under my own strength.

* * * * *

About a month before this, Dr. Noda had informed my parents that there was nothing more he could do.

"I have done everything in my power," he told them. "The only thing left is to amputate both arms and legs, and even then I can't guarantee the results. Maybe, as a final act, you should just give her some food she's particularly fond of."

Hearing this, Mother was beside herself with dismay. For a little girl to lose both arms and legs . . . For the little girl she had given birth to to lose all four limbs, to be robbed of her freedom of movement . . . Just to think of it made her want to scream out in protest. Dr. Noda was a military doctor; maybe that was why he could speak so lightly of amputation. Mother began to have unkind thoughts about Dr. Noda.

In any case, thought Mother, Homare wouldn't even eat the tomato she loved, pushing it out of her mouth. Before she had been fond of bits of tomato sprinkled with sugar, but no more. If it meant a slightly longer life, maybe they should have the amputation done, Mother thought. Or maybe they should just let her pass quietly away as she was, all in one piece. . . .

Whichever choice they made, it was a horrible responsibility, a terrible decision. But they had to choose, Mother knew. Death was approaching. After agonizing over the matter to no end, Mother chose the latter, to forgo the operation. Losing one's arms and legs as the price for a slightly longer life, could Homare really find happiness? She had always been a sensitive child. It was hard to imagine her coolly facing such an awful reality. One day she would ask why we hadn't let her die. Given her personality, she might take her own life. If they were going to put her through such pain and suffering, wouldn't it be better to let her die as she was? At the very least, she wouldn't have to suffer any longer.

Ever since they had entered Qiazi, Homare had been acting strangely, Mother couldn't help thinking. Her unfocused eyes seemed to swim; she had grown oddly mute. That could be due to her extraordinary emaciation, but Mother thought not. Since arriving in Yanji Homare had been operated on a number of times, but she hadn't made a sound, her face expressionless. And that was without an anesthetic. It was as if she had lost the ability to feel pain. If that was true, then this would be the time to let her go. As a mother, this was the last thing she could do for her daughter. Hereafter she herself would have to bear the suffering and pain of her loss.

Mother informed Dr. Noda of her decision.

"I appreciate all you've done for Homare. But I'd like to see her pass on with her body intact."

"I see," said the doctor. "Then we'll call off the operation. She's been very brave, lasting this long. She's been very, very brave."

The doctor wore a grave expression, as though he were

announcing the imminent death of a patient. Then, crossing his arms and sighing, he muttered, "It's too bad you're penniless, so it can't be helped. If only you had the money, something could be done.... It involves more money than any refugee could hope to have, though."

"If only we had the money, something could be done"?

Dr. Noda was referring to the antibiotic drug streptomycin, which had been developed in the United States several years earlier. However, one vial cost the equivalent of Father's salary. As it was, since arriving in Yanji, the family had been hard pressed to support its seven members, and it didn't have a cent of savings. And with streptomycin, one injection wasn't enough; it had to be continued over a fairly long period of time. Cut short, it could make the condition worse and hasten death. Mother knew that the whole family couldn't be sacrificed for one member alone. Which meant, in order for the family to survive, they had to abandon Homare.... On the very day she had come to the gut-wrenching decision to let Homare pass away naturally, she was jerked back to face the same agonizing decision.

"Ah ... if only we had the money."

How ironic! The president of a pharmaceutical company has to let his daughter die because he can't afford the medicine. It was the war, Mother thought. If only there had been no war.

During the food blockade in Changchun, there had been no choice. The whole city was starving, everyone pushed to the limit. If a child died, there was neither the time nor the physical energy for grieving. But now, if you had the money, you could buy food, you could get medicine. Still ...

Mother let out a groan and burst into tears.

Father, of course, knew about streptomycin and had spent many an hour thinking about it. Given their present life, though, it seemed completely beyond their means. That night Father and Mother went sleepless discussing what could be done. They finally came up with the idea of paying for the medicine in monthly installments. This called for getting several years advance on his salary and paying it back over a lifetime. In other words, they proposed to take out a long-term loan.

This meant the family would have to stay permanently in China, give up returning to Japan. They would remain in China and do their best as long as they could. It didn't matter where they were as long as they were together. They didn't want any more deaths in the family. The two of them decided on the streptomycin. When Father immediately went off to the Yanbian Specialist Office about a loan, he was pleasantly surprised to find the office extremely accommodating.

When Dr. Noda heard the news, he was as happy as any member of the family, and he immediately ordered the drug from Shenyang.

The effect of the streptomycin was astounding. Almost like magic, the festering stopped spreading, the will to eat returned, and the swelling of the face, which seemed to presage death, went down. Mother was so happy that she seemed to become slightly unbalanced.

The tomato I had been refusing till now I began eagerly to eat. Even the rice that I had declined to touch before was now welcome. With eggs the story was the same. The little girl who had refused to eat anything was now eating everything. She's coming back, Mother thought; she's coming back from the dead. To Mother the difference between life and death depended on what she gave me to eat. She wanted me to try this, she wanted me to try that. What could she give me next? She was so anxious to give me something good that she apparently became quite befuddled.

Loquats were hard to come by then, but Mother bought some clandestinely and brought them to me, without the other children knowing. Then there was the rice cake vendor who often passed in front of the dorm. The cakes were flattened out several centimeters wide and filled with sweet bean paste. They came in three colors: white, sky blue, and pink. Mother had never called out to the vendor, but she did once, just to try them. I gobbled the rice cake down in no time flat. Mother was so pleased that she always kept one ear cocked for the vendor after that.

By giving birth to me Mother had created my life. Now she was creating my life once again; she felt that very strongly.

Thanks to Mother's selfless efforts and the streptomycin, I began to recover very rapidly. And then came the day I sat up in bed on my own power, when Mother was giving Chiyoji a bath out in the yard. That instant was the first in which I became aware of my surroundings. Everyone looked surprisingly strong and healthy, with full faces.

Had the Eighth Route Army abandoned the blockade of Changchun? No, something was odd. This room looked like no room at the Shinkyo factory. Where was I?

Just this morning it was . . . just this morning . . . we had packed up our belongings and left the factory. We had left the factory, and then . . . What had happened next? We had spent the night somewhere, I was sure. Or maybe we hadn't spent the night anywhere at all, but only this morning had left the factory. Was that it?

No, we had definitely spent the night somewhere. It was dark— dark and cold. Then there was a light. Off in the distance a light. I felt myself being pulled toward that light. And then I was here.

So, so, that meant . . .

Something was wrong. A great deal of time seemed to have passed. We had left the factory. But what had happened after that? I couldn't remember.

As I was trying to remember, I suddenly began to sing.

> *The lark has a house in the wheat.*
> *Newly hatched babies has she five.*
> *Each baby has a cute little face.*
> *But that's a secret.*
> *A secret, a secret.*
> *A secret, a secret, a secret, you know.*

"Oh, Homare is singing, Mother," Father shouted. "Homare is singing. This means she's truly recovered."

Ever since I was small I would break out into song whenever I felt in a good mood. When I ceased singing, it meant I was sick. That's why Father and Mother were overjoyed, hearing my voice. But no one noticed then that that was the only thing I could do, a little girl who could only sing.

I recovered by leaps and bounds. Dr. Noda was astonished, remarked that he had never seen streptomycin have such a remarkable effect. I was recovering that quickly.

Dr. Noda would come to inject the streptomycin, accompanied by a nurse. There were two bottles, each about three centimeters in diameter and six centimeters tall, both made of transparent glass. One of them contained streptomycin powder, the other a solvent. The bottle with the solvent had a tapered end with a light-blue rubber cap. The cap had an aluminum-colored rim and was fixed tightly to the bottle. The liquid would be sucked out of the bottle by piercing the rubber with an injection needle and transferred to the bottle with the powder. Shaking this bottle a number of times produced the streptomycin, which would be injected into my buttock.

"Hey, Homare-chan. You're starting to put on some weight," Dr. Noda would say. "Look, if I pull the skin, it bounces right back. Until now you've been nothing but skin and bones, mighty hard to inject." He laughed as he said this, his lips puckering, his mustache rising and falling.

As soon as Father saw I was on the way to recovery, he began preparing for a trip. There was something he simply had to do. He had to find Mrs. M., who the Eighth Route Army had separated from the group when we left Qiazi. He hadn't been free to do as he pleased until the new Yanbian Depot was on track. But now, just as I was getting better, the Depot decided to send him to Shenyang on some kind of business. He hoped to get permission to drop by Changchun on the way and to look for Mrs. M.

Previously, Father had gotten into contact with a Mr. A., a pharmacist who was still in Changchun, asking if he had any information. A letter arrived saying that he had finally learned something of Mrs. M's whereabouts. If nothing else, it seemed that Mrs. M.'s daughter, Taeko, was still alive. He had learned that much.

Arriving in Changchun, Father and Mr. A. went to the house of a Chinese family where Taeko was said to be. They found the house, and she was there. But as soon as she saw the two of them, she said, "Japanese? I hate the sight of Japanese." She turned and disappeared into the back of the house. Having no other choice, they decided to talk to the man who was head of the house and see what they could learn.

According to the man, Taeko had been adopted into his family. Taeko's younger brother had died in Qiazi. She and her mother had been saved by a certain Chinese man there. Thanks to him, Taeko and her mother had managed to survive until the gate was opened. However, not long after leaving Qiazi, her mother had taken sick and died. That's when he adopted Taeko, he said.

If it was agreeable to Taeko, Father said he would like to take her and raise her as his own daughter. This proposal was met with a curt, negative answer, both by Taeko and her adoptive father. Although Father had half-expected this, he left disappointed, next proceeding to the site of the old Shinkyo factory.

Ma-chan, his youngest child, was buried below the window of the company house facing Xing-an Boulevard. Father went there first of all.

Morning glories were in bloom where Ma-chan was buried. Some were already bearing black seeds. He took one of them in his hand.

He next went to the ether warehouse where Big Brother was buried. It had been turned into a stable.

When Father returned from Changchun, he had large biscuits strung around his neck like a necklace. He raised them above his head to show us. They were the same biscuits that were sold at Jilin Station.

"We couldn't buy them then, but I've got them now. Just look!"

He was trying his best to be cheerful, but his face told a different story: it lacked the vitality it had had when leaving Yanji.

Speaking to Mother, he said, "There were morning glories blooming on Ma-chan's grave."

"My, morning glories you say. On his grave. I see. But what about his remains?"

"Well, the flowers were blooming so prettily, and the land belongs to someone else now, you know."

"But only a little," Mother said. "Only just a very little bit of his remains."

"Now, you see . . . ," Father said, placing a single black kernel in the palm of her hand. It was the morning glory seed. "This is Ma-chan's life. It's proof he's still alive. He's those beautiful morning glories. I couldn't bring myself to dig them up."

"Oh, Father," Mother said. She was holding tightly onto the seed, crying. Father also had tears in his eyes.

"Compared to Ma-chan, I feel so sorry for Isao," Father said, referring to his oldest son. "He's lying under horses' dung."

"But at least he's buried in a tea box. Ma-chan was only wrapped in a blanket."

"That's right," said Father. "But the horses' urine will seep through."

Father looked unbearably sad. Someday he would move them to a proper grave or have them cremated, he said. But for that he would need permission to unearth their remains, and permission would be very slow in coming, he thought.

"And the Chinese don't cremate," he added.

But the "someday" Father spoke of never came.

* * * * *

I got so that I could sit up in bed, stand on my own strength and walk, and finally go out of doors. That day the town was overflowing with festive crowds, almost as if they were celebrating the lunar New Year's. Firecrackers were going off, fireworks rose into the air, gongs and drums resounded, voices sang "March of the Volunteers" and "Without the Communist Party There Would Be No New China," adding to the festive mood.

It was October 1, 1949, the day that Communist China came into being. It was the day that the Five-star Red Flag flew over Tian'anmen Square, the day that Mao Zedong proudly announced the birth of the People's Republic of China.

The siege of Changchun had been for this day. The Eighth Route Army had blockaded food coming into Changchun so that it could emerge victorious on this auspicious day. During the siege Big Brother had died, Big Brother's son had died, Ma-chan had died, and Mrs. M. and her family had been separated from the group. But could it really be said that these deaths, these cruel separations, were for the good of this day? For what reason, for what purpose, had they actually occurred?

Looking up at the night sky shrouded in the smoke of firecrackers, Father had a grim look on his face, his fists tightly clenched, the tips of his fingers quivering ever so slightly. At this momentous moment what thoughts were going through his mind?

I had emerged from the dead on the very same day that China was reborn. My life in Yanji had begun. My first step out into the world occurred when Mother took me to a Korean-operated public bath. There was no bath at the dorm. On our first day in Yanji, we had been told we should take a bath; it was ready. The bath referred to was that in a nearby department store. The area around the dorm was occupied solely by Koreans and Japanese. Most of the Chinese in Yanji lived in a Chinatown on the east side of the city.

The bath was big and brightly lit. The midday sun shone through the skylights.

"It has been quite a while since you've had a bath, hasn't it, Hobo-chan?" said Mother. "I'm just so thankful—you have returned from the doors of death." "Hobo-chan" had been my nickname since I was very small. While Mother continued to be worried about the bandage still on my arm, she was thankfully savoring the fact that her daughter had come back with all her limbs intact.

This was the first time I'd taken a bath with Mother since I could remember. Somehow I felt it was a special treat, and my heart danced with excitement.

This was my first trip to a public bath. Outside of my own family I had never stripped naked before anyone. I felt a little embarrassed. But Mother was with me, and among the bathers there were some naked young girls, all unselfconsciously enjoying themselves. Their laughing voices eased the feeling of embarrassment.

I entered the bathing area cautiously, making sure of each step. The girls were all fair-complexioned and plump of body. Some were sitting on the edge of the tub, dangling their feet in the water; others were in the water but had their arms draped leisurely on the rim of the tub. They were all gathered in a lively group and speaking Korean, their mouths wide in laughter. I squatted down in the area outside the tub for washing, trying not to ruin the mood.

It was then that one of the girls noticed me, saying something in a loud, harsh voice. The laughter stopped immediately, and they began whispering among themselves. They stared at me as if I were some filthy object, frowns on their faces. Mother moved between us, blocking their view.

Even though I had recovered, it only meant that I had escaped death. I still had the emaciated body of a small child. Dr. Noda said that I had put on some weight and that it was easier to give me an injection, but the skin over my thin bones was still covered with wrinkles and colored a dehydrated black. My ribs could be easily counted, one at a time. On top of that, both arms were wrapped in bandages. The wounds were no longer festering, but the skin had not yet closed up. To keep the affected areas from getting wet and worsening, the bandages were carefully covered with oil paper. Just to be on the safe side, I held both arms high above the water, which was bound to draw attention. My legs had completely healed.

Four years had passed since Japan's defeat. Refugees from the immediate postwar period were no longer to be seen. The only city to have suffered from a food blockade during the Civil War period had been Changchun. There had been no starvation in Yanji. To the plump young girls at the bath, accustomed to their present way of life, we must have seemed relics of some bygone era, somewhat creepy, a little weird.

Ignoring the buzz of criticism and hostility at her back, Mother continued doggedly to wash me. Having finished, she picked me up to take me into the tub.

Just at that moment, to our surprise, the girls let out a scream and began splashing me with water, apparently their way of saying I should stay out of the tub. They scooped up the water with both hands, furiously throwing it at me.

Mother was caught with me suspended in her arms, one foot in the tub, one foot out. For a moment she was at a loss what to do. It was already October with winter coming on. My recovering body was cold from the washing, and unless I was warmed up in the tub, I would go into a fit of trembling. With a quick decision Mother stepped in with me in her arms.

This was followed by a body of shouting: "How filthy," "Get out," "Go away." All together the girls jumped out of the tub. This time they picked up the pails used for washing and threw bucketfuls at the two of us.

Placing me in a corner of the tub, Mother put her arms around me and frantically tried to keep the water from hitting my bandaged arms. The deluge only seemed to increase, falling on my head and making it difficult to breathe. Gritting her teeth, Mother's only thought was to protect her child. In both stance and feature she looked absolutely heroic.

Thus my first attempt to step out into the world was rebuffed.

Not wanting to repeat this experience, thereafter the family went to a Chinese public bath in Chinatown. In contrast to the Korean bath, the Chinese bath was divided into separate compartments. Each compartment was further divided into tub and dressing area. The roomy dressing area had a table and some chairs, perfect for relaxing or taking a break. Our weekly visit to this bath was one of the highlights of our life in Yanji. Since that first visit to the Korean public bath, the bond between me and Mother became much stronger.

* * * * *

Chiyoji, now four years old, had started kindergarten. Big Sister had graduated from elementary school in April and was working at the Japanese Residents Administration Committee, to help out the family budget. The next oldest sister, and the youngest as well, were attending the Yanji Japanese Democratic Elementary School. I stayed at home, still in need of convalescence, meaning that I spent the day alone with Mother, the first time this had ever happened. Although this period turned out to be quite short, it was very important to me, since I had been weaned early and felt a certain estrangement from Mother. This period helped fill that gap.

No matter how short the period of time, it is important, I think, for a child to fully experience the love of his or her parents at least once, in order to confidently supersede them.

Among the things that survived the trip from Changchun was a piece of damask cloth about ten centimeters square. Mother removed the threads and made a tiny doll about two centimeters tall, hanging it around my neck. That doll, with its mixture of gold and silver threads, warmed my heart.

At this time Mother was sewing uniforms for the Liberation Army: officially the People's Liberation Army and formerly the Eighth Route Army. Here in the Northeast it was called the

Northeastern People's Liberation Army. There was a period when it was referred to as the Northeastern Democratic Allied Army, albeit rarely. Mother's job consisted of reinforcement stitching on army uniforms. The person who was instrumental in her acquiring this work was a Korean man.

One night this elderly Korean had come uninvited into our room at the dorm. He was unsteady on his feet, obviously drunk. He lowered himself onto the edge of the *ondol*, not saying a word, just glaring up at Father through half-closed eyes. By Father's side lay a silver tobacco pipe, an heirloom from Mother's father, sixteenth lord of the Chosokabe clan. The old man finally opened his mouth. "I want that pipe," he said. Sorry, he was told, but this is a family heirloom.

"Don't be so snooty," he said. "My son's attending Yanbian University, you know. What do you think of that?" He responded somewhat illogically.

Yanbian University was the most illustrious educational institution in the region. What the old man apparently wanted to say was that he may be a mere Korean but his son—*his* son—was attending that wonderful school. So what could Father be thinking, to talk to him like that. Finally he grew irritated with Father's failure to grasp his point, and he went into a long explanation.

According to his account, his son had once worked at a place called Shinkyo. It was run by a Japanese man, but nothing like you, he said. He wasn't a cheapskate, didn't look down on Koreans, but treated them very kindly. Thanks to him, my son was able to graduate from a night school for Korean students. He owes what he is today entirely to that Japanese man.

To make sure of what he had heard Father asked, "What again was the name of that company?"

"Well, let me see. It was . . . you know . . . making medicine, something to cure heroin addiction or the like."

"Oh? Would it be Shinkyo Pharmaceuticals, by any chance?"

"Ah, that's it. Shinkyo Pharmaceuticals it was. How did you know?"

"Well, I don't want to take credit where credit's not due, but actually, you see, I was the president of Shinkyo Pharmaceuticals."

At first the old man was dubious, but when Father produced a slip of paper stating the effectiveness of Giftol, he suddenly changed his attitude. The slip of paper was the same as the one his son had once shown him.

"Ah, so it was you, my son's savior and mentor for life. I can't possibly thank you enough," he said, prostrating himself on the earthen floor in a deep bow, tears streaming down his cheeks. His son was the pride of his life, he said. Before he died he had hoped to meet the man who made his son what he was today and express his gratitude. And now for that to happen . . . there was nothing that could make him happier. If there was something he could do for us, he said, he would be more than happy to do it. Eventually he introduced Mother to the needlework for army uniforms. He revered Father, invariably referring to him as "Professor," and continued to help us out in many little ways.

The army uniforms proved a boon in more ways than one. Lacking proper futons, we slept on the cotton uniforms at night and used them as covers, too. The fluffy uniforms we slept on were compressed by our body weight and turned out just the right thickness—two birds with one stone. Early the next morning the nicely compressed uniforms would be delivered. On the way back we would pick up more uniforms for more needlework. Whenever there was a convenient break in work, Mother would often take me to the Korean market.

The Korean market was on the east side of the dorm, not too far away. The air was fragrant with the smell of hot mustard. Or, rather, more accurately it was the smell of kimchi. Among the goods put out for sale were bright-red cod roe and *tsukudani* with red pepper leaves. Even if you closed your eyes, you could tell you were at the Korean market from the pungent mixture of mustard in the air.

The smell of mustard so stimulated the gastric juices that just approaching the market made me feel hungry. At first, though, I couldn't escape the clutches of malnutrition, and the slightest movement left me out of breath. I wanted to eat a lot and get healthy, but I just didn't feel up to it. When I first sat up in bed and came back to life, I had surprised Mother with my sudden desire to eat, but now, having returned to the living, I had lost most of my appetite.

However, there was one thing I was very fond of. That was *jeon*, a Korean-style pancake similar to Japanese *okonomiyaki*. There were two types: one made of mung bean powder, the other of grated potatos. It was the former that was sold in the arcade at the Korean market, thin and crepe-like and elegant-looking. After frying, a number of them would be put into a deep tube-like pot wrapped in several layers of cloth cord to preserve the heat. The cord was filthy with the grime from human hands. Freshly made *jeon* was best of all. Tightly wrapped, they were eaten with soy sauce and a good pinch of mustard.

The *jeon* made of potato gratings were sold outside the arcade. About five centimeters thick and hefty in the hand, they were somewhat gooey. Some contained chopped kimchi. They were also eaten with mustard soy sauce, but they couldn't compete with the mung bean variety in terms of overall elegance.

This difference may have had something to do with the person who was making them. The woman making the potato *jeon* had thin, upward-slanting eyes, her face puffy and swollen. She seemed to be perpetually angry about something. If you used a little extra soy sauce, she would give you a venomous glare. Large, fat, middle-aged, she presented a very imposing appearance.

In contrast, the little woman selling mung bean *jeon* in the arcade, fairly up in years, always had a friendly look on her face. And her quiet, refined laugh was very cute. It must have been her slender elegance that gave character to the *jeon* she made. The man in the next booth was selling seaweed *tsukudani* and krill *shiokara*, producing another of the distinctive aromas of the market.

Outside the arcade was an open-air market. The vendors sat on the ground next to large baskets selling their goods. The prices were a little lower than those in the arcade, accounting for its greater crowds.

It was the custom of Korean women to carry baskets on their heads. They wrapped a strip of cloth around the top of their heads in the shape of a ring or small hoop and placed a basket with its contents on it. Some carried crocks or water jugs in this way. They kept one hand raised up against the load and maintained their balance by the movement of their hips as they walked. They often wore rubber shoes that curled perkily up at the end. Like a scene out of the *Arabian Nights* they would walk intently through the swarms of people with their tapered shoes flashing from beneath their wraparound *cima* skirts, raising their free hand from time to time to divide the crowd, saying, "Make way, make way."

The way Korean women carried babies on their back was also interesting. They wrapped a broad piece of white cloth around their waists, with the baby's legs sticking out from both sides, their backside acting as a platform for the baby to sit on.

On the right side of the open-air market and its dirt road was a large tree with roots protruding above the ground. A middle-aged woman was squatting there, dressed in a white *cima*. She had pulled up the hem of the ankle-length dress around her waist. Squatting there, she was conversing cheerfully with those around her. It was an unremarkable scene, but there was something about the way the woman was squatting that seemed odd to me. Then suddenly there was a plashing sound as water ran out from beneath the hem of her skirt.

It was hard to believe, but she was urinating out in public, right in front of everyone, while chatting with friends in a loud voice.

Rather than being surprised, I felt sick to my stomach. I might throw up, I thought, and I turned my eyes aside. I felt my heart begin to pound, and I wondered why.

Why was I affected to this extent? As I was trying to figure it out, I got the uneasy feeling that something ominous was approaching me from behind. I shook my head to get rid of that thought, hoping to escape the feeling of uneasiness.

As we went further along, there were many vendors squatting on the ground at the side of the road leading to the right. Some of them were chewing on red mustard in its raw form, as though it were no different from any other food.

Just as the arcade came to an end, the open-air market also ended. Making a U-turn to the left with the arcade at our back, we saw many little booths covered only by roofs. With these on our right hand, we returned to the market's starting point. Then, suddenly, from our right the smell of fresh blood came wafting through the air. Across the way stood the big tree where the middle-aged woman had relieved herself.

The unease I had felt earlier and managed to suppress now renewed its attack. Looking at the shop on the right, I saw three dead pigs, skinned and slung upside down. The pigs had been eviscerated, their eyes sunken. Next door, apparently using the pigs' intestines, there were coils of sausage meat dangling down.

The urge to vomit arose again. There was a ringing in my ears. My chest felt constricted, and my heart began pounding violently. A cold sweat drenched my body. I knew I had to do something, but my arms and legs refused to move. I couldn't utter a sound. My throat felt as though I was being choked; it was difficult to breathe.

Suddenly the forms of the dead pigs, their outlines only, separated themselves from the background of my vision, radiating a brilliant, bizarre light. In the next instant the pigs began to recede into the distance, shrinking smaller and smaller. In their wake was an empty space, itself growing ever smaller. Eventually the pigs became a single point in space and vanished.

Then everything I saw, every sound I heard, disappeared. All that remained was empty space. This space became transformed into glass, glass that continued to spread relentlessly. I became completely enveloped in that endless space.

This vacuous world was hard and inflexible. From beyond it, from beyond its seamless glaze, there appeared a light. A light was welling up from the point at which the pigs had converged and disappeared. What could it be?

The light grew steadily closer. Within it was a mountain. A pale mountain. A shining, unearthly pale-blue mountain.

The mountain grew closer, larger, ever nearer. The glass world pressed on me more insistently. The mountain was now within arm's reach.

No, no!

Fear brought me back to my senses, and in that instant the mountain disappeared. The glass world also vanished. Reality flooded the emptiness of the glass world, and it was suddenly filled with sound. It was as if a film that had been stuck on one frame had started running again. My arms and legs became unfrozen.

"Hobo-chan, is something wrong? Are you okay?" asked Mother, examining my face.

Korean women in *cima* passed by my side, carrying baskets on their heads, balancing themselves with their hips. Vendors were sitting by the roadside, eating raw red pepper. The middle-aged woman was still selling potato *jeon*, still looking angry.

Suddenly I was poked on the shoulder. "Make way there," a middle-aged woman in *cima* told me. Returning to myself, I started walking again.

* * * * *

Always watching my step when I went out for a walk, I eventually managed to go as far as the Yanji Japanese Democratic

Elementary School. Winter had come, and the school grounds were overlaid with a thin film of snow. Students were making briquettes in the playground, chanting as they worked.

> *Let's make briquettes,*
> *Hard and firm.*
> *Let's make a lot of briquettes,*
> *Big and solid.*
> *Then it's study, study, study.*

Working to the rhythm of the chant, they squatted on the ground, compressing the briquettes first with the left hand and then with the right. From the classrooms another song could be heard, the song beginning "The flag of the people, the red flag of China."

In the entrance to the school there were three portraits hung high on the wall. Stalin was in the middle, flanked by Mao Zedong and Kyuichi Tokuda. Kyuichi Tokuda (1894–1953) was the first chairman of the Japanese Communist Party. He served three terms in the House of Representatives, from 1946 to 1950. He had been imprisoned for eighteen years until the end of the war. While he is the subject of criticism in Japan, in China he is regarded as a hero. A little to the side of these portraits was a photograph of Kim Il-sung. The small grade-school students emerged from this entrance in two lines, holding hands, singing at the top of their lungs.

> *Mao Zedong in China.*
> *Stalin in Russia.*
> *Two lights shining, shining, on China and the world.*

Was singing a means of education here, I wondered. There seemed to be a lot of singing. And all the songs seemed to have a political message.

When I went to the teachers' room, I met a teacher wearing

silver-rimmed glasses named Miss Noguchi, who gave me a mimeographed copy of revolutionary songs. If I wasn't ready to attend school regularly, she said, I could just drop by once in a while, or maybe I could take part in the night study groups. If nothing else, I should at least learn the songs. She was an intelligent-looking woman and had a beautiful voice. She looked as though she would be a match for any man, and she referred to me by the masculine second-person pronoun *kimi*.

The songs were very important to me. In fact, they were my only connection with society; essentially, they were my elementary school. I learned every one of them by heart. They were all revolutionary or workers' songs, but the content made little difference to me. I just loved singing, and I sang all the time.

What first attracted me to singing was probably the revolutionary song "Along the Songhua River" (*Songhuajiang shang*). When I realized it had a personal relevance, I was completely dumbfounded. It was the selfsame melody that Zhao used to hum to himself in Changchun when the Eighth Route Army entered the city in April the year after Japan's defeat, bringing the street fighting to an end. He would often whistle that sad, slow song, his rifle over his shoulder, leaning against the windowsill on the second floor, watching the sun go down. Now it brought back memories of myself before the hell of Qiazi. It contained something of myself, something I wanted returned.

"Along the Songhua River" was commonly called "September 18," and it had been translated into Japanese. The Songhua River is also known as the Sungari.

September 18, 1938, is the day on which the Manchurian (Mukden) Incident occurred; in Chinese, it is officially the Liutiaohu Shibian, but most commonly it is called September 18. The song is a lament for the people who were forced from their homes by the Japanese invasion of Northeast China and the establishment of the puppet Manzhouguo Empire. Singing "September 18," and with the hope one day of returning to their homeland, these North-easterners fought and marched alongside the Eighth Route Army. However, the rhythm of the song is not actually suited to marching; it must have been sung while camping at night.

Without knowing the real meaning of the lyrics to "September 18," I just sang all the songs on the mimeograph sheets as they were. The fact is, that was all I was capable of doing. The horrendous scenes at Qiazi had robbed me of the ability to feel fear, had robbed me of all memories of Qiazi, robbed me of any recollection of the trek to Yanji, had even robbed me of the ability to speak. I had turned into a little girl who was incapable of speech. From an early age I had always been rather quiet, and even in Changchun had spent a lot of time gazing at the setting sun, so perhaps it wasn't surprising that my parents didn't notice the change.

Clearly I had suffered some sort of mental impairment. I could comprehend what people were saying. I could understand the situation around me. However, I couldn't communicate with others, couldn't transmit in words what I was thinking. No, it wasn't exactly that. It was that I didn't feel the desire to communicate. I had withdrawn into a world of my own, wandering alone in my desolate wasteland.

I was shrouded in a veil. The veil would allow through it what came from the outside but would cut off anything from the inside. The only exception was eye contact. Eye contact always received an answer. It was my antenna to the outside world. The veil loved beautiful things, bright and cheerful things, and would let them through. But it hated anything sullied or dark, and immediately rejected them. Anything that caused fear or sadness would send me immediately back to that all-enveloping adamantine world of vacuous glass, cut off from all reality.

* * * * *

Our room was on the right just as you came through the entrance to the dorm. Going straight down the corridor, you came to a large inner garden. There was a shared toilet on the left, and the window to Masako's room on the right.

Masako was the younger sister of Miss Noguchi at the elementary school, and she herself taught there. At the time she was recuperating from tuberculosis. At a certain stage of tuberculosis the patient's complexion improves markedly and takes on an extraordinarily beautiful pink. Masako had apparently reached that state, for her pink cheeks and small red lips were radiant below her wide dark-brown eyes. She must have been around twenty. Her smile was especially adorable. All in all, she was an exquisitely beautiful young woman.

Throughout the day the window to Masako's room was full of sunlight. My room was on the east and only received the morning sun. So I could often be found by the window in Masako's sunny room, singing revolutionary songs. Like an older sister Masako always treated me very kindly.

One day she said, "Homare-chan, I can see you really like singing, but why don't you try playing with these for a change?" And she gave me a number of sheets of beautifully patterned *chiyogami* folding paper. They were made of thick Japanese *washi*. She also gave me some German picture postcards, which were made of roughly textured decoupage, showing a blond, blue-eyed little girl playing with a rabbit. Masako's family must have been quite wealthy before the end of the war, to have such expensive things. I treasured these postcards and *chiyogami*, always carrying them with me, clutching them close to my body.

I wonder how I appeared in others' eyes, the little eight-year-old girl who always had postcards and *chiyogami* clutched tight to her breast, who spoke to no one, who was always singing when she could find a place in the sun.

When neighborhood children passed by, they would whisper

the word "Crazy." Sometimes they would surround me, breaking out into song.

> Eliuzi *are good-for-nothings,*
> *Just fooling around,*
> *Their fields running to ruin.* . . .

This was a popular song around this time. An *eliuzi* was someone who was an idler, a sluggard. Communist ideology drove home the idea that those who didn't work shouldn't eat. From the viewpoint of children educated in this way, I was seen as an "extremely bad element" since I neither studied nor worked. Some of them said in no uncertain terms that if I didn't work, I shouldn't be allowed to eat.

This didn't make me sad because I had lost the ability to feel sad. I didn't cry because I had lost the ability to cry. The tears flowed inside, down to my arms and legs and froze them. The sadness ran off my skin like water off a duck's back.

The children's figures receded into the distance, their jeering voices gradually growing smaller. My arms and legs remained frozen in time.

As the children were compressed into a point and disappeared, I was once more pulled into a vacuous world of glass. Into a hard glass world where movement was impossible. A world without sound. Without people. Without sky or earth.

Was I standing vertically, was I lying horizontally, even that I didn't know. There was no means of fixing my position. Then in that endlessly empty world there appeared a light, a light I had seen before.

A pale mountain appeared in the midst of the light. Catastrophically eerie, it ratcheted the pressure of the glass to a new level. Just as the mountain was getting close, just as I was finding it difficult to breathe, the mountain disappeared.

In that instant the glass shattered, and the real world quaked, leaping enlarged into my field of vision. Sound returned, my arms and legs relaxed, blood began to flow. I sighed in relief.

"Homare-chan, are you alright?" asked Masako, gazing into my face.

* * * * *

When spring came to Buehatong River in Yanji, Father would take Chiyoji carp fishing every Sunday. I sometimes went along. It must have reminded Father of the many pleasant days he spent as a young boy in Japan in the hills and streams of Oita, which he often told us about. His eyes, looking into the distance, seemed to be smiling. He would tell us, "Fishing begins with carp and ends with carp; there is nothing better." And he was good at it. Even though the carp were small, he would catch dozens of them.

Chiyoji would be playing around where Father was fishing, catching tadpoles. This was apparently where the tadpoles came from that I saw on a shelf when momentarily regaining consciousness in Yanji.

Whenever Chiyoji waded out into the river, Father would tell him to be careful, recounting the time when he had almost suffered a heart attack from the cold water. There are places where the river becomes unexpectedly deep, he said, like in the gaps between big boulders, and where the temperature of the water suddenly drops. "I got into one of those deep spots and almost lost my life," he said. He served Chiyoji with such warnings any number of times.

Back at home Chiyoji would place the fish on the *ondol* to dry them out, providing the family with a source of protein until the following Sunday.

* * * * *

Thanks to the testimony of Mr. Pak, Father's reputation among Yanji Japanese residents became firmly established around this time, and he served as the leader for the city's study group.

Mother also served as the leader of the women's group, but her principal contribution came in the form of artistic activities. Mother had been a great reader since her younger days, and as long as she had something to read, she didn't mind missing a meal or two.

She was particularly fond of poetry—haiku and tanka. She always kept a slip of paper and a pencil with her, and when a poem came to mind, she would immediately jot it down. Sometimes she would compose ten or twenty poems a day.

She was also very good at the game called Hyakunin Isshu (A Hundred Poets, One Poem Each), in which poems and picture cards are matched. She knew all the poems by heart. Mother and Father cut out cards from scraps of cardboard, and while Mother recited the poems Father wrote them on the cards with a borrowed calligraphy brush. The only thing that remained was to color a purple frame around the edges of the cards with a crayon, producing what was the family's only form of entertainment. Having played this game since I was small, I am still very fond of it today.

The Hyakunin Isshu cards we had left behind in Changchun were exquisitely beautiful. Their colored borders and colorful illustrations were a feast for the eyes. They provided food for my daydreams. By comparison, the cards made in Yanji were simple and crude, but in some ways they were more important to me, more enriching.

I had always liked games that involved memorization and concentration. With regular cards I liked the game Shinkei Suijaku, a type of Concentration. Focusing the mind seemed to bring a kind of inner calm. Exercising the cerebral nerves created a sense of satisfaction, which I dearly loved. Whenever we started a game of Hyakunin Isshu, I would become absolutely revitalized. Noticing this, Mother tried to make time to play the game whenever she could manage it.

However, it wasn't that I simply appeared revitalized to others; I think that my heart, my soul, returned to life in those moments. At the time I wasn't attempting to establish communications with others. My only means of expressing myself was through song. And strangely enough, I rarely sang songs from the past. I sang only the newly learned workers' and revolutionary songs. On the one hand, by singing "September 18" I was trying to return to the innocent past, but on the other hand I was unconsciously trying to distance myself from it. By constantly feeding my brain with new experiences I was subconsciously trying to keep old memories from rising to the surface. This effort devoted to singing also had another function.

In effect, the effort to learn a new song was my response to an external stimulus and resulted in cerebral activity. This means that I still retained some ability to "answer" questions from the outside world. This can also be seen in Hyakunin Isshu, where the player is required to pick up the matching card when a certain poem is read out. This is a clear case of a response to an external stimulus. In this way, singing and poetry games had the function of pulling me back from the wasteland of the dead, a world in which I was already a familiar occupant. Through this stimulus to the brain I was saved from falling completely into a mental stupor.

In Hyakunin Isshu Mother was always the one who recited the poems. If she was one of the players who were competing to see who could be first to pick up the right card, she would always win. She obviously wanted to join in the fun and be one of the pickers, but she agreed to the role of reader, keeping a smile on her face. In the innocent days of my childhood, Mother's voice had the ability to envelop me in her own sweet world. Mother had no need for the reading cards at her side, but I could see the cards' brilliant patterns. The wonderful contrast in color reminded me of the soft crepe dress I wore when I was three. It was my favorite piece of Western clothing, along with the velvet dress that had an arrow pattern of purple, pink, green, and yellow, and the depiction of a crow on the breast.

One of my favorite poems from the Hyakunin Isshu was this one:

> *Oh, thread of my life,*
> *Be torn off now if it must!*
> *I fear in longer life*
> *My secret would be hard to keep.*
> (trans: Yone Noguchi)

I say that it is one of my favorites, but actually I was just curious about its meaning. Regardless of the poem's true meaning, it shows that I had begun to think about the end of life. I was nine at the time.

* * * * *

The Korean women would do their laundry in the river. Placing a laundry basin on their heads, they would head off to the riverbank, steadying the basin with one hand while maintaining their balance by the swivel of their hips. Particularly in spring when the waters of the Buehatong River were warmer, its banks would be crowded with *cima*-clad women. They didn't use soap but rather placed their washing on a flat rock near the shore and beat it with a fifty-centimeter-long mallet. The laundry would be washed by the waves as it was being beaten.

I was a frequent visitor to Buehatong. The simple sound of the beating mallets possessed something sad and solemn, mixed with the rippling of the river, floating up into the firmament overhead. In the blue sky, in the trees, in the fields, spring hovered quietly in the air.

* * * * *

To mark the warm approach of spring the Japanese residents of

Yanji would hold a kind of variety show that combined entertainment with the opportunity for a friendly gathering. The venue was the elementary school lecture hall.

This particular occasion was perhaps to mark International Women's Day. Just inside the lecture hall was a sign pasted on the wall declaring, "Singing is a weapon!" Miss Noguchi was in charge of the singing. One song was "Bound Together, the World Becomes a Flower Wreath"; another was the anthem of the Thirty-eighth International Women's Day.

"Everyone, this has just arrived from Shenyang," Miss Noguchi announced. "Learn it by heart."

She passed out a mimeograph sheet giving the score for the anthem of the Thirty-eighth International Women's Day. On the other side of the sheet was the inaugural issue of "Women's News" put out by the Yanji Japanese Women's Residents Thirty-eighth International Women's Day Struggle Committee. The lyrics were also written out on the blackboard.

This was the first and only song that I was actually taught by someone. The other songs that I sang I had learned on my own, just reading the score. Father had taught me how to read music while we were in Changchun. On this day, at the word "Okay!" I would begin to sing. It was a simple form of communication, but for me it was a big step forward. It meant that, in a very small way, I was able to interact with others. The melody of the anthem of the Thirty-eighth International Women's Day was not like that of revolutionary songs. I especially liked its opening melody.

The last song of the festivities was "The Motherland."

> *This song I sing for those across the seas;*
> *for comrades in my motherland, let it be heard;*
> *for comrades in my motherland, let it be heard.*

While this song may be interpreted in various ways, it is

undeniably redolent with thoughts of returning home. There were many political slogans at the time on the subject: "Down with all those having thoughts of repatriation," "Discard all ideas of repatriation and contribute to the building of a new China," and "Don't be fooled by repatriation rumors." Regardless of its intent, this song was suffused with thoughts of repatriation, something that was undoubtedly on the minds of all Japanese.

Around this time I had the opportunity to go to nearby Pear Mountain to see the trees in bloom. Looking upward, the whole sky was filled with fluttering petals. Translucent against the streaming sun, each and every flower made a home in my heart. Largely white in color they had a touch of yellow resembling the fruit of the tree.

The flowers were singing to me. They were singing the song of life. They were singing of the joy of being alive. These flowers, trembling in the soft breeze, touched something in my heart.

In Baishan Park near our house in Changchun there were blooming apricot trees. Surrounded by red calyxes, the white petals had a faint rosy aura. On holidays we would often take lunch boxes and visit the park. Mother invariably made *maki-zushi*. In early summer the park would be inundated with the blooms of the apricot tree. The whole park became a sweet-smelling cloud, a fragrant garden. At that time in my life I still had a future. I didn't know what it would be, but I knew something was there, far off in the distance, something I couldn't yet quite see.

The pear trees, their beautiful flowers, were trying to show me that future. Their ephemeral beauty, their fluttering in the gentle breeze, would they be taken away from me? Would they be plucked by human hands, would they be rent by the breeze?

With an uneasy heart I stood on Pear Mountain, gazing up at the misting sky.

CHAPTER 6

Outbreak of the Korean War

In April 1950 we moved out of the dorm into a house near the Yanji Japanese Democratic Elementary School. The house had two eight-mat rooms and a garden. Next door on the east side there lived a Korean girl named Yonfee who was very good at singing. She appeared to be two or three years older than I was, maybe eleven or twelve. One of her eyes had a clouded pupil, and her upper lip had a slight cleft so that you could see her front teeth. But more than anything, she had an absolutely beautiful voice and could hit the high notes smoothly, without much effort. She also seemed infatuated with her own voice. She would go out into her garden, turn a bucket upside down, holding it with both hands, and sing with her head inside.

Once she started, she'd keep at it for at least an hour. From among her repertoire she would invariably sing the traditional Korean folk songs "Arirang" and "Doraji." Another of her favorites was a song that began with the words "the Korean people," but I didn't know its title. Sometimes she would sing the national anthem of the Democratic People's Republic of Korea, which was a tribute to Kim Il-sung. Her style was very distinctive, her feet planted firmly on the ground, the bucket pointed up to the sky, her voice full and resonant.

She seemed to be intoxicated by the reverberation of her voice off the sides of the bucket. When she had finished and removed the bucket, her face was shining with a deep sense of satisfaction. For a while she would savor the lingering mood, gazing up at the setting sun.

I was enthralled by Yonfee's singing. I always listened for her evening appearance in the garden when she began her solo performance. The garden had a thick growth of Korean hollyhock, taller than I was. Its small flowers were streaked with light purple and dark reddish lines. It was from behind this hollyhock that I took up my listening post, peering through the open fence.

One day, when Yonfee took the bucket off, our eyes met. Her face at once assumed a dismissive expression, and she turned aside, throwing a fierce glance in my direction. Cold and hard, it was as if she were saying that she wanted nothing to do with the world. She had put up a wall that could not be crossed.

Nevertheless, I liked Yonfee. I liked the way she sang. I liked her voice, so wonderful to hear, and I wanted to be her friend. I wondered if she minded me listening. Maybe it was my watching her that made her mad. But I had simply been enthralled by her voice, that's all.

The next day, out of respect for her feelings, I decided to listen from inside the house. I sat near the window, all ears. As the glass of the window began to turn dark red, her singing began. Her resounding voice from within the bucket seem to be coming from some far-off mountain, mysterious and magical. I focused all my attention on her voice.

Yonfee's recital came to an end as I watched through a crack in the window and saw her remove the bucket from her head. She gave a big sigh and gazed around her. She leaned to one side to peek behind the hollyhock.

She was looking for me! Yonfee was looking for me!

My heart began to pound. Did she want me to hear her singing? Or did she just want to make sure I wasn't there, a furtive listener?

Wanting to know which it was, the next day I decided to go outside. Making sure that she had put the bucket on her head, I sneaked out and hid behind the hollyhock. Her voice was as beautiful as ever, no matter where you heard it from.

The song came to an end. Yonfee removed the bucket, gazing up at the sky. Then she began looking around. Should I come out from behind the hollyhock? Would she look at me dismissively, turning her head aside? Or would she . . .

Taking my fate in my hands, I peeked around the hollyhock, showing only my face. Our eyes locked together. She looked steadily at me, not saying a word.

And then—and then—she smiled, a big, broad, friendly smile.

She had accepted me. She wanted me to hear her singing, after all. I emerged from behind the hollyhock and went toward her, one small step at a time. She raised the bucket in the air with one hand and thumped it soundly with the other. And then she smiled quickly again. We had become "friends."

From then on I went boldly out into the garden to listen to her sing. And then, before long, we were singing together.

Arirang, Arirang, Arariyo . . .

The first time I began to sing, Yonfee hurriedly removed the bucket and glanced at me, startled. But I kept singing. Giving me another quick smile, she replaced the bucket and continued on. It wasn't long before she stopped using the bucket at all.

Facing each other across the fence, we would sing "Arirang" and "Doraji," our voices merging harmoniously, wafting up into the reddening sky.

Sometimes Yonfee would break out into a dance, her wrist and ankles turning neatly to the song's smooth flow in the traditional Korean fashion, her body graceful even in her somewhat worn dress. At times she would leave the singing to me, focusing solely on the dance. There was no longer any sign of the original cold stare.

On the west side of our house lived a Korean father and son

named Kim. The father was approaching seventy, and the son was in his forties. They were both burly men. The neighbors referred to the son as Comrade Kim.

The elder Kim always wore a cloth wrapped around his head, hanging down to his chest. It was said that he had once been a brilliant philosopher, but for some reason or other he had gone a little mad. He was adept at Russian and Japanese, and generally was a very quiet man. Now and then, though, he would begin shouting for no reason at all and turn violent.

I liked the elder Kim. I would often go into his study, where he would let me read his books. The room was a confused jumble of reading material, including some Japanese books and some in Western languages. Aside from those on philosophy, there were others on geometry and astronomy. Not really knowing what I was reading, I went through many of them.

The elder Kim would watch me, a twinkle in his eye. He had very kind eyes. How could such a kind man be mad, I thought. But when he gazed out into the garden, his eyes had something stern in them. Now and then his face would turn angry, and he would mutter to himself.

Mother warned me against visiting the Kim household, saying you could never tell what would happen, but I didn't pay attention. The elder Kim had something that drew me to him. I really didn't understand why he had this power, but it had something to do with his kindness and his inner struggles and sufferings, along with the intellectual world he was apparently familiar with.

Looking back, the people who have most attracted me have had some physical or mental disability: the young woman on the second floor of Shinkyo who had tubercular myositis; Takashi, who was not strong to begin with and became so malnourished that he could only walk by holding on to things; Masako, who, recuperating from tuberculosis, was like a big sister to me; and now this elderly Korean man, who was said to be mad.

I wonder why. What made me choose these people out of all the rest? It may be that such people, standing on the borderline between life and death, having looked into the face of death more than most people, had made use of the opportunity in their short time to think about life. It may be that I was subconsciously searching for an insight into the meaning of life, looking for a kindness in human beings based on the ephemeral nature of life and genuine suffering. Maybe it was just because I felt lonely and was searching for a kindred spirit. Never having been very strong, perhaps I was drawn to the weak like myself.

The elder Kim's thinking had gone beyond Communism. Politically, he was neither on the right nor on the left. But no one could fault him for that; after all, he was crazy. Never once did he tell me that those who don't work shouldn't eat.

Yonfee never said anything like that either. Naturally, she didn't speak Japanese, but her attitude spoke worlds. Neither Yonfee nor the elder Kim attempted to put up a false front of being "progressive." That was one reason I liked them both. Naturally, being Koreans, they had not invaded China, were not enemies of the people. They had no need to prove their innocence.

For Japanese living in liberated Yanji, the story was different. They had to promote Communism, take an active part in the Communist revolution, sing the praises of Mao Zedong and Stalin, and dedicate their lives to the building of a new China.

One day as Mother was hanging out the laundry, Chiyoji, who was turning five, popped up with a question.

"Mother, do you know who the greatest men in the world are?"

"Well, I wonder who they might be. Do you know, Chiyoji?"

"I know. Don't you? Then I'll tell you."

"Please do that."

"Well, first is Marx, then comes Lenin, next is Stalin, next the great comrade Mao Zedong, then Commander-in-Chief Zhu De and Comrade Tokuda. That's all."

"My, you know so much. But why are they so great?"

"That's simple. It's because they're making a better world for us to live in. They're friends of the people. That's why."

"My, you know so much, Chiyoji."

"Yeah, well, I do know a lot. The kindergarten teacher tells us all kinds of things."

Young innocent minds absorb such teachings unquestioningly. And once they are absorbed, they become almost indelible.

* * * * *

After moving into the new house, Mother undertook the task of sealing medicine ampoules. There was a stand in the earthen-floored room next to the *ondol* firebox, and that is where she would seal the ampoules with a burner, working the bellows with her feet. She would also make ampoules from a long glass tube. Turning the ampoule around in her left hand, she would snip off the end with a pair of tweezers in her right. The liquefied glass would make a large arc in the air, thin and threadlike.

I enjoyed gathering up these threads and looking at them as I placed them out into the sun. If you held them up, their ends would open up like a water fountain, the sunlight flowing through them.

It reminded me of the Shinkyo factory in Changchun when I was small, and recalled my beloved red glass bead, the setting sun. That bright-red bead, huge and translucent, which I had gazed upon so many times, seemed to foretell an unlimited future. I recalled Pear Mountain and its canopy of flowers. The lingering hopes for the future I had once had sputtered briefly to life.

However, even these faint hopes for a brighter future were to be dashed by a momentous event. On June 25, 1950, the Korean War broke out.

With the defeat of Japan Korea emerged from thirty-six years of Japanese rule, only to be divided along the 38th parallel by the

Soviet Union in the north and by the United States in the south, both under military rule. In 1948 the Democratic People's Republic of Korea had been established, and in the south the Republic of Korea, confronting one another in open hostility. Then, in 1950 the Cold War became a hot war along the 38th parallel.

Following the birth of Communist China, the United States took the position that the status of Taiwan was an internal Chinese affair and that the U.S. had no intention of interfering, but with the outbreak of war it immediately changed its policy, sending the Seventh Fleet to the Taiwan Straits. However, until the U.S.'s direct intervention, the military advantage lay entirely with North Korea. But when the North threatened Pusan at the southern tip of the peninsula in September, the allied forces countered by landing at Incheon under the aegis of the United Nations. Making use of the latest and most powerful weaponry, the U.N. forces moved the battlefront back to the 38th parallel and even further north, carrying the fighting aggressively to the Yalu River.

The instigator of the Korean War was Kim Il-sung, who was supported by Stalin. Further, China had established the People's Republic of China without first "liberating" Taiwan because it thought this could be done later with the help of the Soviet Union.

The National Revolutionary Army of Jiang Jieshi, which had escaped to Taiwan, had particularly strong naval and air force branches. The air force was most famous for the air corps known as the Flying Tigers, which was established with the help of Song Meiling, Jiang Jieshi's wife.

Mao Zedong was most adept at mountainous guerilla warfare; he didn't have the means to confront Jiang Jieshi on a distant island. Consequently, not long after establishing the new China on October 1, 1948, he requested Soviet aid.

Stalin at first responded positively to Mao's plea to resolve the Taiwan problem immediately, but in the end gave preference to Kim Il-sung's argument that now was the time to unify the Korean peninsula, and that, in any case, the United States had no intention of interfering in Chinese internal affairs.

Why should Stalin take this stance? North Korea shared a border with the Soviet Union; unifying Korea was to the Soviet Union's benefit; Stalin didn't want American influence in South Korea. That was Stalin's thinking.

Stalin was very clever. But that cleverness—Stalin's betrayal of Mao's fervent desire to liberate Taiwan and unify all of China—meant that the situation would remain unchanged into the present century.

China had not viewed the United States as an enemy up to this point, but this changed in April 1951 when the U.S suddenly announced a joint defense pact aimed at containing China. The move was based on the outbreak of the Korean War and China's inevitable involvement. Japan was included in the pact as an ally.

Mao had not wanted a Korean War, and most of all he must have wished to avoid Chinese involvement. Stalin, on the other hand, while remaining in the background, urged Kim Il-sung to get Mao's backing prior to the onset of the war and get him to promise to send in Chinese troops if the situation turned disadvantageous. The ultimate result was the innumerable loss of Chinese lives, including one of Mao's sons.

To repeat myself (because this is an important point), before the conflict began Mao was adamantly opposed to war on the Korean peninsula. He argued strongly that while the United States presently proclaimed no interest in military intervention in East Asian waters, the U.S. position would change once war began, and that it would inevitably intervene. But Stalin and Kim Il-sung were deaf to Mao's pleas. In fact, once the fighting got underway, China had to send in troops while Stalin looked on unconcerned from the side, forfeiting not a single drop of Russian blood.

This period of time was characterized by U.S. army "special procurements" of goods and services from Japan, which provided the impetus for the recovery of the postwar Japanese economy. It also marked the beginning of hostile relations between Japan and China.

Yanji, both geographically and demographically, was a Korean city. Now it became entirely devoted to the war, its nights dismally dark due to the blackouts. North Korean troops flowed into the city, occupying all the elementary and junior high school buildings, making instruction out of the question. The streets were crowded with wounded soldiers. Troops were continually being reorganized and sent back to the front. Some of the troops coming into the city belonged to the Korean Eighth Route Army, which had guarded the southern gate at Qiazi. The officer who was in charge then is said to have been later purged by Kim Il-sung.

Who in the end was responsible for stationing the heavy-handed Korean Eighth Route Army in Qiazi? The responsible parties were Mao Zedong and Lin Biao, as I will discuss later in the Afterword to this book.

It was Mao who gave the order to make Changchun into a "death zone," but he assigned the mission to the Korean Eighth Route Army. When history delivered its verdict, he wanted the responsibility to fall on the shoulders of the "blood-thirsty, cold-hearted Koreans." By purging the officer leading this operation, Kim Il-sung removed a vital witness. It was almost as if Mao and Kim had plotted together to blur the responsibility for the massacre that took place at Changchun.

In the Korean marketplace the number of cima-clad women wailing in grief grew more conspicuous. There were groups of children dressed in grimy rags in the streets. Orphans who had lost their parents in the war, these poor children were emaciated and dazed, recalling the children of the refugees who had escaped the Soviet occupation after Japan's defeat.

It was war again. War had started all over again. How many more children like me would this war produce?

Just as I thought I had found a path leading to a brighter future,

I was being pulled back into chaos and confusion. Urged on by apprehension and fear, I escaped into a world empty of life, only to encounter trepidation and terror and be thrust back again into reality. These two worlds were where I lived, surrounded by unrelieved conflict and endless gloom.

Against the backdrop of chaotic wartime streetscapes, under the nightly blackouts, I was transported back to Changchun during the Civil War between the Communists and Nationalists. Without thinking I began singing a chant popular at that time, which was actually nothing more than a simple play on words.

> *White-eyes, Russkis, barbarians.*

In our dark room with its cloth-covered lamps, I began bemusedly singing this chant. It wasn't long, however, before I was rebuked by a visiting member of the Japanese Residents Association. "It makes it seem as though this house is occupied by antirevolutionary elements," he said.

At this time the skies over Korea were under the sway of the American army. After the U.S. landing at Incheon, the tide had turned against the Communist forces. As if to make up for this, the praise for the Soviet Union rose to new heights.

"The Soviet Union has accomplished some absolutely remarkable things."

"Our ally the Soviet Union has entered a new stage of development."

"In Russia, our Russia, they have achieved wonders unseen elsewhere."

Many people seemed to be laboring under the delusion that if they praised the Soviet Union, they themselves shared in the glory. For such people, this once popular chant surely went against the grain. It was further rumored that Soviet Migs would soon clear the skies of American aircraft. The fact that Russia had successfully carried out an atomic test a year earlier seemed to make this a certainty.

* * * * *

Since the fighting broke out, the elder Kim seemed to become worse. His angry shouting had grown more intense. Mother's warnings that I shouldn't visit his house became more insistent. But I didn't listen.

It was a Sunday morning when I went to his place. He was sitting formally at his desk with his back to me, gazing intently at something on the desk. It was a dead rat. Without moving a muscle, he continued looking at the rat, his face in profile profoundly tranquil. Uncharacteristically, the room was tidy and neat.

"It's a rat our cat caught this morning," he said quietly as if to no one in particular. He didn't turn to look in my direction. He continued to sit primly at the desk, looking at the rat. His back was unmoving, preternaturally quiet.

Around noon on that day, we heard the ear-splitting sound of someone screaming, calling out for help. It was the voice of Comrade Kim.

We all rushed out into the garden, soon joined by the bolting figure of Comrade Kim. There was blood streaming from his head. He had apparently been stabbed in the temple. Father left and instantly came back with a bandage. Mother rushed off to get help from the hospital.

While everyone was feverishly occupied with taking care of Comrade Kim, I slipped away to his house. The elder Kim was standing on the veranda, supporting himself with his left hand on a pillar, breathing heavily. He was glaring out into the garden, his eyes emitting a harsh, sinister light. They were the eyes of Pochi, our dog in Changchun, after it had devoured the babies' bodies.

Where had the quiet elderly man I knew gone? Where his kind eyes? Where his quiet back of that morning?

The headband draping down to his chest was spattered with blood. In his right hand, hanging limply at his side, was a blood-smeared knife.

* * * * *

The elder Kim was not the only one to have his life distorted by the war. The Koreans living in Yanji suffered greatly and in many ways.

When the U.S. and the Soviet Union established a boundary at the 38th parallel, those living below this line automatically became marooned in South Korea. While most of the Koreans in Yanji had their roots in North Korea, a good number of them had relatives in the South.

Families in Yanji who had lost a son or a relative in the fighting indiscriminately hated the South Korean Army. If such families learned that a member of another family was fighting on the Southern side, they deludedly viewed that family as the cause of their son's death. In the eyes of friends and neighbors the son's death came to stand for all that was heinous about the South Korean Army. Consequently, any families who had relatives marooned in the South below the 38th parallel were viewed askance by their neighbors and led rather constricted lives. Not only were such people compelled to worry about the safety of their relatives in the South, but they were also forced to live under insidious social pressure. Some of them became silent and withdrawn. Some, to prove their loyalty, joined the North Korean Army, even though this meant possibly fighting their own kith and kin.

Whatever the circumstances might be, there were some among the many soldiers sent out from Yanji who ended up engaging in a life and death struggle with their own blood relatives.

On October 25, 1950, the Chinese People's Volunteer Army under the command of Peng Dehuai entered the war, just as Stalin had calculated. The next day the American army landed at Wonsan.

Yanji was enveloped in a storm of singing and chanting of the slogan "Resist U.S. Aggression and Aid Korea." In consequence, many young men volunteered for service and were sent off to the frontlines. The casualties were enormous, the result of advanced American weaponry.

When would Yanji be bombed by American planes was a question on all minds. A sense of imminent crisis dominated the city. Day and night the sounds of bombing could be heard, and the city was flooded with wounded soldiers, adding to the overall unease. People evacuating the city, their ox carts piled high with household goods, became an increasingly frequent sight.

Thoughts of evacuation gripped the Japanese population as well. Technical specialists had apparently been advised to evacuate to Shijiazhuang in Hebei Province, and some had followed that advice. Father was urged to join their number.

If that were possible, Father would have been only too happy to leave Yanji. But who, in fact, could tell where it was safe to live in China? Once-safe Yanji had already begun to feel the effects of the war. What must be avoided at all costs were further victims from within the family. Then there was the matter of the streptomycin, for which Father had borrowed several years salary and was honor-bound to return it. He had no choice but to remain in China until that was done. He could not leave Yanji.

The family's destiny, seemingly fixed, was changed radically by a single letter. It was from Zhang Youan, formerly the head of the Shinkyo branch in Beijing. The letter read as follows:

> I have finally found you, Doctor. I am writing to ask that you allow me to reciprocate past indebtedness. If at all possible, please come to Tianjin. I will look after all your daily needs.

The envelope contained an unimaginably large amount of money, together with a note expressing the wish that Father make use of it. It was enough to pay off the streptomycin loan with money to spare. Father didn't hesitate. He instantly decided to set off for Tianjin.

At this period of time the Chinese cooperative managed by

Japanese in Yanji was suffering from a lack of capitalization. Consumers, for their part, were suffering from a lack of daily goods and were attempting to stock up on the necessities of life. The cooperative tried to discourage this movement, for without the proper material they couldn't operate. Given this situation, Father decided to deposit some money in the cooperative, using the funds remaining after paying off the streptomycin loan, and thus help the cooperative regain its financial footing. If this deposit were withdrawn, the cooperative would go under, so Father decided to leave it as it was, in effect making a donation to the cooperative.

Father also tried to get in contact with Mrs. M.'s surviving daughter, Taeko. He asked if she wouldn't be interested in living with the family in Tianjin, with the idea of returning to Japan someday. She didn't write back. Through Mr. A., who had served as a pharmacist in Changchun, he learned that Taeko was married to a Chinese man. There was nothing more that Father could do, and further inquiries would be an imposition. In any case, Taeko had probably become thoroughly acclimated to Chinese ways. Apologizing in his heart to Mrs. M. for not being able to do more, Father finally gave up on being of any help to Taeko.

* * * * *

Now we would be able to escape Yanji. Now we would be able to escape the sounds of aerial bombing. There would be no more dark blacked-out nights.

For me this was a new morning. Tomorrow would be a different day. This thought would rescue me from the desolate wasteland, from confusion and turmoil.

Leaving Yanji meant, I thought, leaving behind what had thrust me into that dark world, leaving behind the uneasy feeling that something vital was missing.

Tianjin—what kind of place would it be?

It was a big city, Father said; it was a wonderful place.

I loved big cities. I hated the earth, the soil. Terror resided in the earth, in the smell of the soil after rain had fallen. There was something sad in that smell. Why I didn't know, but I wanted to escape it.

I recalled the night that had proved my salvation. It was a dark night filled with the smell of withered grass and damp earth, with a single visible ray of light. What could that light be? I felt myself drawn toward it, closer and closer.

Where had that been, and when? In a pitch-black universe there had been a ray of light. That ray, that light, had been my life itself.

Tianjin, too, was a ray of light. The way to Tianjin must lie in that ray. It must, I thought; it must.

Within the light of Tianjin I could see my life. I could glimpse a fragment of my future. There was something there that promised me new life, that promised me a future. I was living in that presentiment, that hope, striving to escape my desolate wasteland.

On December 8, 1950, we set off on another journey. To get from Yanji to Tianjin it was necessary to go through the Shanhai Pass, the gateway to the Northeast region. The pass was located at the eastern terminus of the Great Wall of China and ran along the border of the Northeastern region, dividing the country into those areas within the wall and those without the wall.

The pharmacist Zhang Youan came to meet us at Shanhai Pass. He was sporting a small mustache and had an aristocratic countenance. There was a long wait for the train going to Tianjin, and so Zhang took us down some stone steps to a Chinese restaurant in the back of the station, treating us to a meal of buns with meat filling called *baozi*.

Leaving the restaurant, we strolled around the Wall and found one gate inscribed with the words "First Pass Under Heaven." Going through that gate and climbing the interminable stone steps, we finally emerged on the Wall. It was constructed of large darkish, gray-colored bricks. The stone steps and walls showed the wear and tear of the ages. Grass grew in the gaps between the stone pavement. The Wall wound off into the distance, finally disappearing over the western horizon.

Facing toward the northeast Father placed his hands together in prayer and bowed. He was undoubtedly saying goodbye to his sons in far-off Changchun.

Then, bowing again, he said, "This is farewell. Have a good look. This is the dividing line between north and south. It's a miracle we have come this far. I thank you. I thank you." These last words were undoubtedly directed to the heavens.

The overlapping hills, mottled with dry grass, stretched off into the unlimited distance. Far beyond the grassy haze was Changchun. Changchun, where I had been born, raised, and lived, and had almost been buried. A land mixed with fear and affection. My past.

Like a dragon, the Great Wall could be seen climbing peak after endless peak, cleaving the country into north and south. Would this same Wall cleave my life in two? Would it prove a dividing line between past and future? I was now standing on that line. Where would I find myself next?

Looking in the opposite direction, I could see the earth stretching south, ever south. It was there that lay the coming days of my life. Somewhere out there was Tianjin. Somewhere out there was my future life. The future I had seen in the great translucent glass bead was certainly waiting for me there. I was now setting off on a journey toward the light of Tianjin.

At last the train for Tianjin began to move. Leaving a plume of smoke behind, it began its journey into the light. The smoke, an arrow of time, disappeared into the northern sky.

CHAPTER 7

The Wavering Light of Tianjin

It was night when we arrived at Dongzhan Station in Tianjin. As we left the station, my heart jumped into my throat. Suddenly in the night sky there were clusters of light. Red, blue, yellow, green, pink, purple, orange. Small, brilliantly lit bulbs of light, they flashed on and off, on and off, flying up into the night like bejeweled ping-pong balls. They were little decorative light bulbs festooning a large Christmas tree in the station's rotary.

The surrounding area was dark, with only the rotary being illuminated. The small lights seemed to be floating in the air. With each flash, they flew off in one direction, flew off in another.

I was dumbstruck, frozen to the spot. What beauty, what brilliance!

That the night should have such light, that that light should carpet the sky in such colors. This was not the night sky of Yanji, pitch-dark and blacked out. Did this mean I had escaped the beckoning world of gloom? Each bulb, each flash, was inviting me to climb out of that dark hole.

Crossing a long bridge now known as Liberation Bridge, I was deluged by spectacular illuminations crisscrossing the sky, pervading both body and mind and seeming to take me as their special target.

White lettering hurried across the sky, chased by stripes of red. Green patterns flashed on and off. The frenetic dance of lights seemed to go on forever. The night sky over Tianjin was a virtual canopy of illuminations.

Lights, lights, lights. Their brilliant beams ran through my body like an electric shock—from top to bottom, from side to side, from corner to corner.

"How pretty! How beautiful!" The words burst from my mouth. The Christmas lights floating in the air, the beams of blinding illumination, had apparently made a direct hit on my faculty of speech. For the first time I recovered by ability to talk.

Between the beams of brilliant light could be heard the uplifting sounds of music. It wasn't the music you heard in Yanji, not revolutionary or workers songs. It was the sweet sound of a Chinese violin and the thrumming of a gong. The gong rose and reached a crescendo, then faded amidst the bright illumination.

A man called out: "Here you are! Here you are! Sweet and juicy."

Looking in the direction of this spirited voice, I saw an array of apples and persimmons. The apples were cut in half and aligned side by side, the seeds perfectly symmetrical. Around and between the seeds was an amplitude of frozen apple flesh, which under a spotlight shone red. Sweet chestnuts were being roasted, giving the air a pleasant pungent smell.

Was this still China? Was this the China I knew?

I felt I had been transported to some faraway country. Perhaps this was where I had wanted to go all along. This was perhaps the land I had been searching for in my heart of hearts. Perhaps this land had been waiting for me, waiting forever so long.

I felt intoxicated by the lights, intoxicated by the sounds, intoxicated by the smell of sweet chestnut. I was smitten and besotted by Tianjin.

* * * * *

Before I realized it, we were standing in front of a Russian restaurant named Kelincanting, which was run by Zhang Youan, the man who had invited Father to Tianjin.

On the other side of a glass door stood two slender young men dressed in red suits with gold buttons. They wore army hats at an angle, fringed in gold thread. They looked for all the world like toy soldiers. They moved in perfect unison at the sides of the double doors like mechanical mannequins. Opening the doors, they bowed as one and held out their white-gloved hands to show us the way. In the direction they indicated was a bright-red carpet about a meter wide. From the ceiling hung a resplendent chandelier with numerous glass dewdrops. The dewdrops reflected the red of the carpet and looked weighty, as if they might fall to the floor any minute.

On both sides of the carpet were lines of ladies and gentlemen dressed in evening wear. The women were lipsticked, manicured, and wore jewelry in their ears and around their necks. Their high-heeled shoes looked dangerously fragile. Some wore Chinese dresses slit up the side to reveal their thighs. Others, despite the winter weather, wore nothing on their shoulders. These statuesque women were not mannequins, however, but living, breathing human beings. In proof of this, they all clapped their hands to the rhythm of the Russian folk song "Karinka" as a welcoming gesture.

Zhang Youan had formerly been the Shinkyo branch manager in Beijing. Thanks to this, he had accumulated a fabulous amount of wealth. Now, making elaborate preparations, he had assembled his sometime colleagues to welcome their former company president to Tianjin.

However, surrounded by these resplendent ladies and gentlemen, invited to walk down the bright-red carpet, what kind of figures did we present?

We wore multilayered cotton clothing to keep warm, baggy and patched here and there. Our trousers were stuffed with cotton against the cold, bulging and lumpy. Our scarves were a patchwork of repeated rethreadings. Our shoes were boots for use in winter, oversized and clumpy. Our pathetically meager personal belongings were wrapped in ragged cloth *furoshiki*, dangling at our sides.

To refined eyes, we must have appeared as nothing less than a passel of beggars, children in tow, who had wandered in from barbarous Changchun in the far north. Their sparkling eyes were obviously consternated, unsure of where to look. Their forced smiles and their clapping to "Karinka" were the only things that sustained them.

With numerous popping sounds bottles of champagne were opened, and dinner began. In the center of the table was a bouquet of roses fashioned from deep-purple beets, and around it were arrayed the most luxurious Russian dishes. The pure-white tablecloth was fringed with leavers lace. The metallic dinnerware sparkled with light. The lace-patterned white paper napkins were thin and translucent. The roasted turkey legs were wrapped in threadlike strips of decorative paper. What left a lasting impression on me, however, was not the food, but the overall sheer whiteness and the glimmer of the forks, knives, and spoons.

This brought to mind the days before the Civil War started. It brought back lost memories that continued to shake my inner world. It brought them back and forced them to the surface.

As the party continued, a gentleman wearing black, thick-rimmed glasses performed some magic tricks, and another man, who spoke excellent Japanese and who had the air of an intellectual, sang "Stenka Razin" in a deep baritone. It was just at this point that I felt the need to go to the toilet, which was on the landing leading to the second floor.

As I opened the door to the toilet, time suddenly stopped and I doubted my eyes. It was a flush toilet exactly like the one we had had at Shinkyo. It also had a faint smell of chlorine. Would it really work, I wondered, pulling the chain on the water tank. It did; water came rushing out, bringing with it more chlorine.

I had been waiting for this day, for oh so long. This meant that Changchun had been liberated.

We had always said that the day water ran in the toilet at Shin-kyo, that would be the day the blockade of Changchun would be lifted, the day that food supplies would return, when we would escape the clutches of starvation. If only, we thought, if only water would run in the toilet once again. At Shinkyo I had pulled the chain over and over, but it only clanged dully, producing no water at all. I felt betrayed. While I was doing that, any number of people in Changchun were dying of starvation.

I recalled that fateful day in Changchun in late autumn of 1947, the day when electricity, water, and gas had suddenly been cut off. The day I went to the toilet and found it wouldn't flush, a tremor ran through my body. I was afraid that the electricity would never come on again, afraid that we would run out of food. It was as if I had been thrust into a prison cell, not knowing what would happen, what would befall me next. I was filled with fear and foreboding.

Hoping to find an answer to these questions, I had pulled the chain again and again. Whether the water flowed or not indicated whether the blockade had been lifted or not; it was a signal from the Eighth Route Army. This was my only means of learning the intentions of the Eighth Route Army. In the end, however, the only answer I received was in the negative.

Here and now I saw in front of me a toilet with exactly the same color, the same shape, and the same size as that in Changchun, and it had running water. It had white toilet paper, a shiny paper holder, a shiny chain, shiny pipes, and a pure-white bowl.

For a moment I felt transported back to our house in Chang-chun, more than three years ago. Changchun and Tianjin became inextricably interwoven in my mind.

The toilet at Yanji had been a horror of horrors. Of the earth toilet type, the bottom could be plainly seen. In winter the excrement would freeze, piling up to create a hill. The hill would grow taller and taller, its tip getting closer and closer. At that time I didn't have a menstrual period and didn't know what it meant, so I felt revolted whenever I saw blood on the tip of the hill. Subconsciously it must have reminded me of the time in Qiazi when I had urinated on the skull of a half-buried skeleton. The shock was the same. The memory of that incident had been erased, but even now just the thought of going to the toilet made me feel ill. Just stepping inside would make me retch, feel a chill, break out in a cold sweat. Struggling with these feelings, I would try to finish my business. Looking down would make it all but impossible.

It was around that time that I began to feel a sharp pain on the side of my hand next to my little finger whenever I saw something filthy. If the filthy object remained in my sight, the cramplike pain would gradually pass through my elbow to the base of my ears. Then my ears would begin ringing and I would be transported to the world of glass. The pit toilet caused me to vomit and almost lose consciousness. Exactly why I didn't know, but I felt a deep loathing and terror of excrement.

But now, I thought, I would be freed from that type of toilet, and suddenly I returned to reality.

After all, this was Tianjin. Tianjin, so full of beauty and light. Pitch-black nights, filth, the scary earth were no part of life in Tianjin. It was very much like Changchun before the blockade, very much like life at Shinkyo—the cheerful floral streetcars, the wonderful decorated cakes of the Osaka-ya.

I pulled the chain again. The chlorine-treated water came out in a rush.

Oh, finally, finally, a signal from the Eighth Route Army! They had sent me a signal. The blockage was lifted. Water was flowing. The electricity was on.

Changchun would be liberated. It would no longer be confronted with starvation. Its people would no longer be faced with death. The water was running. The water was running. I burst into tears.

While my mind roller-coastered back and forth between

Changchun and Tianjin, the shock of the running water, the fact that I had been able to cry, caused me to regain normal control of my emotions, excepting those relating to the lost memories of the journey from Qiazi to Yanji.

* * * * *

That night we stayed at a large hotel called the Huizhong. We went up to the third floor in an elevator whose black metal door folded like an accordion, just like the one in the Minakai Department Store in Changchun. You could see outside through the mesh walls. You could also see the chains that pulled the elevator up and down, which was kind of scary.

Once when I rode the elevator at the Minakai Department Store, the elevator floor seemed to tilt when going down, so I clung to Mother's legs to keep from falling. Since Minakai was a Japanese firm then, this must have been before Japan's defeat, which would mean that I was three or four years old. A male employee of the store, who wore a white jacket and black trousers, got into the elevator with us, carrying a tin bucket filled with water. Just as I felt that the floor had started to slant, the water splashed out of the bucket. This could only mean that the floor had truly begun to tilt. But Mother said it hadn't, and we had a good laugh about it as being a product of my imagination. If that was the case, though, then why did the water spill out? Maybe it was due to the clanking and bumping of the chains. And I definitely remember trying hard not to fall. At least about that, there is no mistake.

The next morning at the Huizhong we woke to a voice saying it was time for breakfast. It was one of the boys from the Kelincanting dressed in a white cook's uniform, standing by the side of the bed. He was holding out three stainless cylinders of food, each around twenty centimeters in diameter and ten centimeters high. They contained borscht, salad, and black bread. It was the same as what we had eaten at the restaurant the night before, the meat tender and seeming to melt in the mouth, steeped deliciously in beet juice. It was the most scrumptious borscht you could imagine. Did we deserve all this?

The beds were very high, almost difficult to get on. As it happened, I hated sleeping directly on the floor. I was afraid of sleeping anywhere close to the ground. At this point in time I didn't know why. In Changchun I had most certainly slept on a futon spread on the tatami matting. Why then did just the thought send shivers through my body now, set my heart beating? I tried not to think about it, but my dreams I couldn't control. Since Yanji I had been having strange dreams.

* * * * *

It is terribly bright. I am sleeping on a futon under a glaring sun. There is no ceiling overhead, and when I look up, there is the broad, expansive sky. I seem to be sleeping out of doors.

I am lying on a futon placed directly on the ground. The black earth stretches out endlessly into the distance, without a single blade of grass. I have a premonition of imminent disaster, and at that moment the futon begins to move, swiftly and wildly. It flies over the surface of the ground like a magic carpet. Before I know it, I find myself in a place where a mass of dark-green plants are sprouting out of the black earth. It is apparently Xing-an Hutong, in back of the Shinkyo factory across from the company housing of the Central Bank. It is where we used to pick plants during the blockade of Changchun.

The sunlight is pouring down. Above my head the young leaves of an elm tree are twinkling in a breeze, translucent in the sun. In the distance there is the sound of gunfire. Looking in that direction, I see a soldier with a rifle, his back toward me. What would happen if he turned my way? It would be so embarrassing if he saw me sleeping on the ground like this. I just came to pick plants, so why am I sleeping on the ground?

I have to get up, but I can't. I am sleeping face-up, but I can't seem to move an inch. The futon covering me is as heavy as lead. This time I have to make the magic carpet fly off on its own, but, no, if I do that, I have an idea where it will end up. It will be there—the place where no grass grows, the black sinister earth.

My arms and legs are frozen in time, rigid and immovable. I can't even move my head. It is becoming unbearable.

It is here that I always wake up.

How many years, how many decades, was I tormented by this dream? Before I understood its meaning, how many times did I see it? The memories of Qiazi had become deeply embedded in my subconscious mind—sleeping out in the open side by side with the dead—an everlasting terror, a terror I didn't fully understand.

This is why the high beds at the Huizhong Hotel were such a joy.

* * * * *

Not long after we had finished breakfast, Zhang Youan appeared. He said we were going out to buy some clothes. He must have been mortified by our beggarly appearance the night before.

Behind Huizhong, facing Bangjiangdao Street, was the largest department store in Tianjin, the Quanyechang. This is where we went shopping, and where we were all bought what was considered standard Chinese attire.

This was Haejindao, the heart of the busiest section of Tianjin, with Kelincanting very nearby. We were taken to the restaurant for lunch, but this time we were ushered into a private room on the second floor. The butter, cut into a spiral shape, was especially delicious, and I ate several patties without any bread. There were also tiny *baozi* buns floating in the soup, as well as a dish resembling wonton that was very good. When we had finished eating, we were taken to Zhang's private office.

The reception area had a sofa and a matching furniture set, and in the back was another room, dimly lit, where there appeared to be a Buddhist altar. The aroma of incense pervaded the air. Zhang's father came in, and Zhang quietly beckoned him to enter the room, where he kneeled on a round cushion in front of the altar and began the ritual of three kneelings and five prostrations. Could this be some kind of special religion, I wondered. In Yanji anyone known to have religious inclinations would be castigated as antirevolutionary, maybe even lynched on the spot, lucky to escape with his life. I had thought that religion had been outlawed in the new China, but it seemed that Tianjin was different. Women even wore makeup and had manicures. All of this was unimaginable in Yanji. There you'd be branded a bourgeois and made to rue the day you were born. But this small room was different, albeit mysteriously dark and secluded from inquisitive eyes.

While Zhang and his father were occupied, we were served with dessert on silver plates: Russian cake and ice cream with a side serving of wafers. On the plate with the Russian cake was a special treat, a triangular chocolate waferlike dessert, one side about ten centimeters long. It had a slightly bitter mocha-like aroma.

After lunch we would go out for a walk on the town and then return to the hotel. For dinner we would go back to the restaurant. This constituted our daily routine. In the meantime Father was ensconced in a room on the third floor of the restaurant experimenting with cystine hydrolysis, something he had apparently started the day after we reached Tianjin.

I myself was enjoying the night lights of the city. Going out on the second-floor veranda, I could see the restaurant's illumination close-up. Milky-white neon tubes around 1.5 centimeters thick delineated the name of the restaurant, the letters hurrying across the sign, some places flashing on and off. The scurrying letters, the milky-white neon tubes, were endlessly fascinating. The neon tubes reminded me of the *chitose* candy we got at the Shinkyo Shrine before the end of the war. If you picked out the center of the candy, it became translucent, allowing sunlight to pass through. It seemed as if the restaurant's milky-white light would permeate my whole body. I never got tired of gazing at it.

It was possible that I might spend the entire night watching these lights. I didn't understand why, but they seemed to encourage me to look once again into the future. It was just possible, with fear and trembling, that I was seeing something important through these lights. Compared to the dubious future I has seen in the glass threads held up to the sunlight in Yanji, the neon tubes offered something that was far more trustworthy, far more reliable.

I loved the lights of Tianjin with every fiber of my being.

* * * * *

Life at the Huizhong Hotel was full of interesting and unusual things. There was a little girl who would sit next to the elevator door on the third floor, singing. With a small face and pigtails, she must have been about five or six. She was always singing the same song. It was as if she had transformed the mournful sound of a Chinese violin into its vocal equivalent. I learned later that it was a folk song from the Shanxi region, but in any event I was intrigued by this little girl and her voice.

One day as I got into the elevator on the first floor, I found myself with the little girl, who was holding her mother's hand. Distracted by her, I paid no attention to the floor where they would be getting off. In the back of my mind, I thought she would be getting off on the third, which was my floor, since that is where she was always singing. At this particular time there was no elevator operator.

When they got off the elevator, I got off too, thinking it must be the third floor, but it wasn't. I forget which floor it was, but it was one of the higher ones. When I realized my mistake, the elevator had already started down. I waited for a while, but it didn't come back. Just then, from down the hall to the left, a man appeared wearing only a towel around his waist. He must have just come from the steam bath, for he was sweating profusely, and despite the winter cold, his skin was steaming and red as a beet.

Seeing him, I suddenly remembered that Father had said he would be going to get a haircut. Since I had heard the hotel had a barbershop, I figured it must be on this floor, the same as the steam bath. If I found the barbershop, Father would certainly be there. I decided to look for the barbershop.

Just as I had thought, the barbershop was on this floor, just behind the elevator. But Father wasn't there. Or I should say that I didn't have the time to learn if he was there or not.

When I opened the door, tremendously vociferous voices and a huge volume of steam spewed out. There was a line of ten barber chairs, and the barber and some customers were shouting and laughing in booming voices within a cloud of steam so thick it made it difficult to breathe. The barber was putting a steaming towel on the face of one customer, but this didn't stop the customer from raising his voice vehemently and gesticulating wildly.

There was one person, however, who stood out among all the rest: a woman who was several times taller than I was and built accordingly. She seemed to be the matron of the shop. The man next to her was apparently her husband and the shop owner, with whom she was engaged in a furious argument, despite speaking in the politest language.

The owner was a pink-complexioned portly man wearing short pants and a sleeveless shirt that looked like underwear. The shirt over his flabby belly was stretched as tight as a drum. The woman was wearing a short-sleeved, black Chinese dress. Her hair was drawn up in back, grotesquely accentuating her double chin and pear-shaped head. Her eyes popping out, her thick purple lips distorted out of shape, she was spewing out words like a machine gun. Foam had formed at the corners of her mouth, which she spat out like bullets.

All this clamor and commotion must surely send blood rushing to the head, I thought.

On the woman's forehead there were three dark-purple circles about three centimeters wide, clear signs that she had had moxibustion. A traditional Chinese treatment for headache and shoulder pain, moxibustion calls for creating a fire in a small bottle and placing the mouth of the bottle over the affected area until the fire goes out. This produces a strong suction affect on the skin and supposedly increases blood flow. The woman had apparently had this done, leaving the three dark-purple circles.

When this formidable woman noticed me peeking inside, she opened her already popping eyes even wider and turned them on me, as if I were some kind of small, rare animal. Since she was apparently contributing most to the uproar, when she stopped, the others immediately stopped and turned to focus on the cause—this small, rare creature. The customer with the towel over his face hurriedly removed it, wondering what had happened.

I shrank back from this unwanted attention and closed the door, never learning if Father was there or not.

Surprisingly enough, I didn't find this clamorous commotion, this overheated atmosphere, unpleasant at all.

There was a certain honesty there, a life force, an openness, a sense that what gave vitality to life was not the head but the body. This raw, unpretentious strength was a revelation, a revelation that warmed my inner being. It was infinitely preferable to the insubstantial revolutionary discussions engaged in by the Japanese in Yanji.

I can't help thinking that the formidable woman in the barbershop gazed at my small insignificant self with a certain instinctive tenderness. Even though I would be turning ten in a few days, in her eyes I was nothing but a small fragile creature that had wandered mistakenly into her shop.

* * * * *

There was another aspect to life in the Huizhong.

On the third floor of the hotel, four rooms were assigned to the seven individuals in our family. Each room had two beds and a washstand. Until a suitable house was found, we would be living there.

Across the hall from the room occupied by me and one of my younger sisters lived a quiet, refined older woman and a girl who was apparently her daughter. They were both fair-complexioned and slender, and their quiet demeanor indicated an affluent background. The daughter, who often wore a light-brown fur coat and seemed of marriageable age, had her fingernails manicured in bright red and her lipstick neatly applied in the same color. The mother, who appeared to be over sixty, tottered as she walked on her bound feet.

In their movements and behavior there seemed to be a melancholy air—in the way they would look down when we met, in the incline of their heads. They apparently wished to avoid public attention. This seemed to belie what might appear on the surface as arrogance, as a coldness owing to their superior status. In the past they had probably been among the extremely wealthy, the head of the household killed in the War of Liberation, perhaps arraigned as one of the exploitive classes and incarcerated after the Communist takeover. It had undoubtedly been something of that nature.

One day, the two women happened to hear me and my sister talking. When they realized we were speaking in Japanese, their attitude underwent a remarkable transformation. The off-putting expression in their eyes, their unchanging chilly mien, suddenly took on a look of friendly cheer. From that day on, whenever we met, they would bow in the most polite manner.

We finally left the Huizhong and moved into a new house just shortly after New Year's in 1951. A European brick edifice, it was located in Shandonglu in the French concession. It had a gate supported by pillars made of thirty-centimeter-square bricks, and going through the gate and climbing three flights of stairs brought us to the entrance door, a heavy steel affair framed in curvilinear patterns. Immediately inside was a big hall with a large spiral staircase. Other than that, there were simply three doors leading off to separate rooms. The only distinguishing feature of the hall was the thickly lacquered staircase railings. A stairwell rose up to the ceiling, and high on its walls were small arched windows. The light coming through these windows fell on the staircase railing, creating a beautiful pattern of shadows. Directly in front of the house was a French mission school.

At this time Tianjin was on par with Shanghai as a business center and considered one of the top three Chinese cities. Before the end of World War II it was the site of much competition for hegemony between the imperialistic powers. The city had a port, Tanggu, which served as an outport for Beijing, and was divided into imperial power concessions, the French, the English, the Italian, and so on. A "concession" referred to a territory in an open-port city ceded to and governed by foreign powers, that is, territory where foreign powers had extraterritorial rights; at one time there were eight nations exercising such rights. When we arrived in the city, the word was still being used, but the preference was for "Town": French Town, English Town, etc.

The Quanyechang Department Store, the Huizhong Hotel, and the Kelincanting restaurant were located in what was once the French concession. France had formerly held sway over what was Tianjin's busiest district. The deluge of illumination that had first excited me was precisely that seen on the main street of the former French concession.

Our house in Shandonglu was situated in a high-class residential area, and of course there was no illumination. But when the lunar New Year came around, there were plenty of lively firecrackers. Different from fireworks, which are enjoyed for their colorful effects, firecrackers were to be enjoyed for their sound. They exploded in ear-splitting blasts, and the variety of sounds they made, and how they were ignited, was enormous.

The cook who prepared our meals, the *dashichuan*, lived in the basement of the house. In his forties he was a very kind, gentle man, but one day he inexplicably attached some firecrackers to the front door. It was the lunar New Year, and the sounds outside were so enormous that we went out to see. When we opened the front door, the firecrackers the *dashichuan* had set went off, catching us all by surprise. According to tradition in the cook's hometown, he said, anyone caught off guard like that was assured of good luck in the future.

After moving to the new house in Shandonglu, Zhang would occasionally come visiting, bringing with him a graceful, pretty young woman who was a performer in the Chinese opera called *changhu*. Her supple, manicured, slender fingers were particularly attractive. Whenever Zhang's wife visited from Beijing, they would invariably get into a terrible fight, the cause of which was undoubtedly this young woman.

It was while we were in Tianjin that we began studying Chinese under a tutor. The truth is that while in Changchun we spoke solely in Japanese until most of the Japanese were repatriated, and after that there was no one to talk to. And in Yanji we were surrounded by Korean speakers and attending the Japanese Democratic Elementary School, where we spoke in Japanese. Thus, though we were living in China, we had felt little need to speak Chinese. Our tutor was the man who had sung "Stenka Razin" in a beautiful tenor at the party on our first night in Tianjin.

Father spent his days on the third floor of Kelincanting, making medicine.

During the time spent at the Huizhong, Kelincanting, and now Shandonglu, my wounded heart began to heal. My memories of Qiazi remained lost in time, and there was nothing in my present life that caused them to resurface. I was happy with everything around me.

Surrounded by arched doors, bay windows, high beds and more, my life was European, urban and elegant; there was nothing to associate it with Qiazi, nothing that would force me back into that vacuous glass world. I dearly loved the city of Tianjin. It gave me mental balance, the strength to live, and it made me believe that a future existed. I loved it so much that I wanted to hug it.

If life had continued on like this, I would undoubtedly have lost the memories of Qiazi forever. I would have lived an entirely different life. In actuality, my happiness then was based on the fact that I was leading a life secluded from social reality, something I was totally unaware of.

In early summer that year we moved to #7 Huaanjie, Third District, Tianjin City. It was a large mansion located in what used to be the Austrian concession and bordering the former Italian concession. The iron gate was five or six meters wide, about two and a half meters tall, and sported an openwork cloud pattern. Further in was a large tiled garden that could easily accommodate fifty couples if a dance party were held there. On the right side of the garden were luscious silk trees, and in the center was a wisteria trellis with fragrant flowers. Below the trellis were round porcelain tables and some ten porcelain chairs. To the left of the trellis was a separate building that served as the kitchen and the home of the chef. The house itself was further beyond, a two-story structure, the first floor of which was to function as a pharmaceutical factory, the second story being where we would live.

Going up to the second floor, I could detect the smell of paint. The walls of the enormous landing, about fifteen mats in size, were freshly painted in peppermint blue. Going into the room on the right and opening the bay window, I was immediately startled by the crown of a huge pagoda tree pressing into the room.

Its leaves eagerly brushed up against my face. Its fragrance was

almost overpowering, much like jasmine. Its white petals were swaying gently, blocking out the pure blue sky of early summer. I took a
deep breath of its sweet aroma.

Never had I imagined such a day as this. Wanting to make sure
it was real, I placed a bit of the tree on the palm of my hand. The
small leaves surrounding the petals were shining brilliantly, vibrant
with life.

What a difference there was between the present day and the day
in starving Changchun when I had placed an elm leaf on the palm of
my hand. I didn't want luxury. I didn't envy extravagance. Not at all.
What I wanted was to escape what had laid waste to my life—the
terrible, horrific memories . . . the fear that had buried those memories in a dark corner of my mind. I wanted to escape all the forces
that were trying to pull me back into that desolate wasteland.

Now, here, all I asked was that nothing link me with that world.
That nothing remind me of that terrible time, that nothing insidi-
ously seep through the cracks of time. If there could be something
clean and pure that soothed my soul, I asked for nothing more.

I was being given a break. The heavenly gods were surely giving
me a recess. It was all right to rest up a bit. Finally I didn't have to
be called crazy. If I were, I was capable of feeling sad and shedding
tears. I was now capable of arguing back, "No, I'm not crazy."

I buried my face in the leaves of the pagoda tree. Little did I
know that the real trial was yet to come.

* * * * *

Directly in front of our house was a river called the Haihe (Sea
River), a very wide river that lived up to its name. The local population, however, called it the Baihe (White River). The reason for
this was not because its water was particularly white. The river had
ninety-nine bends in it, one short of a hundred, which number is
written 百 in Chinese. If the horizontal stroke at the top of this

character is removed, you get 白, which means "white." This is the reason locals called it the White River. It was a play on words using Chinese characters.

The Haihe was chock-full of small boats belonging to people who made their living on the river. The boats were mostly junks and sampans, with occasional oceangoing vessels making their way through the smaller craft. These people spent their whole lives on the water, born there and dying there. The boats were their homes.

Looking from our house toward the river, on the right there was a big iron bridge called Jintangqiao. Just on the other side of the bridge was the Public Security Office.

To our left and one street over, along the river, was the former residence of Yuan Shikai, the first president of the Republic of China. While on the one hand he received huge loans from the great powers, on the other he assiduously sought to restore the monarchy and proclaim himself emperor. His grandiose residence was a fitting symbol of his power and authority. Seen through the leaves of the pagoda tree on our second floor, it had all the magnificence and beauty of a modern-day castle.

The house where we were living was formerly the residence of the Chief of General Staff under Yuan Shikai, Feng Quozhang, who was one of a powerful army clique who had graduated from the Baoding Military Academy. With the passing of Yuan Shikai in 1916, he served as vice president and then as acting president of the Republic of China. We were actually living in what had been the residence of this illustrious personage.

How should such an event transpire? It must have been because Zhang Youan had close connections with the Republic of China. The city of Tianjin constituted a strange mixture of frenetic energy, extravagance, and modernism, as well as centuries-old moral degradation, which contained an antirevolutionary element. It was this element that would ultimately prove Zhang's downfall.

* * * * *

The new Chinese school semester started in September. But since summer vacation was almost upon us—vacation began in July—there was little use in my transferring into a new school now, because there would be very little time remaining before school let out. On the other hand, we had finally settled into our new house and I was eager to go to school, so it was decided to have me start immediately.

Instead of going to the nearby district elementary school, we chose the private Peizhi Elementary School in Minshenglu, located in Tianjin's 3rd District. The school was mainly attended by the children of the wealthy and had very high academic standards. Given that, there would probably be little bullying of Japanese students; at least, that was apparently Zhang Youan's opinion.

Since I was born on January 3, 1941, I was already ten years old and should have been in the fifth grade. Up to now, however, my school life consisted of only several months spent at the Changchun School in April 1947 as a first-year student at the elementary level, virtually equivalent to not attending school at all. What with the Revolutionary War and illness, four years had slipped by. It was decided that I would first be enrolled as a third-year student, and if things went well, then placed in the fourth-year class in the following semester.

I could finally go to school. I could finally study like everyone else. I was overjoyed.

Our principal teacher was Miss Liu. She had a fair complexion, a large nose, and although she appeared to be much past her thirtieth birthday, she wore her long hair in braids, which hung down on either side of her head and were tied at the ends with red yarn.

Seating in the classroom was arranged according to academic achievement: the better students sitting at the front and the poorer students at the back. Of course, I was at the very rear since they had no way of judging my ability.

While living in Shandonglu in Tianjin, I had been tutored in Chinese and learned the usual phrases: "Good morning." "Good afternoon." "Please take a seat." "Would you like some tea?" "Excuse me, but how does one get to Kelincanting from here?"

Of course, this level of Chinese wasn't of any use in class. Fortunately, I had learned how to answer when asked my name, carefully explaining the meaning and pronunciation of each of the Chinese characters that my name was written with, a rather convoluted process. I practiced this ahead of time so that I wouldn't embarrass myself.

As expected, the teacher asked me to introduce myself to the class, and I got through most of it without a hitch. Unfortunately, when I got to my personal name, I pronounced it with the second tone instead of the fourth, meaning that I had said my name was "Fish." There was some snickering in the class, finally breaking out into undisguised laughter, and I could only look down at my desk and bear it, my face growing red and hot as I realized my mistake.

Later I learned another reason for all the laughter. Chinese names usually consist of two or three characters. Apart from some rare cases, mostly among minority groups, the Han Chinese, the dominant ethnic group in China, invariably write their surnames with one character, personal names with one or two. In contrast, my name is written with four characters, three for the surname and one for the personal name, making it appear that the last character, my personal name, was a mistake, one character too many. This oddity seemed to be another cause of ridicule. Thereafter, it became a fad among students to attach the character for "fish" after their personal name.

I became anxious about the fact that my name was Japanese. Borrowing one of the characters from my real name, Zhang Youan went so far as to create a more Chinese-sounding name for me, but such sleight of hand had little effect. It was already too late. Apparently the word that a Japanese was living at #7 Huaanjie had spread rather quickly. And they knew what I looked like. On the way to and from school I would be tormented by the cries of neighborhood children.

"Japanese devil!"

"Japanese dog!"

Some threw rocks, or spit on me, or flicked snot from their noses.

In school I was further isolated. Classwork consisted entirely of political education, of ideological indoctrination—how great Mao Zedong was, how wonderful the Chinese Communist Party was, how much the people had suffered under the Japanese invasion, how brave the people had been in resisting the Japanese, how courageous the People's Liberation Army had been in leading the fight, what an exemplary army it was. This same narrative was repeated interminably.

Japanese Imperialism, the Japanese Invasion of China, the scorched-earth Sanguang policy, the War of Resistance against Japan—every time the teacher uttered one of these words, someone or other would turn back and look at me. What hurt me most was the mocking, sniggering expressions on their faces.

But there were other faces as well. Even though all of the students were from affluent families, they had not been left untouched by the Japanese invasion. There was one seventeen-year-old who had lost a leg; there were those who had lost their parents owing to the Japanese army. There were students like that. They didn't look at me mockingly or jeeringly but with absolute hatred. It was my fault, they seemed to say, that things had turned out like this.

* * * * *

Being a Japanese was tantamount to being a criminal. Even a ten-year-old girl had to take full responsibility for the Japanese invasion, had to bear the glaring eyes of the rest of the class. And this culpability didn't apply exclusively to past events.

With the end of the war Japan was occupied by the Allied

powers, one aim of which was the disbandment of the Japanese army. However, in February 1950 the Sino-Soviet Treaty of Friendship was signed, and in June the Korean War broke out. As a result, U.S. policy made a 180-degree turn. The Soviet Union, on the other hand, revoked the Sino-Soviet Treaty of Friendship and Alliance with the Republic of China and replaced it with a new treaty (Sino-Soviet Treaty of Friendship, Alliance, and Mutual Assistance) with the new Communist regime. This was clearly aimed at the United States and U.S.-occupied Japan.

In Japan the United States almost immediately established the National Police Reserve (later the National Safety Forces and still later the Japan Self-Defense Forces), and the U.S. became the only country to maintain troops in Japan on a permanent basis. Fearful that the whole of the Far East might fall under the influence of Chinese and Soviet Communism, the United States began to place its hopes on a liberal democratic Japan as a bulwark against rising socialism.

One of the countries that fought against Japan during World War II was, of course, China. In fact, the People's Republic of China continued to proclaim that, even though it had suffered most from the war, it had not been invited to take part in the Peace Treaty with Japan and that, furthermore, the fact that the peace negotiations proceeded almost solely under American leadership was a violation of the Potsdam Declaration and invalid under international law.

Although one of the professed goals of the occupation of Japan had been the disbandment of the army and demilitarization, in fact the United States continued to station troops in Japan and was attempting through the U.S.-Japan Security Treaty to remilitarize Japan to American benefit. This is the message that Zhou Enlai, the first premier of the People's Republic of China, sent out daily through the mass media.

According to Zhou, the "end of war" peace treaty would not result in compensation for China's huge war losses but unite the

United States and Japan against China. This same message was pounded into our heads in the classroom. "Even though so much Chinese blood was spilled during the war, Japan still refuses to reflect on its past after defeat, but instead joins forces with the United States and sets out again onto the path to militarism."

Throughout China there were violent demonstrations and rallies, an overwhelming reaction on the part of ordinary people. Then, with the outbreak of the Korean War, and America siding with the South, the fear arose that the United States would invade China. Further, the anger over China's being excluded from the peace treaty discussions was now revived and linked to Japan's invidious invasion of China.

At school, this period was one of unrelenting bewilderment and humiliation. It ended up producing groundless feelings of guilt and inferiority at being Japanese. While living in a world of apprehension, there was one good thing: by the end of the semester I had gotten to the point where I had almost completely mastered Chinese. Still, I was excluded from taking academic tests.

During the summer vacation I began on my own to study pronunciation with a vengeance. I had to speak perfect Chinese. A difference in pronunciation was sure proof that I was an outsider, a Japanese, an easy target for bullying and ridicule. And there was no one in the school community who would protect me.

The question of whether or not I could speak perfect Chinese was at the heart of whether or not I could survive life there; it was a question of life or death. Life is supported by the spirit, and my spiritual being had been overjoyed that I would be able to attend school, not knowing that I was actually standing on the edge of a precipitous cliff. Fortunately, I had liked singing since I was small, and singing is vocalization, just as speaking Chinese is vocalization. Memory, language, and vocalization are learned most easily when young, and I was only ten, the age when these three are most easily acquired. Added to this was my own personal preference for these subjects. By the time the new semester started, I had almost perfectly mastered the language. I felt confident. The amount of ridicule I would be subjected to should now be considerably less.

On September 1 the new semester started with hopeful expectations. The main fourth-grade teacher was a man named Ma. The skin on his face was red and slick, and he had a slender nose with a white bridge. His head was close-shaved like a Buddhist priest, and his face was very long like a horse's, in keeping with his name, "Ma" meaning "horse." His eyes were brown. My previous teacher, Miss Liu, had something mean in the look of her eyes, but Mr. Ma had none of that.

My budding expectations, however, didn't work out as hoped. On September 8, 1951, seven days after the new semester had gotten underway, the Security Treaty between the United States and Japan was signed, to go into effect immediately upon being ratified by both countries. To prevent this from happening, a huge wave of chants and slogans swept the length and breadth of China protesting the remilitarization of Japan. The singing and chanting of political slogans had always been an important part of ideological education, but now it reached new heights. Among those heard on a daily basis were "We are against Japanese remilitarization," "We fought for eight years against the Japanese," "The blood of countless people was spilled," "American imperialists are attempting to remilitarize Japan," and "Down with Japanese militarism."

When it came time for the music class under a female teacher, I dreaded entering the music room more than anything else: every minute was devoted to practicing these antimilitarization songs. As they sang, the students would glance back at me. I was sitting at the very back of the room, and so just by looking back, the whole class could see me. Some would furtively peer at me while singing, others would stare with downright hatred. Worst of all were those who smirked and sniggered from beginning to end, never taking their eyes off me.

Their eyes seem to say, "Hey, Japanese. Learned your lesson now?" Or "How do you like singing this song, huh?"

They seemed to derive a sadistic pleasure and sense of superiority from humiliating me, from incessantly watching me suffer, since I had no possible answer to their taunting. It was somewhat like a mischievous child torturing an insect and enjoying its attempts to escape.

If I didn't sing, I would be put through a session of self-criticism during regular class, but if I did, I would be subjected to mocking eyes that seemed to ask how I, a Japanese, could possibly sing along with them.

When one individual directs his gaze upon another, he can send a message of friendly feeling or mutual understanding. Or, by openly appraising the other person's physical being and mentality, and by letting the other person know that he has been the subject of appraisal, this individual's action can be an act of cruelty, one in which he attempts to subsume the being of the other and establish his relative superiority.

By means of such acts of appraisal some people luxuriate in feelings of superiority, which they most commonly express in the form of humiliation. The only thing a person who has been violated in this way can do is to bear it, or to pretend that it has never happened.

Still, the time spent actually singing wasn't bad. The problem was after that, when the singing had stopped and the chant of "Down with Japanese militarism" had been taken up. At this point students were supposed to raise their fists into the air, but what they did was turn and thrust them into my face.

There was nothing I could do to escape this ridicule but sink further down into the depths of humiliation. So this is what a school was? This is what it meant to learn in a group environment?

If I became Chinese, a hundred percent Chinese, would that solve the problem? I had changed my name to a Chinese-sounding name. I had learned to speak Chinese like a native. If I could have a blood transfusion and change all my blood to Chinese blood, should I do that?

But what did it mean to be Chinese or Japanese? What was the difference? What did it mean to be Japanese? Why had Japan invaded China? Why did Japan sign a military treaty with the United States? Why was Japan making weapons for use in the Korean War?

Every move made by Japan pierced the body and soul of a little girl living across the seas like a lethal weapon. Did Japan know that? I began to hate Japan, a country I had never laid eyes on.

Then on November 18, 1951, the U.S.-Security Treaty was quietly ratified, as if all the antimilitaristic singing, chants, and demonstrations had never taken place.

*****

Before entering winter vacation it was customary for the results of final exams to be announced. Usually the focus of everyone's attention was on national events, but since the exams decided the order of seating, the results were awaited with bated breath. For those at the top of the list there was also the possibility of receiving a red scarf (*honglingjin*). This neckerchief signified that the wearer was a Young Pioneer. Young Pioneers were a prestigious group whose role it was to carry on the thought of Mao Zedong and the ideology of the Communist Party. To receive a red scarf was the highest possible accolade, a Young Pioneer being the junior equivalent of a Communist Party member. The Young Pioneers of China were an emulation of a similar organization in Russia, and for every Chinese boy and girl it represented the ultimate in achievement. To be a Young Pioneer meant to be one step from the ultimate honor, that of being a member of the Communist Party. Anyone with a red scarf around their neck had the world at their beck and call.

In my fourth-year class there were only two students wearing red scarves. One was a boy with the best academic record and the class president. The other was a girl with the third-best academic record; her parents were highly placed members in the Communist Party. After these two, there was a boy who was being considered for the Young Pioneers, but academically he was ranked fifth. He was being nominated because of the energetic role he had played in organizing study groups and anti-Japanese marches, but his grades were not outstanding. However, if he finished in the top three in the forthcoming test results, he would be made a Pioneer. Then there was a girl from Fujian Province, fat and puffy-faced, who was ranked second academically. She didn't speak much and didn't take an active part in debates or political activities, and therefore wasn't a candidate for a red scarf.

* * * * *

Mr. Ma began announcing the results of the tests.

"The student who finished first in the exams this time is . . ."

There was absolute silence.

". . . a girl."

A buzz of excitement ran through the class.

Even from the back of the room I could tell that the ears of the boy who always finished first had gone beet red. He must be feeling chagrined, being beaten by a girl. He might even lose his position as class president. The ears of the two girls now ranked second and third were also red. I could tell because one of them had short-cut hair and the other braids. The third-ranked girl flicked her braids behind her shoulders, a clear indication that she thought, just perhaps, she might have finished first.

Mr. Ma continued, enunciating each word slowly and clearly.

"And most surprising of all," he said, looking around the room, "she is not Chinese."

Not Chinese? But that would mean . . . but it couldn't be true!

"Her name is Bao Junxiu," Mr. Ma proclaimed.

Bao Junxiu? He had definitely said Bao Junxiu. That was my Chinese name, Bao Junxiu.

The skin on my face seem to pucker and grow painfully taut. Me! It couldn't be. Me!

The buzz in the classroom grew more heated, inflaming my cheeks, but not a word reached my ears.

The whole class rose to its feet, and I saw Mr. Ma pointing to the top seat and motioning to me with his hand. It seemed the seating arrangements were going to be changed and that I had to move.

My heart was banging in my chest, thrusting up through my throat, a thumping sound that couldn't be held down. Could others hear it, I wondered. Taking a deep breath, I tried to muffle the beating of my heart. Then, as if walking in a dream, I slowly made my way from the back of the room to the front.

The boy who was at the top of the class now became second. The second-ranked student became third, and the girl whose father was a highly placed Communist Party member was fourth. The fifth-ranked boy who was being considered for the Young Pioneers fell to sixth. He would undoubtedly be dropped from consideration.

From my place at the back of the room where I could see everyone, I now moved to a disconcerting position where everyone could see me. I felt as if every eye in the class were drilling into my back.

It was hard to believe. For the first exam ever taken in my life to turn out in this way . . . The future I had seen through the red glass bead, had it been this? I wanted to cry out for joy to the heavens. Humiliated and ridiculed, a new world had been waiting for me, a world I would never relinquish.

* * * * *

With the coming of the New Year, the glaciers in the upper reaches of the Haihe began to melt, sending massive blocks of ice down the river. It was about this time that there was another exam, and again I finished at the top of the class. To a certain extent I began to be accepted. At the same time my desire to learn became even more intense, and I began to frequent bookstores. The school didn't have a library, and I wasn't sure if Tianjin had one either, or where it might be. In any case, at that time I wasn't aware of the usefulness of libraries and thought that bookstores were the only source of knowledge.

There was a big bookstore called Xinhua on Hepinglu, which was the main street running through the business district where the Quanyechang Department Store was located. Whether walking from Peizhi Elementary School or from home in Huaanjie, it took nearly forty minutes. Still, it became my regular routine to walk to the bookstore every day after school let out and read everything I could get my hands on.

Given that the Sino-Soviet Treaty of Friendship had been signed just a year or so earlier, the store was filled with books praising the Soviet Union, the greatest nation on the face of the earth. Among them was *War and Peace*, *Anna Karenina*, and *The Green Arrow*, which was tremendously popular at the time and became a movie. These were the type of books I read at first, and even though I probably didn't fully understand them, they were a great deal of fun. In a biography of Lenin I came across a gravure picture of him as a young boy sitting next to a dog that was as tall as he was. The caption said that Lenin loved animals and they loved him in return, which I found utterly endearing. I also read Lu Xun and looked over some of the books written in praise of Stalin, Mao Zedong, and Kim Il-sung.

I wanted to know more. I wanted to satisfy my intellectual curiosity, to use my mind to the fullest extent. I was hungry for food of the mind.

The wonderful time spent in the bookstore provided me with the most delicious feast I could imagine. This feast was accompanied in the background by the lyrics of the song "Moscow and Beijing."

The People of China and the Soviet Union are forever friends.
The bond between these two brothers is tight.
The two peoples, honest and righteous, rise up together, shoulder to
shoulder.
Honest and righteous, they march forward, a song on their lips.
Stalin and Mao Zedong lead us on.
They lead us on. They lead us on.
Moscow and Beijing. Moscow and Beijing.
The people resolutely march forward.
For the joy of work, for the sake of harmonious relations.
Under the banner of peace, the people march on.

This song and others with similar lyrics were sung as enthusias-tically as the chants opposing the militarization of Japan.

The alliance between China and the Soviet Union, which proved provoking to the United States, was probably one of the reasons for the ratification of the Japan-U.S. security treaty. But the fact that China and the Soviet Union had become allies didn't affect me per-sonally. So I was happy to sing this song in a voice as loud as the rest. There were many similar songs that became popular at this time, all in praise of the Soviet Union and Stalin.

As long as these songs were being sung, things were not so bad, which was around the time that Marxist-Leninist doctrines and other recondite matters were beginning to be taken up. Then the mood shifted in emphasis from friendly alliance to anti-Japanese militarization and anti-American, pro–North Korean thinking, this change being reflected in the daily fare of background music.

There were countless numbers of songs devoted to these sub-jects, such as the "Song of the Chinese People's Volunteer Army," "Anti-American, Pro–North Korea March," "March of Chinese People's Volunteer Army," "Struggle of the People of Korea," "Ad-vance! Heroic Korean People's Army," "Anti-American, Pro–North Korea Duet," and "Ten Eulogies for the People's Volunteer Army."

The most popular was "The Struggle of the Chinese People's Volunteer Army."

> *Fording the Yalu River in high spirits.*
> *Safeguarding the country and preserving peace, protect your*
> *homeland.*
> *O youth of China, come together as one.*
> *Against America, for North Korea, defeat foreign ambitions.*
> *Destroy the American wolves.*

The lyrics of songs are an important means of ideological education. If you know the songs being sung at a particular time, you can get a hint of the mood of the country.

On April 28, 1952, the Sino-Japanese Peace Treaty was concluded between Taiwan and Japan. This was a result of opinion being divided in the United Nations as to which government, the Republic of China or the People's Republic of China, should be invited to San Francisco, where the Peace Treaty with Japan was being drawn up. Since "China" was not included among the countries to which the peace treaty applied, Japan entered into a separate treaty with Taiwan.

For Communist China, which had declared the establishment of a new China without gaining control of Taiwan, the peace treaty with Taiwan was entirely unacceptable, for not only did it formally declare a cessation of hostilities but it in effect recognized Taiwan as the true China, not the People's Republic of China.

Furthermore, China had become inextricably mired in the Korean War, leading to the tragic loss of innumerable Chinese lives. The American army was the enemy, but the weapons it employed were being made in Japan. By becoming a munitions depot for the American army, Japan was trying, it was said, to boost economic growth.

Satirical posters were plastered throughout Tianjin. One showed

President Truman with one leg planted on Japan, the other on the Korean Peninsula, holding a huge bomb in his fingertips, ready to drop it on China. On the map of Japan was a depiction of Prime Minister Shigeru Yoshida, about one-tenth the size of Truman, shouldering a rifle and holding a thick bundle of money, a huge smile on his face. Posters of this type appeared here and there.

Another showed Truman embracing Taiwan and attempting to confine the People's Republic of China to the mainland. It contained the words "Truman, you dastardly villain! Have you lost your mind?"

Another showed a depiction of Japan with the names Mitsui and Mitsubishi written on huge bombs, below which were the words, dripping with blood, "What, Japan, the aggressor again?" This was directed at the Japanese military industry that was profiting from American procurements.

These posters came to be displayed in the confines of the bookstore, and the pushcart at the front was piled high with reprintings of a pamphlet on Japanese aggression. I had an urge to pick up one of the pamphlets, but I didn't have the courage. In any case, I had a good idea of what was in the pamphlet since it was repeatedly drummed into our heads at school. Still, I wanted to get a better idea of why I was bullied to such an extent. In the end it was this feeling that won out, and I reached for one of the pamphlets. In the next instant, I regretted it.

Opening the pamphlet, what should I see but the picture of a Japanese soldier cutting open the belly of a pregnant woman and holding high in the air an embryo skewered on the tip of his bayonet. As he stomped on the woman's face, laughing maniacally, he was captioned as saying, "I have killed the mother of the Eighth Route Army."

At once I hurriedly closed the pamphlet. Then, thinking that someone might have seen how flustered I was, I was tempted to take a quick look around. But then again, thinking that someone might be following the movement of my eyes, I tried to pretend that nothing unusual had happened and peered casually around to see if anyone was watching. No one seemed to have noticed. Like a criminal who had committed some heinous crime, I backed out of the store and left.

My mind was a swirl of emotions. Did Japanese soldiers really do things like that? The picture kept haunting me, relentlessly following me. I erased it from my mind again and again, but it always returned. It began to stir up memories from the past.

I had the feeling that I had experienced something similar to the scene depicted in the picture. I had witnessed something more horrific, sometime in the past. I was almost certain of it.

No, but that couldn't be. Or could it? Yes, I had definitely seen something. But if so, where and when?

Dark things in the recesses of my mind had been disturbed and began to stir.

* * * * *

As you entered the garden to our house, to the right was a large silk tree. In summer it erupted in beautiful pink flowers the size of ping-pong balls. The dark-pink threadlike petals, dewy translucent, were absolutely spellbinding. The contrast between the pink flowers and the dark-green leaves reminded me of the arrow-patterned crepe dress I had worn when I was three or four. It was one of my favorite dresses, along with the velvet piece with an embroidered crow on the breast. I never got tired of gazing at the silk-tree blossoms.

If you touch the leaves of a silk tree, they quickly fold up like wings. One day, wanting to see this phenomenon once again, I touched the tip of a leaf. In that instant a cineramic scene of thistles sprang to mind—purple flowers, threadlike petals, flowing colors, dark-green sturdy leaves, thorns that pricked one's finger.

I was lying on the ground, looking at the thistles; that was certain. I was wandering between life and death, but holding on dearly to life. Why was I lying on the ground then? But, no, it wasn't only that. I seemed to remember lying on the ground somewhere else, too.

That was when . . .

When I had gotten that far, my ears suddenly clammed up, and the silk tree faded into the distance. Just before vanishing completely, the tree suddenly got bigger again, and then smaller and then bigger, over and over, quavering in the air, returning to its normal size in the end.

I didn't enter the world of glass then, but it seemed that the ground was being laid for just that.

* * * * *

In June 1952 there was another round of final exams, and again I finished at the top of the class. The boy who finished second was sitting on my left. He was definitely conscious of my presence, viewing me as a rival. His name was Wang Junguo. Of the three characters that made up his name, the middle one was the same as in my Chinese name, Bao Junxiu. Despite the fact that our desks were right next to each other, and despite the fact that it had been that way for something like half a year, he never looked directly at me and never spoke a word. Sometimes I would feel his eyes on me and glance in his direction, but he would always turn quickly away.

On the day the results of the finals were made known, Mr. Ma said he had an important announcement. Wang Junguo's body gave a faint jerk. He must have thought that he was going to lose his position as class president. Everyone in the room must have thought the same thing. While being the top student wasn't an absolute condition for class president, it was generally required, in addition to being a Youth Pioneer. Since I wasn't a Pioneer, Wang could rest assured on that point, but still he had lost the top seat to me three consecutive times.

"But before that . . . ," Mr. Ma went on: "Wang Junguo, I'm giving you a warning. You've finished second three times in a row. Right? And the gap between you and Bao Junxiu is extreme. And she's a Japanese! She has a handicap, but still there's this gap. How do you explain that? I'll put you down for a session of self-criticism later on. You understand?"

There was no need to be this hard on him, I thought. I turned bright red and lowered my head.

"As I just said," Mr. Ma continued, "Bao is a Japanese. But still, from the very first exam she has done remarkably well. Not only in mathematics and Chinese, but also with perfect scores in social studies and history. She understands the thought of Mao Zedong and is far above anyone else in her comprehension of Party history. This is the reason I am recommending her as a candidate for the Youth Pioneers."

This was beyond anything I had ever imagined. That I, a Japanese, who had been the subject of so much ridicule and humiliation, should become a Youth Pioneer, that I might someday be wearing a red scarf. To think that good grades could produce such a difference. It was true that since finishing at the top of the class, the amount of bullying had diminished day by day. That was why I had studied so hard, the reason I had to finish first. Still, to be appointed a candidate for the Pioneers . . .

However, Mr. Ma had more to say. "Still, she is a Japanese. Whether a Japanese can receive approval or not is unclear, but even if she can't, maybe she can be made an associate member. This summer vacation I would like her to act as leader of the study group. Anyone with an objection to this, please raise your hand."

Mr. Ma surveyed the room. There was a slight pause before someone at the back raised their hand. I wanted to look to see who it was, but I didn't have the courage.

"State your opinion," said Mr. Ma.

"Well, she's a Japanese, one of the invaders! How can a person like that be qualified to carry on the thought of Mao Zedong?"

The strident voice belonged to a boy whose father had been killed by the Japanese Army. He was fourteen. His grades were average, so he sat in the middle of the classroom. From the first he had been one of my worst tormentors, but I didn't hate him for it. It was understandable.

Actually, if the matter was going to become a subject of debate, I wished it hadn't been brought up at all. I'd be happy if they would stop bullying me. I had no interest in becoming class president. If anything, I just wanted to be left alone. Just as I was beginning to regret Mr. Ma's proposal, he spoke up.

"Don't be stupid! Sure she's a Japanese, but did she take part in the invasion of China? On August 15, the date of Japan's defeat, she was only four years old. And her father has contributed to the building of the new China. You heard the May Day broadcast, didn't you?"

As part of the May Day festivities that year Father had been asked to mount the podium and give a speech as the Japanese representative. It had been broadcast by the Tianjin radio station.

Mr. Ma wasn't finished.

"If Japanese were all bad people and Chinese all good people, there wouldn't have been any need for the Chinese Communist Party. There wouldn't have been a need for the War of Liberation, right? It's the same thing. The Japanese Imperialists' invasion of China was one of the most atrocious things imaginable, and it should never be forgotten. But the culprits were a few evil imperialists; the majority of the Japanese people were victims of the war, just like us. That's why we have to join hands with them and fight to build a Communist society. Is that clear? You understand? Never forget this."

This meant that in the War of Liberation and the Revolutionary War, the People's Liberation Army had liberated the country, but even in that we Japanese had been of use.

I lowered my head to my desk and attempted to hold back the tears, but no matter how hard I tried they kept coming. Any minute I thought I would begin to sob. I was glad that I had survived to see this day. I was glad I had put up with the bullying. Never had I thought I would hear such words, no matter how I had thirsted for them. These words were all that I needed to keep me going. In China there were wonderful people who thought like this. As long as there was one such person I could go on living.

Thank you, Mr. Ma.

My heart was full of gratitude. I promised myself that I'd never do anything to disappoint Mr. Ma.

* * * * *

Meeting Mr. Ma's expectations meant joining with the Chinese people to build a Communist society. During the summer vacation I decided to devote all my energy to a study group.

First we would gather in the park for cleaning activities at 6:00. In the crisp morning air there were people doing tai chi, people out for walks carrying birdcages, older people squeezing walnuts in their hands as a guard against ageing. It was quiet but lively. Since there were a lot of older people, everything seemed to be in slow motion. Taking care not to get in the way of these people, we would pick up litter and sweep the grounds with brooms we had brought with us. If there was a bench or anything in need of repair, we would report it to the Public Security Office. Finished with our regular routine we would disband. By then, it would be about 7:00.

After finishing breakfast and miscellaneous errands we would assemble again at 10:00 to listen to the radio broadcast. At that time there weren't many households that had a radio, so we would gather at the home of one of the groups' members that had one. My family had an old radio, its speaker covered with a brown hemp cloth. It was a big apparatus in the shape of a house. We had gotten it thanks to Zhang Youan.

Every night around 8:00 the family would listen to this radio, but what we heard were mostly incomprehensible words dispersed among a lot of static. Still, it was definitely refreshing and exhilarating to hear voices directly from what was supposedly one's home country.

There was another member whose family had a radio, but since I was the group leader, the study group was held at my house. At 10:00 the Tianjin radio station had a political studies program especially for young people. We would listen to that for thirty minutes and then discuss the content until 12:00. By and large this was my daily routine.

Most of the time was spent discussing the Korean War and the anti-Japanese remilitarization movement. However, since the number of casualties from the Korean War had ballooned, and since young Chinese boys from the age of twelve or thirteen to fifteen were being taken into the army as volunteers and sent off to Korea, the focus of discussion turned to opposition to the United States and China's support for North Korea. Boys who volunteered were referred to as "little heroes," and their houses bore a plaque that read "Home of the Renowned." If the boy happened to be killed in the fighting, the words became "Home of Integrity."

The radio programs focused mostly on the background of the Korean War and the present situation, but sometimes they would present a narrative of the Homes of the Renowned. They would follow the psychological process of the families involved: the hesitation, the decision, the courage. "This is a true story," the narrator would say. "Tomorrow this could happen to your family." The narration was meant to be inspiring, but it was also meant to create a feeling of guilt in those who had not yet volunteered for the youth corps. It was meant to make us think what we could do, what we should do, and to put our discussions into action.

No matter what subject was taken up in our political studies, it would almost invariably lead back to Japanese militarism. Japanese militarism was seen as the source of all evil. Although this made political studies extremely distressing, I would unfailingly find solace in Mr. Ma's uplifting words. As long as they remained in my mind,

I had nothing to fear. I couldn't be overwhelmed by guilt. I had to overcome it. Otherwise, I couldn't meet Mr. Ma's expectations.

Telling myself this over and over again, I decided to find out exactly what Japanese militarism was. Every afternoon, as my classmates were engaged in their favorite pastimes, I made the forty-minute trek to the Xinhua bookstore to read the pamphlet on Japanese aggression.

Instead of walking to the store I could have crossed Jintangqiao Bridge, gone past the Public Security Office to the main street, and then taken a streetcar. But for some reason I didn't ask my parents for streetcar money, probably because I didn't want anyone to know about my little secret. Mother and Father were occupied in the factory from morning to night, and the five children were each leading their own life. Never once did I tell any of them what I was really thinking. I suffered on my own, and I struggled on my own.

It never crossed my mind to buy one of the pamphlets. To read one was akin to delving into one's criminal past. If I bought one, the clerk would know what I was reading, an almost terrifying possibility.

I was also afraid that someone would recognize that I was a Japanese. I might successfully strive to overcome feelings of guilt, but I couldn't rid myself of this fear. In the way I approached the pushcart piled with the pamphlets, I still looked for all the world like a petty thief.

What I principally learned from the pamphlet were the terrible atrocities committed during the scorched-earth Sanguang policy and the Nanjing Massacre. Still, if I was going to find out about Japanese militarism, I had to come to terms with these cruel scenes. My heart was racked with pain, but I didn't give up.

The weight of these horrific scenes was perhaps more than I could be expected to bear. Each one, like a single shot of film, was incised deep in the crannies of my mind, disturbing the hidden memories of Qiazi and bringing them slowly to the light.

At night, trying to sleep, these individual shots would be scattered and dispersed into the dark air. The faces of the dead would float to the surface. These images reminded me of something I had seen somewhere, sometime in the past, or had actually experienced.

But when and where? Without realizing it, had I really experienced such horrific, such terrible scenes?

Then I heard a wailing voice. That voice was . . .

At that very instant my ears stopped functioning; the images before my eyes began to fade, reduced to a tiny dot. I was once more in that vacuous glass world where mere breathing was a near impossibility. Apprehension, fear, fright enveloped me. What terrible things were hidden, lurking, in the depths of my mind?

* * * * *

With the end of summer vacation, new fifth-grade classes began. I was happy to learn that my teacher would still be Mr. Ma. I submitted to him a thick report I had prepared on the activities of the study group and what I had learned at the bookstore. He was immensely pleased.

"This is really great," he exclaimed. "No one has ever made a report like this. It's wonderful. It's unfortunate, though—I hate to say this to someone who has submitted a report on political studies like this—I have to convey the news that my recommendation for the Youth Pioneers was turned down. I thought you could at least be made an associate member, but they said that since you're not a Chinese citizen . . ."

So it hadn't worked out. But I really didn't care, not that much. Of course, if I had been made a Youth Pioneer and been able to wear a red scarf, I would have been very proud. It would be a lie to say that I wasn't interested at all, that I didn't yearn in some way for that honor. But as long as I remembered what Mr. Ma had once said, I didn't need anything else. As long as I could pay him back in some way for those words, meet his expectations, I would be perfectly satisfied, heart and soul. He had also thought highly of my report; he recognized my hard work, recognized me as a person. There was nothing more I could possibly ask.

"But I recognize your work," he continued. "You've worked on behalf of a new China; you're a child of the revolution." And then speaking to the class: "How about it, everyone? We're starting a new academic year, so how about conducting an election for class president?"

Wang Junguo went red in the face. Ever since being put though a session of self-criticism, he had looked upon me with harsh, burning eyes. Finishing second had been disgrace enough; he didn't want to lose his position as class president on top of that.

Mr. Ma then said, "In every way, including politics and academic standing, I recommend Bao Junxiu. Speak up if you would like to recommend someone else."

"Mr. Ma . . . ," I said, raising my hand. "I'd like to remove my name from the list of candidates."

"Why in the world would you want to do that?"

"I don't think I'm qualified, not yet. A class president has to be a leader, and I don't have leadership qualities. Wang Junguo is fully qualified to lead the class. I recommend Wang Junguo."

Wang looked over at me, surprised.

"Well, if that's the way you want it . . . ," said Mr. Ma. "What do you say, Wang? You ready to accept this recommendation?"

"Yes, sir."

Wang's voice was rather faint for him, but he looked happy. Everyone started clapping their hands. Wang would continue as class president, just as before.

I felt tremendously relieved. This is the way it should be, all smoothed over, no rough edges. Most of all, I didn't want anyone holding a grudge against me. The most important thing of all was to avoid being bullied.

And Mr. Ma had called me a child of the revolution, hadn't he? What more could I ask? I was happiness itself. I thanked the heavens for giving me this life. The problem was, it didn't last long.

Not only at night but during the daytime too, the scene I saw before me would fade away and shrink to a tiny point, leading to a glassy world. The more I tried to concentrate on what I was doing, the worse it became. This meant it happened most frequently during class.

When Mr. Ma was giving the lesson, I tried to focus every nerve on what he was saying, so as not to miss a single word. Then one day it happened, my ears stopping up, Mr. Ma's voice growing more distant. At first I couldn't believe this was happening in class—there must be something wrong with my eardrums—and I stuck my fingers in my ears and gave a hard push. Still, his voice kept growing smaller. This can't be, I thought, but it was already too late.

Mr. Ma's face began to grow increasingly small. I rubbed my eyes to keep from falling unconscious, but once this kind of thing started, it couldn't be controlled by willpower alone. Mr. Ma's face became as small as a bean, only his mouth moving. I couldn't hear a thing.

Then, in the end, Mr. Ma disappeared altogether.

* * * * *

The social situation and family matters were both undergoing change. For one thing, the Three-anti and Five-anti campaigns had begun. The Three-anti Campaign was a popular movement against the three vices of corruption, waste, and bureaucracy; its principal aim was the thought reform and reeducation of governmental and large enterprise employees. The Five-anti Campaign was similarly a popular movement against bribery and illicit entertainment, theft and privatization of state property, tax evasion and speculation, cheating and cutting corners on government contracts, and stealing

economic information from state organizations and business enterprises by their upper echelons. This campaign mainly targeted capitalists and investors in semiprivate enterprises. The Three Antis had
already commenced by the summer of 1951 and continued until the
end of 1952, but before it could be concluded, it was overtaken and
overlapped by the Five Antis.

The Three-anti Campaign did not have a serious effect on the
family, but the situation underwent a drastic change with the com-
mencement of the Five-anti Campaign.

When we arrived in Tianjin two years earlier, and while we were
living in the Huizhong Hotel, we were astonished by the huge difference between Tianjin and Yanji. Even at this late date Tianjin
society still possessed strong pleasure-seeking, hedonistic aspects.
Aside from that, Tianjin was an industrial center that placed great
emphasis on economic growth, and from the past had been a cradle
of capitalistic ways of thinking. Now it could be called a two-sided
coin with capitalistic thinking on one side and very progressive, revolutionary thinking on the other. There were also said to be reactionary agents working furtively in the background, backed by Jiang
Jieshi, who was profiting from American intervention in the Korean
War.

Throughout the whole of China, the Three-anti and Five-anti
campaigns were perhaps most intense in Tianjin. Ideological education was reinforced, and antirevolutionary elements were exposed,
on a par with the post-liberation period. Some children reported
their parents as possessing antirevolutionary sentiments and were
honored as "little heroes." The religious sect known as Huixindao
came under attack as a propagator of superstition, and this led to
condemnation of religion in general.

In the midst of all this, Zhang Youan was arrested and jailed for
ideological reeducation. Our house was visited by a member of the
Public Security Office, who kept a constant eye on our every move.
He showed up every morning at 8:00 and left every night at 8:00.

Each day was the same. He said he didn't understand Japanese, but this was just a ruse. In fact, he hoped to catch us expressing anti-revolutionary thoughts in Japanese.

It was all wasted effort, in any case, since we no longer spoke Japanese at home. Even our dreams were in Chinese, even when we talked in our sleep.

Never able to relax when away from home, always being watched after coming back, it was sometimes almost difficult to breathe. It was particularly hard on Mother and Father since they were under constant observation all day long. Father was particularly liable to "exposure" by his employees. Even though Father had done nothing wrong, his accusers would make use of the slightest excuse. The best means of self-protection was to accuse the other party first. Attack is the best defense. The old pattern had returned, it seemed. At that time there were only fifteen or sixteen workers in the factory, a small operation. Still, Father was the factory manager, and anyone who was a manager would inevitably come under attack.

Father's greatest crime was that he was living on the premises of the factory. Zhang Youan had provided us with a residence in return for Father's past kindness, and Father had built a factory in one part of the building, to be followed later by the hiring of factory workers. Given this chronology of events, it was only natural that we should be living in the structure where the factory was located. However, this was said to be a grave infringement of the Five-antis' prohibition against "theft and privatization of state property," and hence an egregious example of privileged behavior and in need of thought reform. The workers who brought Father's "crimes" to the notice of the authorities were the same people who had been so deferential when applying for employment. In the end, rather than fighting the accusation, we decided to move to a new house, just catty-corner across the street.

In the midst of a campaign of this sort, the number of crimes that one could be accused of seemed to have no end. As soon as one

was resolved, another would crop up, waiting in a seemingly interminable line. To protect oneself, the essential point was to attack others
before they could attack you.

* * * * *

In any age or era, a person's destiny seems to be decided by
chance encounters. Now, ironically, while the focus of attack was not
Japanese militarism but matters of internal Chinese concern, what
was causing me distress was my own psychological state of mind.
Of course, the roots of the problem ultimately lay in the conflict between the Nationalists and the Eighth Route Army.

Partly perhaps because of the turmoil within the country, the
episodes that caused Mr. Ma's head to grow small and disappear
became more frequent. They seemed to be attempting to bring
something to the surface from the bowels of my mind, something
weighty and resistant.

* * * * *

On the way home from school I would often see a woman who
was slightly mad. She was tall and her body seemed bloated. Her
long hair hung down to her waist, and her skin glistened black, as if
she hadn't washed for years. She had a faint smile on her face as she
walked along, her eyes vacant and unfocused. She was always singing
the same Japanese song.

> Autumn deepens under the traveler's sky.
> Feeling alone, suffering alone.
> My beloved home, my dear old parents.
> Returning home in a dream.

Keeping time with the melody, she would take four tottering

steps to the left, then four tottering steps to the right. Children she passed in the street would make fun of her by scattering in the direction she moved, screaming out in delight. Some children would throw rocks, but she continued to walk on, unconcerned.

Was she Japanese, or did she have some past connection with Japanese residents? Judging from the fact that she would sometimes flourish a stalk of wheat in the air, maybe she had once been a music teacher at a Japanese school before Japan's defeat. I couldn't help wondering what was going through her mind. Maybe she and I were not that different.

* * * * *

In March 1953 Stalin died. At the memorial service held at Peizhi Elementary School in his honor, the weeping Miss Liu thrust her fist into the air and shouted out, "Stalin Banzai," her voice cracking with emotion. Whether her tears and choked voice were the real thing, or merely an ostentatious display of her devotion to the revolution, I wasn't sure. But it is true that the almost violent way she thrust her fist into the air, and the way she wept, caused me to have my doubts.

On the other hand, it may be that she truly revered Stalin as a great revolutionary leader. Under the influence of ideological education it was hard to be objective, and a person might believe that one fanatical individual was actually a great leader. I could understand that. At this point in time Mao Zedong was viewed as a towering figure of almost godlike stature.

I myself sincerely believed in Mao Zedong, that no other person could possibly be as great. The memories of Qiazi, the fact of its reality, were still locked away in my mind. The person who made my faith in Mao Zedong unshakable was undoubtedly Mr. Ma. My whole life was built on his words, and he was a member of the Communist Party. It was only natural that I should honor the ideology that formed the foundation of Mr. Ma's being, and that I should strive to emulate his way of thinking.

At this point in my life it was absolutely necessary that I believe I was trusted by Mr. Ma, that I could rest assured in his understanding, if no one else's. In time, however, our relationship began to crumble.

In April a ceasefire was ratified by the U.N. General Assembly, but fighting did not actually cease until the armistice agreement signed in July. This made the division of Korea into North and South an indisputable fact. The war had played a role in reviving and growing the Japanese economy, creating a Japan-U.S. security treaty, and had been an indirect cause of the Three-anti and Five-anti campaigns. It had lasted over three years and accounted for over 400,000 dead. The line separating the two countries reverted to the 38th parallel, the same as before the war, meaning that neither side had gained a substantial advantage.

With the U.N.'s ratification of the ceasefire, the problem of Japanese returnees resurfaced. Safe passage through the Korean Strait for return to Japan could now be guaranteed, it was said. Another factor was that China was clearly interested in importing Russian technology. Up to this point China had been intent on retaining foreign technicians at whatever cost, but now it did a complete about-face and encouraged repatriation. The man from the Public Security Office, who had been watching Father's every move, now took to urging him to return to Japan.

While this was going on, my mental episodes were growing worse by the day. Any number of times Mr. Ma's voice, and he himself, faded to a tiny dot and vanished during class time. At first, what had occurred only once a week became once every two or three days, then every day, and finally several times during one class.

Mr. Ma asked me: "Bao Junxiu, what's wrong with you? You're acting awfully strange these days. You seem to have your head in the clouds, not even taking notes or anything."

I was sitting directly in front of Mr. Ma. He could see everything I was doing. Whenever my mind went blank, the pages of my notebook would also be blank.

"You're all in a fluster about going home, I bet."

I wanted to say, no, that wasn't it. But even if I explained, who could understand what was going on in my head? I was trapped in a world of self-recrimination, baseless guilt, and feelings of inferiority, unable to move or breathe.

Just once, out of desperation, I asked Mother's advice.

"During class Mr. Ma's face fades into the distance, I can't hear his voice, and in the end his face becomes as small as a bean and disappears. How can that be?"

"That kind of thing often happens when you're young," she said. "It's nothing to worry about."

Perhaps Mother was trying to keep me from being overly anxious, but she didn't pursue the subject any further and never referred to it again.

This short exchange was the one and only time I opened by heart to anyone. Unfortunately, Mother's short words resulted in my feelings of guilt and inferiority growing even more intense. Something must be wrong with me, I thought, since I was agonizing over a phenomenon that everyone commonly experienced.

But no matter how I tried to explain them, no matter how I tried to make sense of them, the episodes never went away.

In the middle of the night an anguished face writhed in the dark, its eyes glazed and glittering. They were the eyes of the skull that had appeared above the ground when I had taken a pee in Qiazi. If I managed to sleep, the futon would begin to move, sweeping me off to unearthly places.

There was one particularly eerie dream I had almost every night. I was trying to go somewhere. I wasn't sure where, but I was trying with all my might. All around me was a vast plain, and I had the feeling there was a mountain lurking in the background. If I tried to go to the right, water would come gushing out and block my path. If I tried to go to the left, more water would assail me. Straight ahead was a large rock. If I tried to climb over it, water from left and right would swirl around it, creating a turbid stream.

Then I remembered the mountain lurking behind me. I could climb that mountain. But looking back toward it, there was no mountain to be seen. Instead I found myself standing on Xing-an Boulevard. I was going home after school, and I had come to the boulevard, which was inundated with water from the recent rain. In the ripples created by the boots of Big Sister and her friend was a small green leaf meandering in the water. While I stood spellbound by that little leaf, I looked up to find myself all alone, all alone in a sea of water, terribly frightened. Then Big Sister's friend fell into the submerged entrance of a bomb shelter and drowned.

Turbulent water. The fear of torrents. Why was I having this dream? I didn't know.

After leaving Qiazi on our way to a train station, we had to cross a fast-rising river, one in a line of refugees. The cart of the family in front of us was upset by the riverbed rocks and was overturned, the family swallowed up in the raging water. Among the family belongings floating on the surface was the hand of a small girl reaching up into the air.

This scene, along with other memories of Qiazi, had vanished from my mind, but somewhere deep down it was still at work, still had the power to terrorize.

In one dream I was walking through town on the way to the bookstore, and suddenly, ahead of me, water gushed up from the ground and came rushing toward me. In the dream I always had the presentiment that this was going to happen. Ah, the water, it's come again. As soon as that thought crossed my mind, the turbulent water materialized without fail. Although I realized that if I took this particular way to the store, the stream of water would come, I still took it, and inevitably the tumultuous waters came.

Together with the dream of the futon skimming over a vast plain, this dream continued to torment me for years on end.

In school Mr. Ma's voice continued to fade away, his figure to disappear into a dot. My existence teetered on the edge of collapse, my heart on the verge of bursting.

It was then that Mr. Ma criticized me for the first time.

"Bao Junxiu, what's going on with you? Always getting good grades, you're not resting on your laurels, are you? Or maybe your thoughts have already turned away from China. All you can think about is going back to Japan. You should reflect on what you're doing. Anyway, turning down the class presidency seems to have been the right choice."

"Seems to have been the right choice," he had said, my Mr. Ma. But who knew what I felt when I turned down being class president? Who knew what suffering I was experiencing? Even Mr. Ma, was it possible for him to understand me?

No one can know the heart of another. Everyone is alone in this world. Living alone and dying alone.

* * * * *

On that particular day the waters of the Haihe were cold. Somehow I found I had gone down the levee and was standing in the river, not a soul in sight. I would go further out, I thought. I would put an end to this struggle. Enough was enough, and I had done my best. I would now find rest. My heart was clear, quiet and unwavering. The water had reached my chest.

It was then that I noticed a capsized boat belonging to one of the water people. Its load of vegetables was bobbing in the river, struggling hands reaching up from among them. Sometimes I could see two faces, the faces of a woman and a child. A man, the husband I supposed, was shouting something as he swam frantically about trying to save them.

Those frantic hands reaching up, the woman and the child. The murky waters.

The swift waters back then had reached my chest. Cold, they were now trying to revive past memories. There was a line of refugees, yes. Clinging to a cart, fighting the strong current, I had crossed that river, the water up to my chest.

The raised hand of the girl swallowed by the river. Her hand. Other hands. Many other hands. A pale mountain where hands moved, only the hands. The mountain was piled high with human bodies. In the pale-blue moonlight the hands of the dead were moving. Wailing voices crawled over the surface of the earth.

The pleading hands on the surface of the river overlapped with memories of moving hands in Qiazi. I was brought back to myself by the wailing siren of a rescue boat from the Public Security Office. I ran back up the levee, screaming aloud, attempting to escape Qiazi. When I reached the road at the top of the levee, another horrendous sight awaited me.

Apparently distracted by the sound of the siren, a cart had hit a little girl. Tossed by the side of the road, her innards had spilled out from the impact, her skull stripped of skin, a shiny pink. Apparently crushed by the tires of the cart, her eyes had popped out of her head.

The child's mother was wailing with grief, frantically trying to replace the girl's spilled innards, trying to push her eyes back into place, as if this would bring her child back to life. Her body shaking with emotion, she repeated her efforts over and over again.

Spilled innards. Rotting corpses. Green bellies, swollen until bursting. The buzzing of hordes of flies dark in the air.

There, on that ground carpeted with bodies, we had spent our nights.

Qiazi!

Qiazi!

Qiazi!

The unbearable memories of Qiazi had finally broken their moorings.

Qiazi, an unearthly hell that shouldn't exist on this earth but did. I had spent many nights there and had left it deranged. After leaving Qiazi there had been days of continuous walking. I had fallen by the side of the road and seen a flowering thistle. I had met with a raging river. On the desolate plain I had seen a light. Among the smells of the wet earth and drying grass, I had seen a light that would prove my savior.

There was the Christmas tree on the night we reached Tianjin Station, brilliant lights floating up into the night air, bulbs of intersecting brilliance. They connected me with the ray of hope I had seen on the wasteland, which had brought me back to life.

A saving light. That must be why I loved the lights of Tianjin so much. Yet that same light that brought me back to life would be the force that would drive me toward death. But since I couldn't bring myself to choose death, there was no choice but to continue to carry the burden of Qiazi.

* * * * *

On September 7, 1953, I was standing on the deck of a ship headed for Japan. Father had finally made the decision to return home after he was betrayed by a Japanese woman whom he and Mother had employed out of pity during the Three-anti and Five-anti campaigns. Having heard Father's May Day speech, she had come to say that she had no family and was desperately in need of work. She sang praises of Father's philosophy of helping out others in times of need, and with tears in her eyes vowed she would remember him for life. However, it turned out that she was not averse to joining with others to accuse her savior if it served her purposes. Father came to the realization he couldn't live a righteous life under the present regime, that it only fostered self-serving attacks upon others. Until now Father had considered it his duty to serve the Chinese people, and he had turned a deaf ear to the Public Security Office's exhortations to repatriate, but this incident changed his mind.

* * * * *

The ship began slowly to slip out to sea. The city of Tianjin grew ever more distant, the houses and the trees taking on the appearance of a miniature garden. In that miniature world were people still feeling joy and sadness? Were they still suffering, fighting among themselves, and loving and killing one another?

Somewhere out there was Changchun, the city where I had been born and raised, the city that had almost been my death. And Yanji and Tianjin, too. There was also the good earth that had given me life and had tried to take it away.

When I next looked around, I found that the ship was out in the middle of a vast expanse of water. Just like the good earth, the ocean was limitless and unending, free of boundaries.

But then, different from the solid earth, the ocean was always moving, somehow unreliable and unsteady, my first experience of this phenomenon. If you tried to stand on it, you would without fail sink beneath the waves. And yet here I was riding on a ship slipping smoothly over its surface.

For the first time in my life I saw a swarm of flying fish skimming over the water. For the first time in my life I was aboard a seagoing vessel that wouldn't sink. Things that shouldn't be happening were happening. I felt a faint glow in my heart, a mixture of uneasiness and hope.

What kind of country was Japan? What kind of people lived there? Maybe, just maybe, an unbelievably wonderful tomorrow was awaiting me.

Deeply I breathed in the salty sea air.

Afterword

In the process of creating a new China, why did Qiazi have to take place and why in Changchun? To answer this question objectively two historical facts have to considered. The first is the Cairo Declaration, the second Mao Zedong's strategy of "encircling the cities from the countryside."

On November 22, 1943, a meeting was held in Cairo, Egypt, attended by American president Franklin Roosevelt, British prime minister Winston Churchill, and Jiang Jieshi, president of the Republic of China. The purpose of the meeting was to discuss postwar arrangements in Asia, as the war neared its end. The principal subject of discussion was Allied policy vis-à-vis Japan.

The underlying reason for the Cairo Conference was that Jiang Jieshi wished to consider the possibility of calling a halt to the conflict between the Republic of China and Imperialistic Japan and concluding a separate peace treaty.

World War II was fought between the Allied powers (the United States, Great Britain, France, the Soviet Union, the Republic of China, and others) on the one side and the Axis powers (Germany, Italy, and Japan; the Tripartite Alliance) on the other. The Republic of China was dissatisfied with the support it was receiving from the U.S. and Britain. The wife of Jiang Jieshi, Song Meiling, had been very active as Secretary-General of the Chinese Aeronautical Affairs Commission, and in 1941 she had succeeded in gaining the aid of the

American Flying Tigers. However, this group was disbanded in 1942 in the face of overwhelming Japanese air power. Jiang Jieshi's position had become increasingly untenable.

The government of the Republic of China at the time was split into the pro-Japanese Nanjing regime and the pro-U.S., pro-British Chongqing (Chungking) regime. The dominant force in Nanjing was Wang Zhaoming (Wang Chaoming), and in Chongqing, Jiang Jieshi. The Nanjing regime was backed by Japan and was where the father of Jiang Zemin served, later president of the People's Republic. Wang Zhaoming had no desire to continue the fight with Japan.

In 1910 Jiang Jieshi had graduated from the Tokyo Shinbu Gakko, a Japanese military academy for Chinese students, and for a time was a cadet in the 19th regiment, 13th division of the Japanese Imperial Army. Fundamentally, he was a Japanophile. He wavered between continuing the war of resistance against Japan and calling a halt to the fighting and signing a separate peace treaty. In particular, the rumor had reached Allied ears that his principal interest was in driving out the Communist Party and defeating Wang Zhaoming.

With this in mind President Roosevelt invited Jiang Jieshi to Cairo as one of the "Three Great Allies." Roosevelt was wary of the Communist Party under Stalin gaining an advantageous position in the postwar world. Overcoming Churchill's opposition, he gave preferential treatment to Jiang and promised him further support. Roosevelt urged him to continue the fight until Japan's unconditional surrender, essentially proscribing a cessation of hostilities and a separate peace treaty.

Jiang Jieshi was delighted. The Republic of China had been selected as one of the top three, not France or the Soviet Union. Further, the U.S. and Britain had chosen not Nanjing's Wang Zhaoming but he himself, Jiang Jieshi. For this he would agree to anything demanded of him.

On December 1, 1943, the Cairo Declaration was released to the public. It was unsigned, and Churchill later declared it without legal efficacy. However, for Jiang Jieshi the Declaration was of utmost importance. The passage to which he attached particular significance read as follows:

> It is their [Three Great Allies'] purpose that Japan shall be stripped of all the islands in the Pacific which she has seized or occupied since the beginning of the first World War in 1914, and that all the territories Japan has stolen from the Chinese, such as Manchuria, Formosa, and The Pescadores, shall be restored to the Republic of China.

In Jiang Jieshi's mind, this passage made it unequivocally clear to the international community that the Republic of China held sovereignty over these territories.

The base of the Japanese military invasion of China was the capital of the Manchurian puppet State of Manzhouguo, namely, the city of Changchun (then called Hsinking or Xinjing in Chinese, Shinkyo in Japanese). Who occupied Changchun, who controlled it, was thus an indispensable indicator of the territorial authority of the Republic of China. It could not be abandoned to the Communist Army.

This is how the siege of Changchun came into being. If Changchun had not been the capital of Manzhouguo, there would have undoubtedly been no siege. If it had not held this strategic importance, Jiang Jieshi would undoubtedly have abandoned it and quickly moved his base of operations to the more advantageous Shenyang.

On September 18, 1945, the Communist Party set up a Northeastern Bureau in Shenyang, with Peng Zhen at its head. On October 23, 1945, Lin Feng, with whom my father was to form a tight bond in Changchun in 1946, arrived in Shenyang to work with Peng Zhen. On March 12, 1946, however, Shenyang was occupied by the Nationalist Army.

Once the siege of Changchun commenced, Shenyang became

the source of all provisions for the Nationalist Army in the city, brought in by air. Given that the principal supply depots were there, Shenyang was best situated to serve as a Nationalist base of operations. In addition to air traffic, contact with the Nanjing regime could be easily maintained by train and through the port of Huludao. Furthermore, Shenyang was the site of imperial palaces and villas dating from the Ming and Qing dynasties. From the viewpoint of the Republic of China, which had toppled the Qing dynasty in the Xinhai (Hsin-hai) Revolution, Shenyang was a natural choice for the base of its operations. The Northeastern Bureau established in Shenyang by the Communist Party had been overrun, which was all the more reason for the Nationalists to headquarter at Shenyang.

Nevertheless, the site the Nationalists chose to make a stand was difficult-to-defend Changchun. Clearly Jiang Jieshi wished to adhere to the wording of the Cairo Declaration, stating that "all the territories Japan has stolen from the Chinese, such as Manchuria, Formosa, and The Pescadores, shall be restored to the Republic of China." It seems certain that if Changchun had not become established as the capital of the State of Manzhouguo, the siege of Changchun would have not occurred. There may have been a siege of Shenyang, but not Changchun.

In the defense of Changchun, supply of food and other provisions by air was a dire necessity. In time, however, airborne delivery became more difficult, and when reinforcements by ethnic soldiers from Yunnan Province, the Sixtieth Army of the National Revolutionary Army, were brought in, they suffered discrimination in the sharing of food. This led to desertion to the Communist side and the eventual defeat of the Nationalist Army on October 17, 1948. The actual "liberation" of Changchun took place two days later, on October 19, one month after my family's escape from the city. In this case the word "liberation" is a term used by the Communist Party to indicate the victory of the People's Liberation Army over the Nationalist Army and the freeing of the people from the oppression of the Nationalist government.

With the fall of Changchun the Revolutionary War quickly turned to the Communists' advantage, and as the People's Liberation Army moved south, one region after another fell under its control, resulting in the creation of the People's Republic of China on October 1, 1949.

*****

Meanwhile, Mao Zedong had called for the implementation of his grand strategy of "encircling the cities from the countryside." His chief rationale for this approach was that he was suffering from a shortage of weaponry. Stalin, for his part, thought the Communist bloc did not need two leaders. One was enough. Stalin belittled the fact that Mao Zedong was trying to use Marxist-Leninist thought to create a revolution in the Chinese countryside rather than in the cities as had been the case in Russia.

Stalin continued to consolidate his position in the Soviet Union, humiliating and betraying Lenin, who had played a leading role in the Revolution of 1917; once Lenin died, Stalin would become the overwhelmingly dominant political figure. When Mao Zedong appeared on the scene as the leader of the Chinese Communist Party, Stalin couldn't help vilifying him as a leader of peasants. To his mind, even given that ninety percent of the Chinese people were farmers, it would be impossible to create a successful revolution in China.

On August 14, 1945, the Sino-Soviet Treaty of Friendship and Alliance with the Republic of China was signed. In accordance with this treaty, the Soviets would supply munitions only to the Republic of China (Jiang Jieshi), not to the Communist Party of Mao Zedong.

Thus, without Stalin's aid, Mao was compelled to use munitions that had been abandoned by the Japanese Army.

Until October 1, 1949, China was officially known as the Republic of China, an ally of the Soviet Union in the prosecution of World War II. The Soviet Union had no intention of supplying munitions to the Republic's enemy, the Chinese Communist Party. After the disarmament of Japanese troops, it is said that the Soviet Union passed some of their weaponry on to the Communist Party, but even if so, the amount was infinitesimally small. As a consequence, the Communists avoided head-to-head confrontations, hiding in the mountains and villages, indoctrinating the farmers, and of necessity engaging chiefly in guerrilla warfare.

The strategy at Changchun was to cut off all food supplies, demoralize the Nationalist troops in the city, and encourage defections. It was a triumphant success.

This conflict mirrored in miniature the conflict between American anti-Communist policies and Stalin's ambitions. The fact that Stalin was not invited to the Cairo Conference is a direct reflection of this state of affairs.

In the 1990s I interviewed a former member of the People's Liberation Army who had entered Changchun on the day it was liberated. He stated, "There were so many emaciated bodies on the streets that it was difficult to thread your way through them. But there wasn't a single Nationalist soldier among the dead. They were all innocent civilians."

According to the Chinese Communist government, the number of dead was between 120,000 and 150,000 people, whereas the government of the Republic of China calculates the dead to be between 600,000 and 650,000. My own estimate, based on personal interviews of survivors in 1983 and calculations from the demographics of Changchun around 1947, is approximately 300,000. While hard facts are difficult to come by, it seems certain that the number was in the range of several hundred thousand people.

In correspondence exchanged between Mao and Lin Biao during the siege of Changchun, Mao directed the marshal to make

Changchun into a "death zone." But surprisingly, when my family escaped Qiazi, the People's Liberation Army provided us with gruel to eat. This was in keeping with Mao's directive that the people should be made aware of who was providing them food, for the people would then adhere to that side. This is still the overriding principle of the Communist Party today: China has become wealthy and economically powerful owing to the governance of the Communist Party, and for that reason the people should be loyal to the Party.

* * * * *

Sixty years have passed since crossing the sea, sixty years since seeing the flying fish and arriving at Maizuru Harbor in Japan. In China I was reviled as a "Japanese devil"; after returning to Japan I was called a "red." I began to reflect on the difficulty of living, on the meaning of this world, and ultimately confronted the philosophical question of the meaning of existence. From there I entered the world of theoretical physics. However, times had changed, from an era when you could solve an equation with pencil and paper to a period of computer simulations. Moreover, the university campus was overflowing with Chinese exchange students. The "China" I had tried so hard to forget, the China I thought I had forgotten, had now returned.

But this time the situation was different. If these young Chinese students asked for help and I responded, I could contribute to making their lives easier both mentally and in terms of daily needs, creating the space for them to study.

While there are undoubtedly a great many people who have studied theoretical physics, there are not many university teachers who know China and can speak almost perfect Chinese. This fact led me to abandon the field of theoretical physics and devote myself to helping Chinese students. Each time a student's problem was solved, I felt the gaping holes in my heart begin to heal. The emotions that filled these gaps—the sadness, the rancor, the anger, and the fear of the land that had given me birth and almost led to my death—disappeared a little at a time. This proved to be an important step in the process of attaining mental well-being.

In 1983 I wrote a small 100-page booklet called *Fujori no kanata* (Beyond the Unthinkable), followed in 1984 by the book *Chazu: Deguchi naki daichi* (Qiazi: The Land of No Escape). It was after finishing these two works that I noticed a momentous change. I no longer had the horrible dream that had been my constant nightly torment—the dream in which I was sleeping on a futon on the ground, in which the futon would begin skimming over the earth, in which, preceded by a premonition of imminent disaster, torrents of water would gush from the ground. Every time I had that dream I would wake with an unearthly scream, causing no end of concern to my family.

This dream abruptly stopped. It was then I realized that writing, by giving concrete form to one's inner world and providing a means of escape, can be an excellent means of mental therapy.

In order to provide a greater appreciation of the problems faced by the Japanese Ministry of Education and Japanese universities concerning the conditions and special problems of Chinese students in Japan, I made a personal visit to the Ministry of Education of the People's Republic of China. At that time known as the Committee of Education, the Ministry is one of the highest organs of the Chinese government. The Committee gave me a warm welcome and told me, "This is the first time this has ever happened, for an individual to come visit us with such a purpose in mind."

This was also the first time for me to return to China, and it marked the beginning of a cordial relationship with the Chinese government.

On one such occasion something unexpected occurred. I located Taeko, whom I had never quite given up hope of finding. This was entirely due to the kindness of a certain woman, a former resident of

Changchun, who was actively engaged in supporting Japanese children orphaned in China.

At our first meeting in half a century, for a while Taeko and I simply hugged one another in silence and wept. There was no need for words.

* * * * *

What caused me to write this book were the final words Father spoke to Mother.

"Qiazi was really terrible, wasn't it, Mother. I can't forget Mrs. M."

Holding Mother's hand, he forced the words from his mouth. These words, which he had never uttered since returning to Japan, were his final ones. Realizing how heartbreaking that experience must have been for him, I decided to write this book in his honor.

* * * * *

Taeko's husband had already passed away, and all her married children and her grandchildren wanted earnestly to come to Japan. There were more than twenty individuals in all.

What proved a godsend in this case was my involvement in the administration of international student affairs. One result of this was the publication of *Chugoku daigaku soran* (Comprehensive Guide to Chinese Universities), compiled in cooperation with the Chinese Committee of Education and the first publication of its kind. This guide was not only found useful by the Japanese Ministry of Education and Japanese universities but became an invaluable reference for the Japanese Immigration Bureau. In consequence, I was appointed a member of the Immigration Policy Committee of the Immigration Bureau and thus able to speak to the director-general of the Bureau on an equal footing.

As evidence of my relationship with Taeko since 1947 I attached a copy of the documentary *Chazu: Deguchi naki daichi* (Qiazi: The Land of No Escape) and frantically completed all the paperwork required for entry into Japan for more than twenty people. In the end I was successful, without a single person being left behind.

I visited Father's grave and reported the happy outcome, something that would have pleased him enormously, since the incident with Mrs. M. had long been eating away at his heart. For me this marked the end of an era filled with rancor and resentment at the injustices of history.

* * * * *

Even when on the verge of starvation, Father never sold the invaluable screen belonging to Empress Dowager Cixi that he had bought from a thief. He had promised it to Lin Feng. He wanted to see this precious work of art in the hands of someone who could appreciate its worth. In fact, though, did Lin find the screen carefully hidden on the second floor of the Shinkyo factory? Did he realize that Father had tried to the very end to keep his promise? Did he appreciate the good faith embodied in the hidden screen?

History is full of ironic twists. During the Cultural Revolution, when Lin Feng was working in tandem with Liu Shaoqi, once president of the People's Republic of China, he was arrested and incarcerated owing to his connection with Liu. Among the crimes he was accused of committing was that of treasuring cultural properties from the Shenyang Palace. If this is true, then it may be that Lin found the six-panel screen and the hanging scrolls and kept them as precious relics of the palace.

Years later, in Changchun, I happened to meet Lin Feng's son, Lin Yanzhi (1948–), who had just assumed the post of associate secretary at the Communist Party Jilin Provincial Committee in 2000. We met at the former headquarters of the Kanto Army, which was then housing the Committee. Lin resembled his father, a tall man with a mild but intelligent mien. He had studied physics at Qinghua (Tsinghua) University, and I had served on the Board of Education in Japan. As a senior civil servant he had published on education. That the children of two former friends should tread a similar course in life, that we should meet at the headquarters of the Kanto Army, a place that my father had so often frequented, was very moving.

Lin Yanzhi, who is seven years younger than myself, knew nothing about his father's activities during the Cultural Revolution. He wept when he heard about our fathers' friendship. He said that his surviving older sister was also entirely ignorant of this period, and asked that I write down what I had told him. Removing the impolitic passages about Qiazi, I presented him with a Chinese translation of *Chazu: Deguchi naki daichi*.

* * * * *

In the early 1990s I screwed up my courage and revisited Qiazi. The barbed wire that had separated the area occupied by the refugees from the liberated zone was now replaced by a white fence. Inside the fence the ground was still stark and bare, but now converted into a garbage dump. There were a few shanties on the verge of collapse. The area outside the fence, the former liberated zone, was now a flourishing shopping area, a different world. The Eighth Route Army's checkpoint had been replaced by a police box performing similar functions.

Where the mountain of corpses had once been was an open-air toilet exposed to the elements. Luscious green trees, extraordinarily green, covered the hill, benefiting no doubt from the countless bodies lying under the ground. Tens of thousands of bodies pushed the verdant trees upward as if to block out the sky, the last cry of the vindictive spirits of the dead.

The ravenous scarlet flames that once engulfed Qiazi were still burning. The spirits of the wandering souls of Qiazi were still alive, the glowing embers of a great conflagration. The lives that had been tossed aside as so much trash still sought a final requiem. Or so it seemed to me.

* * * * *

The survivors of Qiazi are passing from this world one after another, their stories untold. A memorial must be erected to their lives. That is precisely why I survived.

Sometimes I think that to go on living is not necessarily a good thing. To continue living means to assume the unbearable burden of pain of one's loved ones. We didn't choose to live, and we don't choose when to die. Still we go on living. And as long as we are alive, we want to live without regret, doing our best. For me this means bringing to the light of day one hidden incident in Chinese history. After that, my job will be done.

Homare Endo
November 15, 2012

Note and Acknowledgments

The present English translation is based on my *Chazu: Chugoku ken-koku no zanka* (Qiazi: The Burning Embers at China's Foundation) published by Asahi Shimbun Publications. It is one of four books I have written on the subject. Since each of these books varies in subject matter and length, they can be considered separate publications. The Chinese version published in Taiwan in June 2014 is based on the same version as this book.

In the 1990s a team of volunteers, out of the kindness of their hearts, undertook the task of translating part of my *Chazu: Chugoku kakumei-sen o kugurinuketa Nihonjin shojo* (Qiazi: A Japanese Girl Who Lived through the Chinese Revolutionary War), published by Bungeishunju. Unfortunately, this project never reached book form, but I would like to sincerely thank the following people for their valiant efforts: Dr. Hiroshi Maruta, Dr. Han-Seung Yoon, Dr. Kenneth S. S. Chang, Dr. Katsuko Shimokawa, and Mr. Raymond Spencer.

For the present translation I wish to express my heartfelt thanks to Mr. Michael Brase for undertaking this time-consuming translation from scratch. Mr. Brase was kindly introduced to me by Mr. Kuniaki Ura of IBC Publishing.

The story of Qiazi (romanized as "Chazu" in Japanese) is now available in three languages—Japanese, Chinese, and English—and should reach a wider audience. As a survivor of Qiazi, I now feel that I have done my duty in honoring and commemorating the dead. I offer my sincere thanks to all those who took part in making this book a reality.

For the publication of *Chazu: Chugoku kenkoku no zanka* by Asahi Shimbun Publications in 2012, I owe many thanks to Director Kojima of the Business Department as well as to Mr. Taro Saito, the editor in charge of the book; to Mr. Shigenobu Tamura, Advisor, Policy Research Council, the Liberal Democratic Party; to Mr. Michihiko Kunihiro, former Japanese ambassador to China; and to Mr. Junpei Kato, former Japanese Ambassador to Belgium.

In particular, Mr. Saito was always a source of warm encouragement. Without him it is unlikely that the book would have reached completion. I owe him my deepest thanks for making this particular dream of mine come true.

At the time of the publication of *Chazu: Deguchi naki daichi* by the Yomiura Shimbunsha in 1984, I was indebted to many more people, to all of whom I offer my heartfelt appreciation.

Dr. Homare Endo was born in China in 1941, lived through the Chinese Revolutionary War, and returned to Japan in 1953. She is a Doctor of Science, director of the Center of International Relations at Tokyo University and Graduate School of Social Welfare, and professor emeritus at the University of Tsukuba. She was a visiting researcher and professor at the Chinese Academy of Social Sciences. Among her published works are *Mo Takuto: Nihongun to kyobo shita otoko* (Mao Zedong: The Man who Conspired with the Japanese Army; in Japanese and Chinese), *Chaina Sebun: Akai kotei Shu Kinpei* (The China Seven: The Red Emperor Xi Jinping), *Chaina nain: Chugoku o ogokasu kyunin no otoko-tachi* (The China Nine: The Nine Men who Move China), *Netto taikoku Chugoku: Genron o meguru kobo* (Internet Superpower China: The Battle over Freedom of Speech), *Chaina Jajji: Mo Takuto ni narenakatta otoko* (Bo Xilai: The Man who Failed to Become a Second Mao Zedong), *Kanzen kaidoku: Chugoku gaiko senryaku no nerai* (An In-depth Study: The Aims of Chinese Foreign Policy), *Chugoku-jin ga eranda wasuto Chugoku-jin banzuke: Yahari akai Chugoku wa fuhai de horobiru* (The Worst Chinese as Selected by the Chinese: Corruption Will Bring Red China Down in the End), and *Chugoku doman shinjin-rui: Nihon no anime to manga ga Chugoku o ugokasu* (The Chinese Anime-Manga Tribe: Japanese Anime and Manga Shake China).

OTHER TRANSLATIONS OF INTEREST FROM STONE BRIDGE PRESS

The Pearl Jacket and Other Stories:
Flash Fiction from Contemporary China
edited and translated by Shouhua Qi

The Cape and Other Stories
by Kenji Nakagami; translated by Eve Zimmerman

In the Woods of Memory
by Shun Medoruma; translated by Takuma Sminkey

The Silver Spoon
by Kansuke Naka; translated by Hiroaki Sato

Wind and Stone
by Masaaki Tachihara; translated by Stephen W. Kohl

Still Life and Other Stories
by Junzo Shono; translated by Wayne P. Lammers

The Milky Way Railroad
by Kenji Miyazawa; translated by Joseph Sigrist and D. M. Stroud